TOM FOLEY

CONGRESSIONAL LEADERS

Jeffrey Crouch and Matthew N. Green
Series Editors

Burdett A. Loomis
Founding Editor

TOM FOLEY

THE MAN IN THE MIDDLE

R. Kenton Bird and John C. Pierce

University Press of Kansas

Published by the University Press of Kansas (Lawrence, Kansas 66045), which was organized by the Kansas Board of Regents and is operated and funded by Emporia State University, Fort Hays State University, Kansas State University, Pittsburg State University, the University of Kansas, and Wichita State University.

Library of Congress Cataloging-in-Publication Data

Names: Bird, R. Kenton, 1954– author. | Pierce, John C., author.
Title: Tom Foley : the man in the middle / R. Kenton Bird, John C. Pierce.
Description: Lawrence, Kansas : University Press of Kansas, 2023. |
   Series: Congressional leaders | Includes bibliographical references and
   index.
Identifiers: LCCN 2022038413 (print) | LCCN 2022038414 (ebook)
   ISBN 9780700634651 (cloth) | ISBN 9780700634668 (ebook)
Subjects: LCSH: Foley, Thomas S. | United States. Congress.
   House—Speakers—Biography. | United States—Politics and
   government—1945–1989. | United States—Politics and government—1989–
Classification: LCC E840.8.F65 B57 2023 (print) | LCC E840.8.F65 (ebook)
   | DDC 328.73/092 [B]—dc23/eng/20220812
LC record available at https://lccn.loc.gov/2022038413.
LC ebook record available at https://lccn.loc.gov/2022038414.

British Library Cataloguing-in-Publication Data is available.

Printed in the United States of America

10 9 8 7 6 5 4 3 2 1

The paper used in this publication is acid free and meets the minimum requirements of the American National Standard for Permanence of Paper for Printed Library Materials Z39.48-1992.

CONTENTS

A photo gallery follows page 128.

SERIES FOREWORD

Over twelve thousand people have served in the US Congress since the beginning of the American Republic. Only a fraction of these lawmakers have distinguished themselves from their peers and shaped the direction of the country through their leadership. The Congressional Leaders series is dedicated to telling their stories.

Tom Foley, the subject of this latest entry in the series, is probably best known as the first Speaker of the US House of Representatives since the mid-nineteenth century to lose his bid for reelection. Yet it would be a mistake to define Foley's long congressional career by that single election. As R. Kenton Bird and John C. Pierce explain in the pages that follow, Foley was a powerful advocate for his district, an institutionalist who cared deeply about Congress, and a Speaker who helped pass major Democratic bills while striving to maintain comity in an increasingly partisan political environment.

Foley had demonstrated his leadership acumen years before becoming Speaker of the House in 1989. First as a member, and later as the elected chair of the Democratic Study Group—an influential organization within the Democratic Caucus—he helped institute several important reforms that spread power more widely within the chamber. Foley also chaired the House Agriculture Committee for six years, then became party whip in 1980, a job that required him to build support for major party bills. Six years after that, he ascended to the number two spot on the leadership ladder and served as majority leader until Speaker Jim Wright stepped down and Foley took his place.

The authors argue persuasively that, as Speaker, Foley was a transitional leader. He bridged the gap between an older, more cooperative, decentralized, policy-oriented era of congressional politics and a new one that concentrated power at the top of the leadership ladder and emphasized political conflict and sharp partisan rhetoric.

Transitional leaders face unique challenges, and Foley was no exception. Increasing polarization and growing bad blood between the two political parties made it harder for him to build majorities for legislation. Emboldened members of the minority party were willing to attack not only the chamber but also Foley himself, sometimes in starkly personal terms.

Foley also entered the speakership under especially difficult circumstances. Speaker Wright's forceful leadership style had rubbed members of both parties the wrong way, and as the minority party, Republicans felt particularly embittered by how the Democratic majority ruled the House. Wright had resigned under a cloud of ethical charges brought by Georgia Republican Newt Gingrich, an event that left Democrats angry and eager for retribution.

Nonetheless, Foley managed to navigate these obstacles with aplomb. His accommodating leadership style helped lower the temperature of the House, and he could take credit for many of Congress's subsequent accomplishments, including the Americans with Disabilities Act, reauthorization of the Clean Air Act, deficit reduction legislation, and the passage of the North American Free Trade Agreement. A firm believer in protecting Congress's institutional authority and integrity, he steered his chamber through several scandals and successfully demanded that President George H. W. Bush seek legislative approval before deploying troops in combat against Iraqi forces that had invaded Kuwait.

In short, Bird and Pierce have written an impressive biography of a man whose many contributions made him one of the most important individuals to ever serve in the House of Representatives. Tom Foley showed how a congressional leader can represent the nation and the legislature without sacrificing his partisan principles.

On a final note, this is our first foreword as the new coeditors of the Congressional Leaders series. Our predecessor, Burdett A. "Bird" Loomis, who passed away in 2021, was the founding editor of the series and a beloved member of the community of congressional scholars. By continuing this series, we hope to honor his memory.

Jeffrey Crouch
Matthew N. Green
Series Editors

PROLOGUE AND ACKNOWLEDGMENTS

John Pierce: On a warm spring afternoon in 1971, two young men were talking quietly in a hallway of the Longworth House Office Building of the US House of Representatives in Washington, DC. I was one of those young men. We both worked in the Longworth building, albeit only temporarily. While still early in our careers, we were American Political Science Association (APSA) congressional fellows, university faculty members, and PhD-trained political scientists. Along with several journalists and administrative fellows, we had been selected to be part of a small group of junior academics and professionals to work for half a year for a member of the House and half a year for a member of the Senate, usually as the only APSA fellow in an office. After a year on Capitol Hill, the faculty fellows were expected to return to their campuses and carry their newfound knowledge of the legislative process with them into their classrooms and research programs.

In the month preceding that conversation in the Longworth hallway, we had quickly become good friends; we both were from the West and had conducted our graduate studies at large state universities in the Upper Midwest. Moreover, both members of the House for whom we worked were also from the western United States. This particular conversation focused on our positive experiences in the members' offices. I was assigned to the office of Congressman Thomas S. Foley, Democrat of eastern Washington State. The other fellow's member of Congress was from California. The talk turned to our experiences with the members themselves. My colleague from the Californian's office spoke about the high regard in which Tom Foley was held by the California representative. Indeed, the fellow's member had recently said he expected that someday Tom Foley would become Speaker of the House.

While, in the long run, the rise to the speakership turned out to be an accurate prediction for Tom Foley, it was quite a surprising hypothesis at that particular time. Never before had there been a Speaker of the House from west of Texas. (Texan Sam Rayburn was Speaker for seventeen years, 1940–1947, 1949–1953, and 1955–1961.) Regardless of the geographic region of Foley's home district, it was premature to make such a bold forecast about a junior member of Congress—Foley was then only in his fourth two-year term. It was an even bolder statement about a Democrat from an agricultural district in eastern Washington that had sent a Republican to Congress for eleven terms before Foley's election in 1964. But, as it turned out, the California congressman was correct. Even though Foley's ascent to the speakership did not happen for another eighteen years, his path to that position was sure and steady. Once he was in the Speaker's office, his values, priorities, and actions were distinct from those of both his predecessors and his successors.

Kenton Bird: As I stood outside the House of Representatives' gallery at the US Capitol on May 31, 1989, I knew that timing would be critical. The ushers typically rotated groups of visitors in and out of the gallery every fifteen minutes, but once a major speech began, seated spectators could remain. That day's *Washington Post* gave a hint of the drama that was about to unfold: "The timetable for House Speaker Jim Wright's anticipated resignation remained unclear yesterday, but sources close to the Texas Democrat said he is likely to announce his intention to resign today or Thursday."[1]

As a participant in the same congressional fellowship program as John Pierce but nearly two decades later, I worked that spring in the office of Representative Lee Hamilton of Indiana. I closely followed press reports of the House Ethics Committee's investigation of Wright over a questionable book deal. When word spread through the halls of the Rayburn House Office Building on the afternoon of May 31 that Wright planned to address the House of Representatives, I rode the subway to the Capitol, took the elevator to the gallery, and found a place in line. My hunch was correct. House members poured onto the floor, while spectators filled the gallery. As soon as I was seated, the ushers closed the doors. Foley, then the House's majority leader, assumed the speaker's chair and called the House to order. A little after 4:00 p.m., he recognized Wright to address the assembled members. "I don't want to be a party to tearing up the institution; I love it," Wright said, declaring his intent to step down as Speaker once a successor was chosen.[2] A week later, Foley was elected to the position, fulfilling the prediction that Pierce's colleague had made in 1971. My firsthand witness to this transition heightened my curiosity about leadership in Congress, particularly the qualities Foley demonstrated in the weeks following Wright's resignation. After my fellowship ended that summer and I returned to my newspaper job in Idaho, I found numerous opportunities to observe Foley's leadership style during the next five years, both in Washington, DC, and in his home district in eastern Washington.

Pierce: Less than six years after he had reached the pinnacle of power, I sat down with Speaker Foley and a few others in his Washington, DC, office. This particular meeting occurred soon after the election in which Foley was defeated for reelection to his own congressional seat. This stunning electoral outcome was the first loss by a sitting Speaker since the time of Abraham Lincoln.[3] On this particular day, those gathered in the Speaker's office lamented Foley's unexpected rejection by his constituents, tried to understand the cause of his defeat, and speculated about what this development might portend for the future of the Democratic Party, for the House of Representatives, and for the country.[4] During this meeting, we also discussed the possibility of Speaker Foley donating his congressional papers to Washington State University, the major public university in Foley's home district, where we planned to establish a center honoring him and his career.

Understanding Tom Foley's Defeat

The surprising outcome of the 1994 election raised many questions. Did Foley's loss stem from the same attributes and values that had led him to become Speaker? Or, more narrowly, was the outcome the result of his opposition to term limits for members of the House or from his support for restrictions on the sale of assault-style firearms? Or was he simply swept away by much larger national political currents? Had Foley's successive leadership positions diverted his attention from his constituents' needs? In this vein, two observers of Congress commented:

> When Tom Foley (D-Wash.) lost to George Nethercutt in 1994, Foley's defeat appeared to occur in large part because of public perceptions that he was more concerned with national politics than with local representation. But after Foley received an alarmingly

low 35 percent of the vote in an open primary in 1994, his campaign "tried to show that the 15-term incumbent was still listening
to his constituents and that, as Speaker, he had the power to amplify the response."[5]

That message apparently was neither sufficiently powerful nor convincing enough to carry Tom Foley back to the House of Representatives for
a sixteenth term. Foley's defeat also reflected the context of an increasingly
polarized Congress and country, along with a leadership style strikingly different from that of both his predecessors and his successor. Whatever the
reason for his defeat, Speaker Foley clearly was stunned by the outcome.
At the same time, though, consistent with Foley's values and the behavior
and personality that had taken him to the office, he lashed out neither at
the politics that produced the outcome nor at Newt Gingrich, the Georgia
Republican who had engineered the Republican takeover of the House and
was likely to become the next Speaker.

This book examines Foley's rise to Speaker of the House, his service as
Speaker, and his eventual electoral defeat, along with the Democratic Party's
loss of the majority in the House for the first time since 1955. We suggest
Foley exhibited a career-long commitment to sustain a vibrant and responsive House of Representatives as an institution, but that he also eventually
faced criticism from within his own party, deep partisan polarization, and
difficult social and political challenges in the country at large.

Acknowledgments

The authors are grateful to the American Political Science Association,
which supported each of us as congressional fellows at different stages of
our careers. The APSA fellowship program brings journalists, political scientists, federal employees, health professionals, and others to Capitol Hill
to work in congressional offices.

At Washington State University (WSU), the repository for Tom Foley's
congressional papers, the staff of Manuscripts, Archives and Special Collections at the WSU Library has been helpful, beginning with Kenton Bird's
dissertation research in the 1990s. Research for the current book was facil-
itated by Trevor Bond, assistant dean of the library, and Gayle O'Hara and
Cheryl Gunselman, archivists.

The Foley Institute for Public Policy and Public Service at WSU continues Tom Foley's legacy through internships, research fellowships, lectures,

panels, and symposia. We are grateful to Cornell Clayton, director, and Richard Elgar, assistant director, for their assistance with tracking down documents and photographs.

The University of Idaho's Office of Research and Economic Development awarded Bird a travel grant for two trips to Washington, DC, while the College of Letters, Arts and Social Sciences supported Bird's work through a social sciences fellowship.

Former members of Congress were generous with their time and candid in their recollections of events during Foley's thirty years in Congress, especially his speakership. The authors are grateful to David Bonior, Don Bonker, Norm Dicks, Richard Gephardt, Dan Glickman, Mike Kreidler, Larry LaRocco, Jim McDermott, and Leon Panetta for sharing their insights.

Foley's success as a congressional leader was partially the result of his talented staff. Among those who helped the authors better understand events of the 1980s and 1990s are Jeff Biggs, George Kundanis, and Mary Beth Schultheis. Heather Foley, the Speaker's wife, political adviser, and unpaid chief of staff, kindly shared anecdotes and referred the authors to other sources. Bruce Reed provided valuable insights into Foley's relationship with the Clinton White House.

Many journalists, historians, and political scientists advised the authors on lines of inquiry or provided access to interviews and archived articles. They included LeRoy Ashby, Sarah Binder, Jim Camden, Juliet Eilperin, Zusha Elinson, Ron Elving, Rick Eskil, John C. Hughes, Marc Johnson, Nicholas Lovrich, Thomas Mann, Ken Olsen, James Thurber, and Martin Wattenberg.

In preparing the manuscript, the authors relied on the careful reading of Diana Armstrong and Kerry Darnall. At the University Press of Kansas, Burdett Loomis, the series editor, made the initial contact with John Pierce about this book, and helped bring the idea to fruition. Senior editor David Congdon helped focus the authors' research, while managing director Kelly Chrisman Jacques responded to multiple style and formatting questions. Copy editor Susan Ecklund polished the final manuscript and assured consistency throughout. The book that emerged from this long process reflects their insights and attention to detail. The authors also thank Brian Beesley and Emmett Mayer III, who created maps and figures for chapters 4 and 5.

Burdett Loomis died unexpectedly in Lawrence, Kansas, on September 25, 2021. He left a deep legacy of intelligence, civic commitment, and profound values. An accomplished scholar in his own right, he published widely adopted books on Congress and on interest groups. He wrote a regular column about Kansas politics that appeared in many of the state's newspapers. Most important, though, Burdett Loomis was a strikingly good person who enhanced all who were privileged to be in his presence.

Finally, the authors wish to thank their wives, Ardith Pierce and Gerri Sayler, for their encouragement and support as the many stories of Tom Foley came together over the past four years.

TOM FOLEY

CHAPTER 1

THE MAN IN THE MIDDLE

There's no question that there may have been some luck of the Irish operating when it came to Tom Foley, as well as incredible stamina. But what led him to make history as the first Speaker of the House from west of the Rockies was not luck. It was his hard work, his deep integrity, his powerful intellect, and, as Bob Michel so eloquently and movingly stated, his ability to find common ground with his colleagues across the aisle. And it was his personal decency that helped him bring civility and order to a Congress that demanded both—and still does.

—President Barack Obama, speaking at the memorial service for Tom Foley, US Capitol, October 29, 2013

I n 1989, Thomas Stephen Foley, a Democratic representative from a traditionally Republican district in eastern Washington, became the first Speaker of the US House of Representatives from a district west of Texas. Foley served in Congress for thirty years, from 1965 to 1995. Over that three-decade span, he moved steadily up the Democratic Party's leadership ladder. During the last five and a half years of his congressional career,

Foley was Speaker of the House, sitting second in the line of succession to the president of the United States. Throughout his time in Congress, Tom Foley persistently demonstrated a deep commitment to the House of Representatives as a civil, collaborative, and bipartisan democratic institution, while still promoting and facilitating the Democrats' role as the majority party. That particular institutional perspective made Foley largely unlike Thomas P. "Tip" O'Neill and Jim Wright, the Democratic Speakers who immediately preceded him. But Foley stood in even greater contrast to the contentious and highly polarizing Newt Gingrich, the Republican from Georgia who succeeded him in 1995.

To be sure, Foley confronted significant challenges throughout his time as Speaker. His responses to those challenges resulted in occasional criticism, sometimes sharp, of his leadership style from both within and outside his party. But Foley weathered that disapproval until 1994, when the Democratic Party suffered catastrophic losses in national elections. The Democrats lost their majority in the House of Representatives, and Foley himself lost, albeit very narrowly, his seat in the House, as well as the speakership. Some of Foley's setbacks stemmed from personal choices resulting from his bipartisan, inclusive, institution-building leadership style and personal values. At the same time, other forces were seemingly beyond his control, such as the Gingrich-led Republican "revolution" that had begun in the late 1980s. This movement both reflected and contributed to a growing ideological polarization between the two political parties in Congress and in the country's electorate—a pattern that continues today.

In this book, we examine Foley's rise to Speaker of the House, his service as Speaker, and his eventual electoral defeat. The following pages will address a set of major themes in his career—and especially in his speakership—and how they played out on various policy and institutional stages. We suggest that based on his long-held personal and political values, Foley exhibited a strong motivation to sustain a vibrant and responsive House of Representatives as a democratic institution. But he eventually faced deep partisan polarization, pockets of criticism from within his own party, and difficult social and political challenges in the country at large.

We view Tom Foley as a "man in the middle," frequently (but not always) a policy centrist. Perhaps more important, we also see him as a leader in a context in which his values positioned him between political forces, institutional norms, personal styles, and individual loyalties. Providing a window into Foley's career in the House and placing his speakership in the context of congressional leaders of the late twentieth century, the book will address the following themes and contextual sources of that "middleness."

First and most obvious, Foley was a transitional leader, literally in the middle between, on the one hand, the preceding long line of Democratic Speakers dating back to Sam Rayburn (whose first of three terms as Speaker began in 1940) and, on the other, the subsequent partisan, polarizing approach exhibited by his successor, Newt Gingrich, and other Republican Speakers after 1994. Foley had been a leader of the reform-oriented Democratic Study Group (DSG) in the 1970s, but by the 1990s Gingrich painted him as the symbol of old-school Democratic politics in Congress that needed to be rooted out to achieve the Republicans' policy goals. In addition to the presence of heightened partisan polarization in the House, this transition also occurred in the context of enhanced partisan "sorting" in the electorate. That sorting was found in the allegiances of voters for the two major parties, such that "the constituencies that have comprised the respective party caucuses have become more homogeneous."[1] In large measure, the resulting party polarization and sorting at both congressional and constituency levels created a dissonance between Foley's roles as representative of a conservative district, on the one hand, and as the leader of a progressive party caucus in the House of Representatives, on the other hand. The consequences of that dissonance surely contributed to Foley's defeat in 1994.

Second, throughout his career, Foley was largely an institutionalist, reflected in his values-based commitment to the House of Representatives as a strong, bipartisan, Constitution-derived, procedurally consistent, and democratic legislative body. Foley's deep institutional commitments appeared early in his career when he chaired the progressive DSG, which produced major changes in the process of selecting committee chairs, diminishing the importance of seniority. Foley himself benefited from that change when he was elected chair of the Committee on Agriculture, dislodging the senior member, Democrat William R. "Bob" Poage of Texas. Working from the middle, between reformers and seniority-affirming traditionalists, he could defuse opposition from those senior members of his party, thereby enabling his advancement up the leadership ladder. Likewise, early in his speakership, Foley was able to work well with Republicans, especially with the minority leader, Robert Michel (R-IL), even while he enjoyed strong support from his own party. That bridging of the parties enabled Speaker Foley to change the tenor and climate of the House. Later, though, the polarization and sorting just noted, along with other pressures, made his commitment to the institution's strength as a bipartisan corporate body less tenable politically, both in the House and in the nation. Ironically, Foley was in the middle between some of the younger progressive members of his party (a cohort to which he once belonged) and his commitment to the traditional Democratic party leadership in Congress.

Third, Foley's distinctive personal background and resulting sets of values were expressed both in his path to the speakership and in his leadership actions while Speaker. To be sure, later in his speakership, the political expressions of those personal values often were at odds with the increasing polarization of the institution, as in his support in early 1989 for his predecessor, Speaker Jim Wright. Foley was raised in a Roman Catholic home and educated in Jesuit schools, resulting in strongly held beliefs that were expressed in his personal life and political career. The political edges of those values were honed by the mentorship and support of two of the most powerful Democratic members of the US Senate, Henry "Scoop" Jackson and Warren Magnuson, both from his home state of Washington. After his election to the House in 1964, Foley turned often to Jackson, and to a lesser degree Magnuson, for advice.

Fourth, Tom Foley surely was personally uncomfortable in the strident political climate that emerged in the early 1990s, a climate fueled by harsh talk radio and other conservative media and successfully exploited by Gingrich and his fellow partisans. In retrospect, Foley had difficulty reconciling his personal and institutional values with the ways voters obtained news about Congress and made decisions on Election Day. In all of this, his education and natural instincts epitomized values of collegiality, collaboration, and bipartisanship, even in the face of the polarizing partisan reality; indeed, he made strategic partnerships with Republicans throughout his career (e.g., Senator Dan Evans and Representative Sid Morrison from his home state and later Robert Michel of Illinois, the House GOP leader) to advance legislation to benefit his district, state, and the nation. Foley was the last Speaker of the House in the era when Congress functioned as a bipartisan legislative body—a bipartisanship that ebbed away in the last years of his speakership and has appeared only rarely since then.

Fifth, as suggested earlier, Foley built his reputation as a reformer in the 1970s. Ironically, though, by the 1990s he was seen by some as an impediment to further reform of the House. He defended Congress as an important democratic institution and the House in particular against charges it was corrupt (e.g., the so-called House bank scandal), rebutting claims that it needed new (Republican) leadership. However, Foley apparently did not recognize how much the polarizing accusations of Gingrich, other Republicans, and the conservative media resonated with the American public. He also seemed to underestimate the depth of the anti-incumbent sentiment that led to the Republican takeover of both chambers of Congress in 1994.

Sixth, in the last five years of his three decades in Congress, consistent with the partisan sorting processes, Tom Foley was caught between the conservative values of his district and the increasingly liberal Democratic Caucus. He surely struggled to find balance among his duties as Speaker, his personal values, and his responsibilities as a member representing a single district, which itself was undergoing demographic changes. Viewed by most observers as a moderate Democrat, Foley had been elected in 1964 from a district that had been held by a Republican for the preceding twenty-two years—and has been held by two Republicans since his defeat in 1994. Selected as chair of the House Committee on Agriculture in 1975, early in his congressional career, Foley could attend to the expectations of his agricultural constituency. Simultaneously, he was active in the reform-oriented DSG, a group of progressive Democratic House members that took the lead in limiting the powers of entrenched committee chairs.[2] Then, in 1977, Foley became chair of the Democratic Caucus, and in 1981 Speaker Tip O'Neill chose him to be the last appointed Democratic whip, a position from which he broadened the base of the Democratic whip system. That process underscored his inclusive values and enhanced his political prominence in the party. Foley was elected majority leader in 1987 and became Speaker in 1989 after Jim Wright's contentious resignation.

During his more than five years as Speaker, though, Foley's values and style increasingly were seen as inconsistent with the expectations of many of his more conservative constituents but also with some in his own caucus as well. As Foley told a reporter in 1990: "There are people who think I should be more partisan, . . . should be more aggressive, should be more combative. More hard-edged. I know they're there. I know they think that. But I don't tend to agree with it."[3] Nonetheless, he became a lightning rod for public discontent with Congress, a theme reinforced by Gingrich and the nascent Republican majority. That dissonance and Foley's response to it surely contributed to his defeat in 1994—the first electoral loss for a sitting Speaker in his home district since the days of Abraham Lincoln. His defeat, along with the Republican Party's seizure of control of the House of Representatives, represented a seismic transition in the landscape of American politics. The aftershocks, including the heightened partisan polarization in the House and the partisan sorting in the US electorate, continue today.

In a broad view, this work suggests that across those six themes, Tom Foley's leadership as Speaker of the House of Representatives can be seen through two frames. One frame is *transitional*. Foley was a bridge between the old-school partisan leadership styles of Jim Wright and Tip O'Neill and the polarizing politics of Newt Gingrich. He exhibited a commitment to the goal of bipartisanship in "holding the center."[4] He maintained this generally conciliatory posture amid an onrushing transition in the House from decades-long Democratic domination to a polarized partisan environment, personified by Gingrich, Speaker from 1995 to 1999. The polarizing challenges also surfaced in Foley's own Democratic Party, but from an entirely different ideological direction. Foley was caught up in that transition, even as he tried to occupy the middle ground.

The second frame, while less obvious, is a view of Foley as a *transformational* leader. Political scientists Sarah Binder and Thomas Mann wrote:

> James McGregor Burns, in his classic book on leadership, distinguishes two types. Transactional leadership, based on exchanges between leaders and followers, is characteristic of leader-follower relationships in groups, legislatures, and followers. Its primary mode of operation is bargaining to produce a discrete outcome. Transformational leadership, on the other hand, involves a fusing of purpose among previously disconnected or conflicting individuals that produces a mutual and continuing pursuit of a higher purpose. . . . The quest for better, more effective leadership in American politics today sometimes focuses on more skillful transactional leadership. Often, however, it imagines the possibilities of visionary, courageous, inspiring leadership at all levels of government that can transform the bitter partisan and ideological divides and render our public life more productive and satisfying.[5]

Ronald Peters and Craig Williams echo Burns, Binder, and Mann with the following observation:

> This transformational leadership model is far more complex than the contingent reward-based transactional style. In it the leader tries to demonstrate that organizational objectives transcend the self-interests of the follower—that is, he instills in the follower a desire to work hard for the over-arching organizational goals. The

leader does so through a process of confidence-building in the follower and emphasizing the importance of achieving organizational goals as beneficial to all members within the organization. He pursues paths of intellect, knowledge, benevolence, understanding, trust, commitment, and joint responsibility among all individuals.[6]

As Peters and Williams also note, Burns suggests that legislative leaders are much more likely to operate in a transactional mode, while transformational leaders are more likely to be found in the executive/presidential domain. Transformational legislative leaders thus may face different and more complex challenges than those for whom transactional behavior is the mode. In addition to the patterns of behavior that best describe transformational leadership, Burns elaborates on what he sees as the value base for transformational leadership:

> Leaders embrace values; values grip leaders. The stronger the value systems, the more strongly leaders can be empowered and the more deeply leaders can empower followers. The transformational dynamic that mutually empowers leaders and followers involves, as we have seen, wants and needs, motivation and creativity, conflict and power. But at its heart lie values.[7]

For Burns, "the mobilizing and kindling power of transforming values is the most essential and durable factor in leadership."[8]

It is our view that Tom Foley's implicit goal was to be a value-based, process-oriented *transformational* leader even in a legislative context that emphasizes and rewards transactional behavior. What characterizes such an aspirational approach? Theresa Bullard has written that among the values that distinguish transformational leaders are seeking "to foster a sense of community via collaboration with peers and amongst their peers."[9] We suggest that Foley generally exhibited a commitment to that transformational value, even if he did not act perfectly in accordance with it at all times. The political world is far too contentious and complicated for that to be true for anyone. Very real cross-pressures were produced by his values resting in a context distinguished by the transactional values of many in the House of Representatives, by a constituency more conservative than Foley himself, by some members of his own party who wanted him to move faster and with more central control than his values allowed, and by the polarizing activity of the minority party leadership. However, Foley's transformational leadership was founded on by very different value sets.

These elements of transformational leadership style contrasted with Foley's Democratic predecessors Tip O'Neill and Jim Wright, who acted more in the traditional transactional style of legislative leaders. Foley also contrasted with his Republican successor, Newt Gingrich, who was seen by some as transformational, but with different goals: partisan polarization, hierarchical party organization, and tight party unity.[10] Foley did not ignore the transactional obligations of legislative leadership or constituency representation, but he put greater emphasis on producing a legislative community with a collaborative culture committed to a higher purpose. The transformational purposes that guided Foley in the House often accompanied transaction-infused policy goals that would benefit his constituency. The dissonance between his largely transformational approach to internal congressional processes and the transactional constituency-based expectations of his representative role ultimately contributed to his electoral defeat. Examples of that dissonance included issues of term limits, a constitutional amendment to ban flag burning, and a ban on assault weapons as a crime-fighting measure.

Unlike the Democratic leaders who preceded him, Foley was not a partisan policy ideologue; rather, he often worked across the aisle to make the legislative process function, giving both parties an opportunity to participate. His transformational vision contained a different philosophy of leadership, focused on the processes that produced legislative outcomes. Reflecting that value, Foley once said: "Sometimes to pass a bill, you have to change the attitude of the country."[11] As House majority leader in 1987, he claimed, "The House of Representatives probably provides more opportunities for minority expression and participation in a meaningful sense than any other legislative body in the world."[12] After Foley succeeded Jim Wright as Speaker, congressional scholar Roger Davidson noted: "While the new team—Speaker Thomas S. Foley (D-WA) and Majority Leader Richard A. Gephardt (D-MO)—betokened a 'kinder, gentler' House leadership, the change was more one of style than substance."[13] We would argue, though, that style is not without substance when that style itself is based on clear and distinct values about processes and participation that had been previously ignored or are seen to be in significant decline.

In a postspeakership book by Foley and his former press secretary, Jeffrey Biggs, Biggs wrote of the Speaker's fundamental philosophy:

Foley believed the House needed a sense of comity, a respect for procedure, and a sense of mutual forbearance. A legislative body was, after all, a venue of representative government, a place where disagreement, debate and deliberation about the public good was possible. Power without judgment was worse than judgment without power. A good Speaker had to have both and use both. But when the majority couldn't count on Republican support, and couldn't muster a majority among its own, Foley's unwillingness to exert a heavy hand was not without criticism by some party members who wanted discipline meted out as an object lesson.[14]

Foley responded to critics on that point: "It's so obvious that what they want is that their opponents, or their philosophical adversaries, or their not-too-friendly committee or subcommittee chairmen be sanctioned, punished, or criticized."[15] That was not Tom Foley's leadership style.

Where did Foley's approach to a speakership with significant transformational elements come from? How did that approach develop before and throughout his congressional career? Chapter 2, "You Can Get There from Here!," focuses on Foley's early life and the forces that shaped him to aspire to be a transformational leader. These forces included his value-based family background, his Jesuit education, and his mentorship by two of the most powerful people in Washington, DC, Senators Henry "Scoop" Jackson and Warren Magnuson, from his home state of Washington. Foley's leadership style, comprised largely of the transformational values of comity, intelligence, and goodwill, was evidenced in his first political campaign in which he defeated a long-standing Republican incumbent. After that first election, all sides agreed that Foley had conducted his campaign with integrity and evenhandedness. Early in his congressional career, those same attributes led colleagues and journalists to forecast his surprising rise to power from a district geographically distant from the seat of American government.

Chapter 3, "A Bipartisan Speaker," provides an overview of Foley's steady movement up the congressional leadership ladder to the top rung, where he sat in the Speaker's chair. We highlight the crucial contexts in which Foley excelled as a leader, reaching across the aisle to the Republicans and cementing his close relations with minority leader Robert Michel. While Foley embraced his predecessors, O'Neill and Wright, despite their style differences from his own, Newt Gingrich rejected Robert Michel's conciliatory relationship with Foley, fueling the hyperpartisanship and polarization that have characterized the House in the decades that followed.

Chapter 4, "Mapping the Fifth District Landscape," begins with an overview of redistricting that resulted in major changes to the district's boundaries during Foley's fourth term in the House. It addresses support for Foley in the various counties of the district, including how he fared in contrast to the Democratic presidential candidate in those elections. This chapter also analyzes the district's political culture and policy preferences as potential explanations for his electoral success and eventual defeat. It examines Foley's career-long positioning within the House, especially in terms of his roll call voting support for his party, for the president, and for the "conservative coalition." This analysis provides insights into changes across time that affected Foley's political destiny.

Chapter 5, "Holding the Center," begins with Foley's long-standing support for agriculture's central importance in the Fifth Congressional District. It then turns to the controversy over the North American Free Trade Agreement (NAFTA) with Mexico and Canada as an example of Foley's "man in the middle" dilemma. While NAFTA offered potential benefits for agricultural interests in Foley's district, it also threatened a negative impact on labor, especially in the Spokane area. How Foley resolved that personal conflict, along with tensions within the House Democratic leadership over NAFTA, reflected his conciliatory style.

Chapter 6, "The Pinnacle of Power," describes how Foley exercised power and influence as Speaker. It examines two foreign policy confrontations between Congress and President George H. W. Bush: US support for the authoritarian government of El Salvador and the buildup to the first Persian Gulf War of 1991. Domestically, this period saw Foley's principled stand against a proposed constitutional amendment to prohibit burning of the American flag, a position that prevailed when the House failed to give the amendment two-thirds approval. These years also saw a cordial relationship between Foley and Bush, even as they disagreed on issues.

Chapter 7, "Defending the Reputation of the House," reviews a series of scandals that cast Congress in a negative light in the early 1990s. A bipartisan deal to raise congressional pay drew unfavorable attention to congressional salaries and perquisites. The House bank and post office controversies resulted from long-standing practices on Capitol Hill, but they came to a head on Foley's watch. Ethics scandals affecting key members of the House Democratic Caucus (such as House Democratic whip Tony Coelho and Ways and Means chair Dan Rostenkowski) put Foley on the defensive, even though he was not directly associated with either colleague's questionable (and, in Rostenkowski's case, illegal) behavior.

Republican insurgents, led by Newt Gingrich, intensified their attacks on the institution, seeking to portray Congress as a corrupt institution that could be fixed only by Republican majorities—a strategy that ultimately succeeded in 1994.

Chapter 8, "The Perfect Storm," focuses on the 1994 election. It synthesizes earlier chapters that examine the electoral history of the Fifth Congressional District to provide context for the 1994 outcome. These include the effects of redistricting, widely varying margins in support for Foley and his opponents across time, national political trends, the district's political culture, and the public policy positions taken by Foley. We suggest that in 1994, these forces coalesced in a perfect storm, sweeping Foley out of public office after three decades.

Chapter 9, "His Own Stamp?," examines the significance of Tom Foley as a twentieth-century transitional congressional leader who possessed both transactional and transformational dimensions. We argue that Foley's tenure as Speaker (from June 6, 1989, to January 3, 1995) represented the last time the House of Representatives was a collegial legislative body. Finally, we place Foley in the context of the Speakers who followed him, establishing him as "the man in the middle"—chronologically, ideologically, and stylistically. An epilogue gives an overview of Foley's life after he left Congress in 1995, including his service as US ambassador to Japan.

CHAPTER 2

YOU CAN GET THERE FROM HERE!

Thomas Stephen Foley was the first Speaker of the US House of Representatives from a district in one of the country's most western states. Foley's home in Spokane, Washington, was twenty-five hundred miles from Washington, DC. This *geographic distance* clearly made it difficult for Representative Foley to stay in touch with his constituency, especially while sitting in the Speaker's chair. But the *political distance* from a first-term Democratic member of Congress representing a conservative, remote, and Republican-leaning district to that of Speaker of the House may have been even farther. But Foley successfully traveled both of these roads. His route to the Speaker's chair took a steady, career-spanning trajectory that reflected a combination of his fundamental values, intellectual and political acumen, and personal leadership style. Those values, intelligence, and style provided Foley with the tools to express his distinct approach to leadership during a time of major transitions in American politics, both in the country and in the House of Representatives.

Throughout his time in Congress, Foley's transformational leadership style was deeply rooted in his upbringing and education. In the face of partisan polarization and personal attacks, his political instincts and behavior were consistent with the transformational values described in chapter 1. He was inclusive, bipartisan, and committed to cooperation, comity, evenhandedness, and institutional effectiveness of the legislative process. To be sure, Foley's leadership style was severely challenged by political currents in the country and in Congress, and by the disjunction between his own values and those of many of his constituents.

How did Tom Foley emerge as one of the most powerful leaders in the US government? Why did he aspire to such an unusual unifying transformational role in the midst of an era in the throes of transition to significant partisan polarization? Much of the answer is found in the family and community cultures in which he was raised.

The Spokane where Tom Foley was born on March 6, 1929, was a city of 115,000. Its downtown of bustling department stores and rising office buildings hugged the south bank of the Spokane River at a point where it drops nearly one hundred feet. Train whistles competed with the roar of the falls; three transcontinental railroads passed through the city, and several regional rail lines originated in Spokane as well. Spokane was the primary trading and supply center of a rich farming, logging, and mining region its boosters proclaimed as the "Inland Empire."[1] The "empire" stretched west to the Columbia River, north to Canada, east to the Rocky Mountains of western Montana, and south to Oregon. Spokane and its neighboring counties eventually became Washington's Fifth Congressional District.

Tom Foley's deep roots in Spokane surely contributed to his political success. The railroads, which had brought both sets of his grandparents to eastern Washington, supported one branch of the family directly and the other indirectly. Foley's father's family settled in Spokane, his mother's family in the wheat-growing region to the west. The city and its agricultural hinterland became the twin cornerstones of Foley's political foundation. As a student, lawyer, candidate, and member of Congress, he consistently reflected the values of the region in which he was raised: hard work, patience, and respect for other viewpoints.

Foley's education in Roman Catholic schools, Gonzaga University in Spokane, and the University of Washington in Seattle gave him the intellectual skills he needed to excel as a member of Congress. He had a knack for making friends who eventually would aid his political career, along with a gift for spotting and taking advantage of opportunities. The events in the summer of 1964 that took him from congressional aide to congressional candidate in little more than twenty-four hours—decisions that launched his thirty-year congressional career—illustrated Foley's personality, political instincts, and good fortune.

Tom Foley's interest in politics and public issues came from his father, Ralph Foley, Spokane County prosecutor and later a superior court judge. "I started going out on his election campaigns quite early in life, when I was a little boy," Foley said. "Also, through his associations and friends, I met people in politics and public life that I wouldn't have met."[2] Ralph Foley gave his wife, Helen, credit for their son's personality. "He has great principles, judgment, compassion and great ability," the elder Foley said in 1980, when Congressman Foley was advancing in congressional leadership. "He gets most of it from his mother."[3]

Foley attended a public elementary school, Hutton, before transferring to Sacred Heart, a Roman Catholic school.[4] There, he completed seventh and eighth grades before enrolling at Gonzaga Preparatory School, Spokane's Jesuit school for boys. He was a member of the debate team and earned the nickname "Senator," foreshadowing his congressional career. "We knew that he might be interested in public affairs because he was . . . a star debater in high school and in college," Ralph Foley recalled. Tom Foley also had a "keen sense of justice, even as a young boy," and he "read avidly and he had a remarkable memory—what he read, he could retain."[5]

As a high school debater, Foley was knowledgeable, articulate, and witty. Most student debaters relied on note cards, but Foley was comfortable speaking without notes—"not even a pencil," teammate David Robinson said.[6] To understand an opponent's motivation and evidence, the Gonzaga debaters practiced both sides of an argument, an approach Foley would put to effective use decades later in the House of Representatives.[7] "He was a legend," his former debate coach, Dan Lyons, said. "He was one of the best in the country. He never tired of debating."[8]

An incident during Foley's high school years in the mid-1940s also demonstrated his sensitivity to injustice, reflecting his nascent commitment to the transformational values of equality and diversity. On their way to Seattle, Tom and his parents stopped for a meal at a diner in central Washington. While his parents looked over the menu, Tom became agitated after noticing a sign that read, "We Don't Serve Negroes." "We've got to get out of here," he told his parents. "I won't eat in a place like that." Ralph Foley was proud of his son's insistence that the family not patronize the restaurant.[9] As an Irish Catholic, an ethnic group that once had been discriminated against in the United States, Ralph Foley was sensitive to prejudicial treatment of others, although according to Tom's sister, Maureen Latimer, "Dad had a moderate temperament—he didn't rant and rave about injustices done to the Irish."[10]

Like many of his high school classmates, Foley enrolled at Gonzaga University, where his father had attended law school. In his third year, his grades began to slip, and the dean called him in.[11] "We differed," Foley recalled, "and he observed that with my kind of attitude, maybe I shouldn't be there anyway. I said, 'I guess you're right about that.'"[12] Nonetheless,

Foley praised his Gonzaga teachers for stimulating his intellectual curiosity. "The pride of Jesuit teaching was to teach people to think, to analyze, to question," he later said.[13] Foley finished his undergraduate education at the University of Washington, across the state in Seattle. Maureen Latimer said the circumstances of her brother's decision to leave Gonzaga were never openly talked about at home. "There had been a falling-out of some sort, some disagreement with one of the priests over an administrative matter," she recalled. But also, "He'd gone to Gonzaga for prep school and college and wanted to go somewhere more liberal."[14]

Tom Foley found a different intellectual climate at the University of Washington. There, he studied history, earning a bachelor's degree in 1951.[15] After finishing his undergraduate degree, Foley was prepared to follow his father into law. But at the orientation for new law students, Foley was bothered by the dean's speech, which equated studying law with learning a trade. Longtime friend Scott Lukins said Foley's approach to the law was more philosophical, a posture that also appeared in his approach to politics.[16] Before the semester began, Foley switched to graduate studies in international relations, concentrating on the Soviet Union.

The early 1950s were turbulent times at the University of Washington. Foley, who liked to debate politics with friends, was involved in the Young Democrats. A state senator from Spokane wrote to Foley warning him against getting too closely aligned with liberal student groups, Lukins remembered.[17] For a time, Foley considered becoming a teacher, remembering a period of indecision in the mid-1950s about what to do next. "I was really trying to analyze whether I wanted to continue with that [graduate school] or go back to law school. For a couple of years there was a sort of a sense of uncertainty and drifting that I look back on as somewhat of a down period in my life."[18] He reapplied to law school in 1954, finishing in 1957. As a law student he worked at the King County Juvenile Court's detention facility, attending classes during the day and working evening or night shifts.[19]

After passing the bar exam, Foley went into law practice with his cousin Henry Higgins, opening small offices in Spokane and Wilbur, a small town sixty-five miles to the west. He also taught a constitutional law class at Gonzaga University. He joined the Spokane County prosecutor's office in 1958. Two years later, Washington attorney general John O'Connell appointed Foley to be an assistant attorney general in O'Connell's Spokane office.[20] Herb Legg of Olympia, a former Washington State Democratic chair, knew Foley from his work in the Attorney General's Office. He remembered Foley reading the *Catholic Worker*, a religious magazine with liberal political leanings founded in the 1930s by activists Dorothy Day and Henry Maurin. Legg said that Day's writings reinforced the social justice message that Foley had received a decade earlier at Gonzaga University.[21]

Then, in October 1961, Senator Henry Jackson offered him a job as counsel to the Senate Interior Committee. A year later, when Jackson became chair of the committee, he appointed Foley special counsel and assistant chief clerk. His duties included legislation relating to agriculture, public works, Indian affairs, and the Bureau of Reclamation, which oversaw irrigation projects in eastern Washington.[22]

In 1963, Foley asked Senator Jackson, who became an important political and personal mentor, for advice about running for the US House against incumbent Republican Walt Horan, then in his eleventh term. The senator dismissed Foley's prospects because the next election was only a year away. "Well, it's getting kind of late," Jackson scolded.[23] In March 1964, a six-paragraph article in the *Spokane Daily Chronicle* gave the first hint of Foley's political ambitions. Quoting unnamed Spokane friends of the family, it reported Foley's interest in running for Congress.[24]

Foley relished retelling the story of how he decided at the last minute to become a candidate—and how circumstances nearly prevented him from filing his nomination papers. On a visit to Spokane in the summer of 1964, Foley had lunch at the Spokane Club, the city's exclusive men's club. He told a Democratic businessman, Joseph Drumheller, that he probably would wait until 1966 to run for Congress. As Foley recalled the conversation, Drumheller then declared: "You're just like everyone else these days—you think the party's going to come with a silver tray and an engraved invitation and beg you to run for Congress, and that's not going to happen. You're either going to seize the opportunity and do it, or you're not."[25] After a testy exchange, Drumheller told Foley he would support him, even if he faced a primary challenger. Drumheller's encouragement, or perhaps his testiness, moved Foley to act. He left the table and sent a telegram to Senator Jackson's offices and home, declaring his intention to run.

That afternoon, Foley drove to Seattle, meeting friends and well-wishers at a popular political watering hole owned by the brother of the Democratic governor, Albert Rosellini. By one account, the celebration lasted until 3:00 a.m. The next day, the friend who was to drive Foley to Olympia overslept, and the two men left Seattle for Olympia, the state capital, about sixty miles away. Compounding the late departure, a tire on the car blew out, and the spare was flat. On the outskirts of Olympia, the car ran out of gas. Foley arrived at the election superintendent's office just twenty-five minutes before the filing deadline. "I've got to be a little bit lucky for all of those things to happen in the space of twenty-nine hours," Foley recalled years later. "Suddenly, I had decided to run, gone to Olympia, filed and found myself the nominee."[26]

Believing 1964 would be a good year for Democrats, Jackson recruited three candidates besides Foley to challenge Republicans for House seats in Washington State. While pressing for his own reelection, Jackson used every campaign appearance to boost the chances of Foley, Brock Adams of Seattle, Lloyd Meeds of Everett, and Floyd Hicks of Tacoma. Most of Jackson's television commercials in eastern Washington also endorsed Foley. The commercials were extremely helpful, Foley said, not only because of Jackson's popularity but also because they "gave me all kinds of television exposure I couldn't otherwise afford. And he [Jackson] had a big budget."[27] One campaign brochure capitalized on Foley's work for the Senate Interior Committee; it included pictures of Foley with Jackson, President Lyndon Johnson, and Senate majority leader Mike Mansfield of Montana. Other photos showed Foley in a suit standing in front of the US Capitol and in a windbreaker and jeans with a cattle rancher, reflecting the dual nature of his constituency. Foley so adroitly took advantage of his association with Jackson that after the election, his office received mail addressed to "Congressman Jackson Foley."[28]

As the campaign entered its last two weeks, a United Press International reporter observed: "In this year of the political mud bath a strange campaign is underway in Eastern Washington. . . . Two gentlemen are battling for the Fifth District congressional seat; the most insulting statement to date is Democrat Tom Foley's 'My opponent has a negative voting record.'"[29] Republican Walt Horan, the long-term incumbent, campaigned on his own record and rarely mentioned his challenger. Foley recalled that Horan "would go around saying that he had known my father and mother, and they were fine people, and that I was a fine young man. . . . It was not bitter in any way, and compared to today's campaigns, it is remarkable to look back upon."[30]

President Lyndon Johnson led the Democratic landslide over Republican Barry Goldwater; in Washington State, Johnson prevailed in thirty-five of the thirty-nine counties. His long coattails included Henry Jackson, reelected to the Senate by more than four hundred thousand votes, and Tom Foley, who defeated Horan by nearly eleven thousand votes. Three other Democrats recruited by Jackson also won House seats.[31] Foley returned to Washington, DC, with advantages that few new members of Congress shared: he knew his way around Capitol Hill, and he had two powerful mentors, Jackson and Senator Warren Magnuson. Together, the two senators (nicknamed "Scoop" and "Maggie") eased Foley's entry into Congress and also worked to assure his reelection in 1966 and subsequent years.

During Foley's second term, his staff noticed a frequent visitor in the congressman's Capitol Hill office, Heather Strachan, a law student at George Washington University. Strachan and Foley met in the early 1960s when both worked in Jackson's office. Foley, twelve years her senior, was the special counsel for the Senate Interior Committee, which Jackson chaired, and Strachan was a clerk, handling correspondence for Jackson. She later worked for the Democratic National Committee and for Representative John Dingell (D-MI).[32] Foley and Strachan dated for almost six years before announcing their engagement in August 1968. They were married on December 19, 1968, at St. Mary's Roman Catholic Church in Colombo, Ceylon (now Sri Lanka), where Strachan's father worked for the US Agency of International Development.[33]

Heather Foley received her law degree in June 1969 and passed the District of Columbia's bar exam. After Richard Larsen stepped down as Foley's administrative assistant to return to a newspaper job in Washington State, Heather Foley replaced him as an unpaid chief of staff. "I have no ambitions to be a politician," she said five years after their marriage. "I'd much rather stay in the background, although I've always intended to practice law someday."[34] Because of concerns of a possible conflict of interest, she never practiced law, instead tending to administrative details for which Tom Foley had no aptitude or interest. She also took a role in managing her husband's reelection campaigns, moving to Spokane for six to eight weeks during election years while he remained in Washington, DC.[35]

By the mid-1970s, Foley demonstrated the leadership style that would enable him to advance in the House leadership. One opportunity came in the Democratic Study Group (DSG), founded in the 1950s by a handful of moderate and liberal members. By 1970, it had grown to include nearly half of the House Democrats. It took on new visibility and importance after Representative Phillip Burton of California was elected chairman in February 1971. "Almost overnight, the DSG became an important center of House activities, the engine of reform and the instrument of Burton's power," Burton's biographer wrote.[36] Foley started attending DSG meetings soon after his election to the House in 1964, probably at the invitation of Representative Julia Butler Hansen of Washington's Third District. Perhaps out of concern that the DSG would be seen as too liberal in his home district,

Foley didn't trumpet his membership. Records of the DSG showed that in 1965, Representative Mo Udall (D-AZ) assured Foley his association with the group need not be made public. In a letter thanking him for a check for his membership dues, Udall said, "As I told you this morning, the DSG officers are keenly aware of the nature of your district and the special problems that you face. There are no DSG membership lists, but we are happy to provide you with the benefit of research and assistance of our group."[37]

Herb Legg, the former state party chair, spent the summer of 1972 working for Hansen at the DSG. He attended some of the leadership's late-afternoon meetings. "The thing I noticed about Tom is that when he said something, everybody listened," Legg said. "Tom had a capacity then—which some of us who were more liberal than Tom would tend to scorn—to stay in the middle of the people he was working with. . . . Foley and the other reformers were already talking about how they would reorganize the House once they took over."[38]

In January 1974, the DSG elected Foley as chair, succeeding Burton. At the time, the group claimed 170 members, more than two-thirds of the Democrats in the House. Under Foley's leadership, the group adopted a strategy of incremental reform that Foley later called "the salami approach"—one slice at a time. In the wake of Richard Nixon's resignation, the election of seventy-five new Democrats in November 1974 gave the reformers the clout they needed to act. "It was not so much because of that class, but that class provided enough votes for the reform agenda," Foley said. As a result, "we achieved all at once what it would take several Congresses to achieve."[39] Tim Wirth of Colorado, elected to the House in that election and later a US senator, said the freshmen provided the "shock troops" to challenge the authority of entrenched committee chairmen.[40] John Lawrence, who went to Washington in 1974 as chief of staff to newly elected Representative George Miller of California, called Foley a catalyst for the procedural changes that the incoming class helped bring about. In an interview, Lawrence described Foley as "a different cut than the old southern Democrats. He was perceived as scholarly and thoughtful. It didn't hurt that he was attuned to younger members, the reformers, who were comfortable with him."[41]

As a result of DSG-sponsored reforms, the senior member of the majority party on each committee no longer was automatically in line to become chair. Instead, all committee chairs were subject to a secret vote of the Democratic (majority) Caucus. Although this seemed contrary to the reformers' goal of opening up the process, Foley said the secret ballot was essential because an open ballot would put junior members at risk of retribution.[42] A no-confidence vote would prompt an election by the caucus in which the deposed chair could run again.

The same month Foley became DSG chair, a report by the nonpartisan citizens group Common Cause gave ammunition to the reformers. The report assessed House committee chairs in three areas: fairness; use of power; and compliance with House, caucus, and committee rules. The report was especially critical of Edward Hebert, chair of the Armed Services Committee, who (in the report's words) "flagrantly violates all three areas" examined by Common Cause.[43] The group also found "a pattern of serious abuse" in the leadership of three other chairs: George Mahon (Texas) of Appropriations, Wayne Hayes (Ohio) of Administration, and William R. "Bob" Poage (Texas) of Agriculture. The liberal group Americans for Democratic Action gave Poage, first elected to the House in 1936, six points out of a possible one hundred.[44] Liberals criticized his willingness to provide federal subsidies to sugar and cotton growers while opposing measures to expand food stamps and food distribution programs.[45]

Foley, by then vice-chair of the Agriculture Committee, had a cordial relationship with Poage, as was the case throughout his career in similar circumstances. Foley quietly lobbied colleagues in support of Poage's bid to retain the chair position. Representative Mike McCormack, a Democrat who represented Washington's neighboring Fourth District, reported that Foley gave a spirited defense of Poage. "He stood on the floor [at the caucus meeting] and asked them not to" oust the chair, McCormack recalled.[46] In Foley's judgment, Poage "wasn't guilty of the worst abuses that some committee chairmen were."[47] Representative Bob Bergland (D-MN), a friend of both Poage and Foley, believed the push to strip Poage of the chair position came from outside of the Agriculture Committee. "To newcomers, he was a symbol of the seniority system," said Bergland, who later became secretary of agriculture under President Jimmy Carter.[48]

The Democratic Steering and Policy Committee, a leadership group appointed by the Speaker, voted 14 to 10 on January 15 to retain Poage as chair.[49] But when the caucus took up the appointment the next day, it rejected Poage by a vote of 146 to 141.[50] The Steering Committee then turned to Foley. Poage could have run again, but he decided not to challenge Foley. The following week, the caucus ratified Foley's nomination by a vote of 257 to 9. Presaging his rise to the speakership, Foley became the first House member from Washington State to chair a major committee and the first chair of the Agriculture Committee from outside the South in ninety-five years.

Poage subsequently replaced Foley as vice-chair of the committee and quietly served in that position for his last four years in the House. In a letter written just before he left office in 1978, Poage thanked Foley for his fairness and courtesy. "I will always be proud to tell my friends that the committee is in good hands," he wrote. "I fully recognize that my position on the committee for the last four years has often been a source of embarrassment to you, although you have never given any indication to that effect."[51]

In retrospect, Foley called his work to reform House procedures one of his major accomplishments, clearly an outcome based on his transformational values. In Foley's own words: "The reforms . . . made the institution more open to participation by members and gave it a more 'small-d' democratic cast and prevented the domination of the institution by senior members."[52] By reducing the power of committee chairs, the reforms also strengthened the Speaker's position—a change that worked to Foley's advantage fourteen years later when he became Speaker. By focusing on process as well as substance, Foley aligned himself with what political analyst William Schneider later called the "problem solvers" rather than the "advocates" within the Democratic Party.[53] At this point in his career, Foley clearly was more comfortable in that faction, which gave priority to institutional reforms rather than to policy initiatives. His goal was to transform the House and the role of its members in institutional governance.

CHAPTER 3

A BIPARTISAN SPEAKER

Reflecting a consistent set of personal and political values, Tom Foley built a remarkable career in Congress. In his first term, he was part of the huge Democratic majorities in Congress that passed President Lyndon Johnson's Great Society package of anti-poverty programs into law. Foley's first national platform was the House Agriculture Committee, where he was able to shape legislation to benefit farmers in his district. As a member and, after 1974, chair of the committee, he worked tirelessly on behalf of his constituents, a strategy that succeeded as long as his district's economy relied on farming, ranching, logging, and mining.

The 1980 election thrust Foley into the top ranks of congressional leaders and put him on track to become Speaker in less than a decade. He became more visible at the national level, frequently articulating the Democratic position in response to presidential speeches. As he rose in the House leadership, Foley no doubt benefited from being in the right place at the right time. But that was far from the only thing that worked in his favor. To move up, "you have to have smarts, timing and luck," observed former representative Pat Williams (D-MT), and Foley "had a measure of all three."[1] Yet Foley did not simply wait for good fortune to strike; instead, he positioned himself for the House leadership by developing expertise on issues that went beyond the Agriculture Committee, particularly on defense and foreign policy. Moreover, as chair of the House Democratic Caucus from 1977 to 1981, he established a reputation for fairness and a willingness to listen to other members' concerns, traits that earned the respect and allegiance of his colleagues.

To some, Foley gave the appearance of climbing effortlessly to the top of the House. Indeed, when he finally reached the most visible leadership position in the legislative branch in 1989, a news magazine mistakenly described him as "The Accidental Speaker."[2] Another article called him "the Accidental Tourist of American Politics."[3] In fact, Foley carefully anticipated and quietly seized opportunities to move up the leadership ladder. People who thought he lacked ambition did not understand the way he worked. That myth developed because Foley was reluctant to call attention to himself or to his accomplishments, said Werner Brandt, his longtime executive assistant.[4] Reinforcing this image, a biographer of Representative Jim Wright (D-TX), who preceded Foley as Speaker, said of Foley, "There was no obvious press of ambition and yet he was ambitious, no driving passion and yet he had arrived."[5]

But to get there, he had to overcome the fallout of the 1980 election, which was a disaster for the Democrats. Not only did Ronald Reagan swamp incumbent President Jimmy Carter—carrying all but five states and the District of Columbia—but the Republicans also took control of the Senate for the first time since 1954.[6] The Democrats lost thirty-three seats in the House but still held a 243–192 majority. The members' party affiliation, though, did not fully explain the political challenges for the leadership. Southern Democrats, many of them conservative, held the balance of power, and those from districts where Reagan had run strongly tended to support his agenda, at least in the first two years of the new president's term.[7] Foley himself had a close call; Republican challenger John Sonneland held him to less than 52 percent of the vote in the Fifth District.

The 1980 election results also reshuffled the House Democratic leadership. Indiana's John Brademas, the Democratic whip, fell victim to a well-financed independent campaign by the National Conservative Political Action Committee (NCPAC), an organization founded by young conservative political activists to defeat liberal members of Congress.[8] Brademas's logical successor as whip was Representative Dan Rostenkowski of Illinois. However, Rostenkowsi, the chief deputy whip, was also the second-ranking Democrat on the Ways and Means Committee. When Oregon voters ousted Representative Al Ullman, the Ways and Means Committee chair's position was unexpectedly vacant. For a time, Rostenkowski hoped to hold both jobs. Speaker Tip O'Neill of Massachusetts and majority leader Jim Wright of Texas vetoed the idea. "Both of us thought that was absolutely wrong," Wright recalled. "Either job was a full-time job. It would have been altogether bad to allow one individual to handle both jobs and do justice to either, and probably wield more power than any one individual should."⁹ They told Rostenkowski to choose one or the other; he chose Ways and Means. "Tip wanted me to be the [Ways and Means] chairman," Rostenkowski later said. "It had a higher public profile. No one knew who the whip was." Rostenkowski also feared that because of the relatively young age (fifty-five) of Jim Wright, O'Neill's likely successor, it might be a decade or more before the Speaker's job opened again," closing off that destination for Rostenkowski.¹⁰

Another factor in Speaker O'Neill's decision may have been his dislike for Representative Sam Gibbons of Florida, who ranked behind Rostenkowski on Ways and Means. Gibbons had challenged O'Neill for majority leader in 1972, which obviously did not endear him to the Massachusetts congressman. Other Democrats also encouraged Rostenkowski to chair the Ways and Means Committee, arguing that the party needed a strong advocate to resist Reagan's tax-cutting agenda.¹¹ "From the standpoint of wielding influence in the legislative process, it [choosing Ways and Means] may have been a wise choice—if you weren't interested in becoming Speaker someday," Wright said.¹²

Rostenkowski's decision to take the Ways and Means chair position left Foley as the leading contender for the whip's job. As whip, Foley was responsible for assessing House members' positions on issues and rounding up support for legislation backed by the leadership. Foley was then finishing his second two-year term as chair of the Democratic Caucus, and under caucus rules, he could not run again. In Foley, O'Neill saw "a bright guy who had the capacity to make a lot of friends, persuade people and win votes," said Foley aide and confidant Werner Brandt. Surviving the Reagan landslide of 1980, in which Republicans gained thirty-five seats in the House, made Foley a stronger candidate for leadership, Brandt believed. "He told others who won by narrow margins, 'I know what it feels like.'" Foley often demonstrated sensitivity to the needs of members from marginally Democratic districts like his own by allowing them to vote against the leadership's position on legislation if their vote was not essential to a bill's final passage.¹³

Once Rostenkowski chose Ways and Means, Foley was the only serious contender for whip. "Tip and I had absolutely no problem in agreeing on the appointment of Tom Foley," Wright recalled. "Almost everyone [in the caucus] had been impressed with his skill, his judicious temperament, his manner, his nonabrasive but sometimes persuasive advocacy on issues. He was an easy choice. I don't think anyone really complained about that, except maybe one or two other guys who would have liked to have been whip."[14]

O'Neill and Wright announced Foley's appointment as whip December 8, 1980, in Washington, DC, where the new Congress was holding organizing sessions. "I am very honored that the majority leader and the speaker have decided to give me this responsibility," Foley said. Anticipating possible negative feedback from constituents who might see Foley's new job as a loss of attention to them, he added, "I think it will enhance my ability to represent the people of the Fifth District in general and enhance my ability to represent farmers."[15] Foley intended the reference to farmers to allay concerns about his potential loss of influence on agricultural issues; by accepting the whip's job, he agreed to step down as chair of the Agriculture Committee. But he was allowed to resume his position as chair of the Livestock and Grains Subcommittee, which he had held before taking the helm of the full committee in 1974, a strategic move to maintain a transactional connection to the wheat growers in his home district.

O'Neill and Wright found Foley to be an informed and articulate voice for the Democrats' positions. In August 1982, they asked him to give a nationally televised speech in support of a tax increase that President Reagan had requested. After Reagan attacked them during the 1980 campaign as the tax-and-spend party, rank-and-file Democrats were in no mood to support a three-year, $98 billion tax package made necessary by what they saw as the failure of Reagan's economic policies.[16] As further evidence of the personal and political values underpinning his leadership style, Foley appealed to the American people, and, indirectly, to his colleagues, to be fiscally responsible, confront the deficits, and protect programs that otherwise would be cut. "I support the revenue bill because it is fair and because it brings some long-overdue moderation to the administration's economic program," Foley said.[17]

The Foley speech helped convince as many as fifty uneasy House Democrats to support the bill, which on August 19 passed the House by a 226–207 vote.[18] "Tom was terrific; he did a super job," said Representative Bill Alexander (D-AR), the chief deputy whip. Foley's Washington State colleague Al Swift agreed: "It's worth about sixty or seventy votes on an issue like this to have a guy as respected as Tom Foley on your side."[19] At the next leadership meeting after the tax bill passed, O'Neill proclaimed, "A star is born."[20] The speech also played well in Foley's home district. Luke Williams, a prominent Spokane Republican, said people asked him, "Boy, did you see Foley supporting the president?" Williams, who had been involved in several attempts to recruit challengers to Foley, acknowledged the congressman's popularity. "Tom is [a] very well-liked person in this town. It's kind of like everyone liking Reagan, but not his policies," Williams observed. Perhaps presaging the politics of a decade later, he suggested that "Foley's voting hasn't necessarily represented the feelings of the people. But they've been tolerant of him."[21]

Foley undoubtedly faced dissonance between his leadership values in the congressional setting and the perceived transactional obligations inherent in representation of his congressional district. His newfound national prominence opened him to criticism from opponents who attacked him for spending too much time in Washington, DC, and for neglecting his district's interests. Looking back on that period, Foley said he was frustrated when his Republican opponents in eastern Washington accused him of being less helpful to the needs of the Fifth District after he became whip. "The ability to do things for the district is enhanced and amplified by being in leadership; there's no question," he insisted.[22] In the next decade, though, Foley sometimes failed to demonstrate to his constituents how he used his influence to help their interests, possibly contributing to his eventual defeat in 1994.

Nationally, Democrats gained twenty-six House seats in the 1982 elections, including thirteen that had been lost two years earlier. The result gave the Democratic leadership a working majority, enabling O'Neill, Foley, and Wright to overcome the alliance of Republicans and southern Democrats that had supported Reagan's initiatives. "I had gambled that the meanness of America in the first two years of Reagan's administration was a fad that wouldn't stick and that you couldn't hurt people long without there being a reaction," Tip O'Neill reflected later.[23]

In early 1984, O'Neill told a reporter he intended to retire from Congress at the end of the year if voters elected a Democratic president. Otherwise, he would stay until the end of 1986.[24] O'Neill had not intended to make a public announcement that early, but a remark he thought to be off the record showed up in print.[25] By giving so much advance notice of his retirement, O'Neill allowed Wright sufficient time to line up supporters for his own speakership bid. Similarly, Foley was able to win commitments from enough colleagues over the next two years that he went unchallenged for majority leader.

Eight years earlier, in 1976, Jim Wright had won a heated four-way race for majority leader by defeating California's Phil Burton by a single vote.[26] Foley might have faced similar competition for majority leader, but again, timing, good fortune, and good strategy were on his side. Richard Gephardt, the caucus chair, planned to seek the Democratic nomination for president in 1988. Tony Coelho, the energetic chair of the Democratic Congressional Campaign Committee, was too young to leapfrog over Foley. Powerful committee chairs, such as Rostenkowski at Ways and Means and John Dingell at Energy and Commerce, showed no interest in being majority leader—"speaker, yes, majority leader, no," as Wright biographer John Barry put it, apparently ignoring the importance of the majority leader position as a stepping stone to the Speaker's office.[27] "Rosty wanted to be speaker, then and earlier," said Rostenkowski biographer Richard E. Cohen. "But he was satisfied as Ways and Means chair and never seriously undertook a campaign for the top spot."[28]

Foley's amiable personality, intelligence, and fairness in dealing with colleagues partly explained the absence of opposition. Another reason was his decision to more than double the number of deputy whips, from thirty-six to eighty-three. Thus, intentionally or not, Foley had co-opted some potential challengers by making them part of his leadership team.[29] In early 1985, to forestall any potential opposition, Wright began by asking House Democrats to support Foley for Speaker in 1986. He announced in February that he had commitments from 184 Democrats, a comfortable majority of the caucus. Foley had no potential challengers for majority leader, either, but he knew his elevation to the number two spot was not automatic. He contacted all House Democrats to express his interest in succeeding Wright. He called on members in their offices, asking their opinions on issues facing Congress and the nation.[30] "Given that Foley had thoroughly canvassed the caucus, my sense is that it would have been difficult—if not impossible—for someone lower down the power grid to challenge him," Cohen observed. By fall, Foley had spoken with about half of his colleagues, describing their responses as "very, very favorable and encouraging."[31]

Among those not committed to Foley was Representative Henry Waxman (D-CA), who believed Foley might not be sufficiently aggressive to be majority leader: "I want to look at the whole leadership team and evaluate where we are going in the House on issues I consider important before I decide whether to support him."[32] The concerns behind Waxman's comment would surface later from a faction of the House Democratic Caucus during Foley's speakership as well, especially after the contentious Newt Gingrich (R-GA) rose in visibility as the House Republican whip.

While much of Foley's approach to leadership focused on the values of fairness in the legislative process and organization of the House, Foley also used his leadership position to benefit the interests of his district and state. Thus, when a bill to create a national scenic area in the Columbia River Gorge hit a legislative roadblock in October 1986, Foley worked behind the scenes to overcome it. Representative Don Bonker (D-WA), whose district included most of the north side of the gorge, called Foley to advise him of the problem. Foley then spoke to House Rules Committee chair Claude Pepper of Florida, who called his committee together after midnight to send the bill to the floor. It passed the House the next day. "We would never have gotten the bill without Tom Foley," said Bowen Blair, a leading backer of the scenic area. Asked later about his influence, Foley explained, "That's an example of the kind of thing I can do for the region that would be difficult for me to do as a back-bencher." But Foley acknowledged the limits of his power: "Can you make bricks without straw because you are a majority leader? No. This is a collegial body."[33]

In the fall of 1986, a glowing profile of Foley in the *Seattle Post-Intelligencer* suggested that his move to majority leader was all but certain. In comparison to the feisty and partisan Jim Wright, "Foley, the incoming majority leader, is cerebral and generous toward 'worthy foes,' attributes associated with the lofty speaker's office," the paper's longtime political reporter Joel Connelly wrote.[34] When the Democratic Caucus met on December 8, 1986, Wright was the unanimous choice of Democrats to succeed O'Neill as Speaker. In his acceptance speech, Wright drew a contrast between his own style and Foley's: "I am sometimes impatient; I want things done yesterday. But I know to listen to Tom Foley when he plays the devil's advocate because I know I will learn something." Richard Gephardt of Missouri, reelected chair of the caucus, nominated Foley for majority leader. Four House members seconded Foley's nomination, praising his public speaking, his parliamentary skills, and "his ability to craft a unified party position," according to a press release from Foley's office. He won the unanimous endorsement of the caucus.[35] In the only contested leadership race, Tony Coelho of California comfortably defeated Charles Rangel of New York for whip.

In 1987–1989, the trio of Wright, Foley, and Coelho led the House Democrats. "I thought it was a pretty good combination," Wright recalled a decade later. "Each of us brought to the table some distinctive traits and skills, and we probably complemented each other." Foley was especially helpful in mediating jurisdictional disputes between House committee chairs. "If it was a major leadership initiative, I would ask Tom to sit in on the conference," Wright said. "There was a general division of labor, but a willingness to play any position on the team on the part of all three of us."[36]

Foley also won praise from his Democratic colleagues for his attention to detail and the long-term consequences of legislation, rather than only to the short-term transactional benefits that might obtain. "It is essential for good public policy to have a Foley," said Representative Leon Panetta (D-CA), later White House chief of staff for President Bill Clinton. "The House needs someone who says, 'Wait a minute.' There's a natural inclination of leadership to try and slam dunk issues. . . . If you always let your gut instincts control the issues and the institution it would not take much to walk off a cliff."[37]

After the Democrats regained control of the Senate in 1986, they challenged the Reagan administration on domestic issues as well as foreign policy, stalling White House initiatives and offering legislation of their own. Some observers compared their legislative productivity to that of Congress in 1965–1966, Foley's first two years in the House. As commentator Fred Barnes wrote in the *New Republic*, "My bet is that liberals will one day look back at 1987 and 1988 as a golden age (a brief one, I admit)." While Tip O'Neill was Speaker, Reagan had succeeded in cutting taxes, boosting military spending, and slowing the growth of domestic programs. In contrast, Barnes wrote, "On Wright's [watch], Reagan got nothing but liberal bills he didn't like (spending for the homeless, plant closing legislation, the Civil Rights Restoration Act, arms control amendments, etc.)."[38] Among the other major accomplishments of 1988 were bills dealing with trade, welfare reform, and catastrophic health insurance (repealed in 1989 after a massive lobbying campaign by senior citizen groups).

A month after the 1988 election, the House Democratic Caucus unanimously reelected Foley as majority leader. In a nominating speech, Indiana representative Lee Hamilton (like Foley, first elected in 1964) praised him as a conciliator who worked well with all factions of the House. Tom Foley "leads not with raw power but with his wit and with his power of persuasion," Hamilton said. In response, Foley thanked the voters of the Fifth District and challenged his colleagues to work with President-Elect George H. W. Bush to reduce the size of the federal budget deficit.[39]

In the spring of 1989, days before he became Speaker, a lengthy and flattering profile of Foley appeared in the *New Yorker*. Montana representative Pat Williams used a nautical metaphor to describe the roles of the three House leaders: "Jim is the captain, Tony the oar drummer, and Tom the navigator. Democrats in the House and most of the Republicans have great respect for the navigator."[40] By the time the profile was published in April, Jim Wright's days as captain were numbered. Under the decks, a mutiny was afoot, and its agitator was the calculating and ambitious House Republican whip, Newt Gingrich.

Wright paid a price for his sweeping legislative agenda. When he met with Central American presidents and diplomats, Republicans asserted that he (Wright) was usurping the prerogatives of the secretary of state. When he used House rules to the Democrats' advantage, they accused him of disregarding the rights of the minority party. One particular incident galled the Republicans. In October 1987, Wright invoked an obscure parliamentary procedure to hold open a roll call to allow Democrats to round up enough votes to pass a budget reconciliation bill. To get around a requirement that two-thirds of the House must consent to reconsideration of the same bill, Wright asked the House to adjourn and then reconvene on a new legislative day.[41]

Years later, former representative Richard "Dick" Cheney (R-WY), chair of the Republican Conference in 1987, still seethed about the maneuver.[42] "It was really outrageous behavior, a gross bending of the rules," Cheney said. Although O'Neill and Foley were Democrats, they treated everyone in the House with respect, regardless of party. "You'd gone out there and earned the right to represent your constituents just like anybody else," Cheney believed. After Wright became Speaker in 1987, however, "a feeling developed on the part of the minority, that if you were a Republican, you were dirt. Your views didn't matter."[43]

Meanwhile, Newt Gingrich, elected to the House in 1978 from a suburban Atlanta district, began to attract attention for his criticism of Wright. In the early 1980s Gingrich began using to Republicans' advantage a section of the House agenda known as special orders. Under House rules, once the House finished its business, any member could speak on any topic for up to one hour. Even though the House chamber was usually empty, television cameras would carry the member's words and picture across the country on C-SPAN, the Cable-Satellite Public Affairs Network. "What really infuriated me about those guys," O'Neill later complained, "is that they had no real interest in legislation. As far as they were concerned, the House was no more than a pulpit, a sound stage from which to reach the people at home. If the TV cameras were facing the city dump, that's where they would be speaking."[44]

O'Neill became particularly incensed when Gingrich used this forum to criticize O'Neill's Massachusetts colleague Representative Edward Boland for voting against military aid to the Contras, the US-backed military groups seeking to overthrow the left-leaning Sandinista government in Nicaragua. O'Neill viewed Gingrich's remarks as an attack on Boland's patriotism and went to the floor of the House a few days later to chastise Gingrich. "You deliberately stood in that well before an empty House and challenged these people when you knew they would not be there," he scolded. "It is the lowest thing that I have ever seen in my thirty-two years in Congress."[45]

Gingrich stepped up his criticism of the Democratic leadership after Wright became Speaker in 1987. Political historian Julian Zelizer's account of Gingrich's rise to power suggests that Wright didn't recognize the threat posed by Gingrich's aggressive style. "Though the Speaker and his closest associates continued to think of Gingrich as a historical outlier, conservatives were becoming more antiestablishment in their outlook about Washington," Zelizer wrote. "The Republicans were determined to tear down the political status quo by whatever means necessary."[46] Wright was Gingrich's obvious target, owing largely to his attempt to use sales of a book to get around House limits on outside income. In May 1988, Gingrich filed the first of a series of complaints about Wright with the House Ethics Committee. Later, Common Cause, the nonpartisan watchdog group, raised other questions about Wright's actions. On June 9, 1988, the House Ethics Committee opened a formal inquiry. Ten months later, the twelve-member committee (composed of equal numbers of Democrats and Republicans) formally accused Wright of sixty-nine violations of House rules over the previous ten years. The committee said that a Texas developer's hiring of Wright's wife for an $18,000-a-year job constituted an improper gift to Wright. In addition, Wright had arranged for the publisher of his political memoir, *Reflections of a Public Man*, to sell bulk copies to lobbyists. That deal, too, represented a violation of House rules, the committee's report said. Wright's lawyers unsuccessfully attempted to have the key charges against him dismissed.[47] Wright's troubles were deeper than book sales and a salary for his wife. Political analyst Norman Ornstein assessed the Speaker's predicament this way:

> Wright effectively used House rules and his own partisan majority
> to set and pursue an aggressive legislative agenda, often ignoring
> and sometimes exploiting the outrage voiced by House minority

Republicans. While legislation passed, one side effect of Wright's strong and assertive leadership was sharply heightened partisan conflict, exacerbated by frayed tempers and personal clashes. Partisan tension in the House was a major factor in Wright's eventual resignation.[48]

On the other side of Capitol Hill, a partisan fight over confirmation of a cabinet nominee indirectly heightened House Republicans' resolve to press the ethics charges against Wright. In March 1989, the Senate, on a near-party-line vote, rejected President Bush's nomination of former Texas senator John Tower to be secretary of defense.[49] Democratic senators argued that Tower's history of alcohol abuse and his close relationship with military contractors disqualified him from leading the Department of Defense. After the Senate refused to confirm Tower's appointment, Bush nominated Representative Dick Cheney for the Pentagon job. Cheney, who had been White House chief of staff fifteen years earlier for President Gerald Ford, easily won Senate confirmation.

Cheney's departure for the Pentagon left a power vacuum among House Republicans that Gingrich filled, narrowly defeating Representative Edward Madigan (R-IL), a traditional conservative, for whip in March 1989 after a contentious campaign.[50] Gingrich soon began to upstage his nominal superior, Robert Michel of Illinois, the minority leader, with whom Foley had a positive, amicable relationship. On a visit to Boston soon after his election as whip, Gingrich presciently predicted the House would expel Wright (or that he would resign as Speaker) by June. Gingrich also took a swipe at Foley, saying the majority leader would have to choose between reforming the House or defending it. "Foley has to decide," he told a reporter. "Either way the Republican Party is going to be a winner and the current Democratic machine is a loser."[51]

Foley chose to defend the House, even while trying to bring greater civility and comity to it, a decision that shaped his time as Speaker. Foley's approach also may have contributed to Gingrich becoming Speaker six years later. Indeed, as the Wright scandal deepened, Foley found himself in an increasingly awkward position. He and Tony Coelho, the Democratic whip, dutifully appeared with Wright at a press conference during which hostile reporters questioned the Speaker about his ethics. "Right now, they are going through a tribal loyalty dance," said Representative Vin Weber (R-MN), mocking the Democratic leaders.[52]

When "Foley for Speaker" buttons appeared in March 1989, Foley and his staff quickly disassociated themselves from what presumably was a Republican prank. Although he stood to advance as a result of Wright's misfortune, Foley's loyalty to the man who had supported his appointment as whip eight years earlier did not waver. Whatever his private thoughts about Wright's conduct, Foley's public statements remained supportive. He told reporters in early April that he expected Wright, several years his senior, to be Speaker "for a long time." And, he warned Gingrich, "If the House breaks out into partisanship—it's pikes, guns and grenades on the House floor—it will only hurt President Bush."[53]

Foley's efforts to dispel speculation about his becoming Speaker were fruitless. Newspaper and magazine articles reviewing Foley's career were full of compliments from colleagues and constituents. This description from Representative Barney Frank (D-MA) was typical: "He's very, very smart; he has enormously good judgment; he combines very good political skills with first-rate intellectual skills. Also, he's a nice guy." Other House members praised Foley's accessibility, congeniality, and knowledge of the legislative process and his good relations with Republicans and the press.[54]

To his dismay, Foley learned that Tony Coelho planned to resign his congressional seat on June 15. Coelho, the "oar drummer" of the Democratic leadership team (as described in the New Yorker profile of Foley), had been the subject of a Justice Department investigation into whether he improperly profited from a 1986 "junk bond" transaction.[55] The turn of events disappointed Foley. "It's a loss of a friend and colleague in the Congress," he said.[56] Coelho's departure left Foley as the only member of the Democratic leadership trio untainted by scandal. It also removed a potential rival to Foley for Speaker when some Democrats wanted a more aggressive approach to dealing with Republican president George H. W. Bush.

Returning to Washington, DC, after a holiday, Foley learned that Wright had decided to resign rather than continue to fight the ethics charges. Looking back eight years later, Wright praised Foley's loyalty: "He was supportive in reality, not just in words. When I decided that I wanted to retire, the only person I talked with before going out on the floor was Tom. His instinctive reaction was 'Don't do it, Mr. Speaker, don't do it.' He tried to dissuade me from it. There never was any question as to his loyalty."[57]

On Wednesday, May 31, Wright addressed the House of Representatives for the last time as Speaker. In an hour-long speech, Wright lamented the spirit of "mindless cannibalism" that had invaded the House, a comment that drew applause from his colleagues. He acknowledged making mistakes but said he could have cleared his name, given enough time and money to mount a defense. He said he was resigning because reporters insisted on asking him about "petty personal finances" rather than problems facing the nation. "Have I made mistakes? Oh, boy. How many!" he acknowledged. And he apologized to the Republicans for the way he had run the House. "If I have offended anybody in the other party, I am sorry. I never meant to."[58] Wright's troubles also stemmed from the fact that he was unpopular among some of his fellow Democrats. His hard-edged style rubbed many of them the wrong way, especially given the affability of O'Neill and Foley.

As Wright stood in the well of the House, Foley sat behind him in the large leather chair of the presiding officer. A reporter wrote of Foley: "He looked stoic, somber in a gray suit and ready to applaud, as he has all these months, the explanations and defense of his embattled colleague." Concluding his lamentation, Wright said he would step down as Speaker as soon as a successor could be elected and would resign from the House by the end of June. "Let me give you back this job you gave to me as a propitiation for all of this season of bad will that has grown up among us," he told his House colleagues. "Let that be a total payment for the anger and hostility we feel toward each other."[59] Afterward, Foley declined requests for interviews and released a brief statement: "For 40 years in public service, Jim Wright has been a symbol of constancy, courage and commitment to principle. . . . History will remember him as a great member and a great speaker."[60] That same week, Foley distanced himself from the combative rhetoric of Wright and Gingrich. He told a *New York Times* reporter: "I'm proud to be a Democrat. But I don't particularly like to bash Republicans." In Foley's view, "the best partisanship is to try to persuade the unpersuaded of your point of view, to attract voters to the party, to attract support to the party and its principles and policies and not just to have a donnybrook of trashing Republicans."[61]

On Tuesday, June 6, the Democratic Caucus met in the House chamber. Wright nominated Foley for Speaker; Tony Coehlo and Lee Hamilton were among the House members who made seconding speeches. No one else was nominated, and the Democrats chose Foley by acclamation to be their candidate. He was not yet Speaker—that honor would come later in the day when Republicans would join Democrats in the House chamber. After a brief tribute to Wright, Foley told his colleagues why he had chosen a career of public service. When the House formally convened, Thomas Stephen Foley was nominated to be the forty-ninth Speaker of the House of Representatives. All 251 Democrats on the floor voted for Foley; follow-ing tradition, the 164 Republicans voted for minority leader Robert Michel. Foley and Michel each voted "present."[62]

Foley's opening remarks as Speaker were conciliatory; he wanted to transform the tone of the House. "We need to debate and decide with rea-son and without rancor," he said.[63] Turning to the Republican side of the chamber, Foley extended an olive branch. Again, calling on his transfor-mational values, Foley said, "After 24 years in the House, there should be no doubt that I am proud to be a Democrat." He continued, "I am deeply conscious, however, of the obligation I bear as speaker of the House. I am speaker of the whole House, not of one party, but to each and every member of the House, undivided by the center aisle, I pledge to protect the rights and privileges of all members."[64] In the months that followed, Foley won respect from many Republicans for his commitment to that principle. He continued the cordial relationship with Michel he had enjoyed as major-ity leader, which Michel reciprocated. Assessing Michel's time as minority leader, Douglas Harris and Matthew Green noted that Michel and Gingrich disagreed over strategy and tactics. "Gingrich did try to stay in Michel's good graces, and Michel saw some utility in allowing Gingrich to pursue partisan messaging and aggressive tactics in the name of a shared goal: getting the Republicans into the majority," Harris and Green wrote.[65]

On his first full day as Speaker, Foley acknowledged the validity of some Republican complaints about Wright's speakership. In a meeting with re-porters, he recalled Wright's decision of the previous September to hold open the roll call on the budget bill long enough for Democrats to round up enough votes to win. "I think we went too far on that day," he said. Referring to the Democratic Party's control of the House, which had been continuous since 1954, Foley said, "Thirty-five years of uninterrupted power can act like a corrosive acid upon the restraints of civility and comity." Foley promised to respect the rights of Republicans and to concentrate on governing—not seeking political advantage.[66]

Foley's election as Speaker was the beginning of a brief era of tran-quility and legislative productivity in the House; his fairness, knowledge of issues, and belief in bipartisanship ideally qualified him to lead the Demo-cratic-controlled Congress during the administration of a Republican pres-ident. For most of the next two years, Foley enjoyed the confidence of fellow Democrats, the respect of President George H. W. Bush and Republicans in Congress, and the appreciation of his constituents. Foley's constituents in eastern Washington recognized his visibility and power. They received him warmly during his visits to the district and reelected him by a comfortable margin in 1990.

Perhaps as a reflection of his proclivity to work more quietly with members, Speaker Foley made fewer than the average number of floor statements of any other Speaker from 1940 to 2006. On average, Foley spoke from the floor 6.4 times per Congress, compared, for example, with John McCormack's average of 27.3, Carl Albert's 20.3, and Newt Gingrich's 21.0. Political scientist Matthew Green quoted a Foley staffer as saying Foley was "more likely to address the floor if people felt that the vote was close or the people with us were a little shaky." Green added, "Even if speakers do not, in their spoken words, explicitly connect a particular result with future benefits, they may commit other passive or active leadership activities in conjunction with floor statements that do draw such a connection."[67]

Foley's first three years as Speaker of the House, although not free of difficulties, confirmed his place as one of the nation's most influential elected officials. By most accounts, he led the House with style, grace, and a commitment to make government work. But it was during this period that the values and patterns expressed in his statesmanlike approach may have begun to seem out of keeping with the hardball politics of the 1990s. Increasingly, Foley found it difficult to balance his conciliatory nature with the demands of his Democratic colleagues to confront the president.

After the partisan sniping that marked the last six months of Jim Wright's speakership, Foley saw his first task as restoring civility and fairness to what he described as a "very divided and surly House of Representatives."[68] To do so, he had to assure Republican members that their voices—and votes—counted. "My overwhelming desire is to return the House to an atmosphere of collegiality, comity and respect," Foley said shortly after becoming Speaker.[69] Wright, who remained in the House for several months after resigning as Speaker, had nothing but compliments for his successor. "Thoughtful, friendly, patient, conciliatory, and a fine lawyer, Foley was uniquely well-suited to the effort," Wright later wrote.[70] His comments echoed the praise for Foley by another Texan, William Poage, after Foley succeeded Poage as chair of the Agriculture Committee in 1975.[71]

The House responded to Foley's gentle persuasion on several occasions in 1989, including setting aside money for cleaning up waste sites at the Hanford Nuclear Reservation in central Washington. Foley explained: "Any speaker has an opportunity to convey to members his interests in his district, state and region, and usually that's persuasive if it doesn't involve impossible requests."[72] Foley's sophisticated response masked the real power and influence that he could exert as Speaker to influence legislation.

The early years of Foley's speakership thus exhibited his career-long approach to comity and bipartisan leadership, even while remaining a committed Democrat. Later chapters will show how Foley's personal and political values, his institutional and party leadership roles, and his sense of representational responsibilities meshed, albeit not always comfortably. These transformational concerns pushed him in the direction of a desire to move away from the leadership styles of his predecessors and to take on a different posture. Ornstein noted the contrast between Foley and Jim Wright:

> With a personality in dramatic contrast to his predecessor's, Tom Foley moved quickly and effectively as speaker to heal the partisan wounds. While Foley did not have any stunning legislative victories in his first months as speaker, his personal qualities—a mastery of the House, including its rules, history, and policies, the universal respect he commanded from the Washington community, and his breadth—raised the intriguing possibility that he could be as productive and powerful a speaker as Wright but with a radically different style of leadership.[73]

That "radically different style of leadership" did not, however, bode well for smooth going in the face of increasing ideological polarization. In his 2013 obituary of Foley, *New York Times* writer Adam Clymer wrote:

> Upon his selection as Speaker, Mr. Foley immediately appealed to "our friends on the Republican side to come together and put away bitterness and division and hostility." He promised to treat "each and every member" fairly, regardless of party, and by most estimations he lived up to that promise to a degree unmatched by his successors. For a time, he succeeded in making the House a more civil place, winning praise from many Republicans for his fairness.[74]

Foley's style can be seen as placing a "greater emphasis on the House-wide duties of the speakership," especially in comparison to Wright.[75] This difference was not a short-term, opportunistic maneuver on Foley's part. He transformed not only the way the person holding the speakership was perceived but also the way his district perceived him. Although Foley spent nearly as much time in the district after 1980 as he had previously, leadership duties competed with constituents' concerns for his time and attention. Indeed, during his last decade in Congress, Foley performed a political balancing act. As the Fifth District's demographics and economy changed, discerning the middle ground became more difficult. His oft-described middle-of-the-road position often frustrated both sides. Yet his desire for compromise was consistent with his moderate ideology and his transformational view of how the legislative process should work. After leaving Congress, Foley argued:

> The House of Representatives probably needs to have a strong speakership today as much as it has at any time in its history because the pressures on members, the diversity of influences from outside the Congress, and the complexity of legislative proposals is greater than in the past. I want to emphasize that there is need for a centralizing, organizing principle in the House of Representatives that is best expressed by the Speakership. . . . If you don't have a speaker who is able to bring some kind of organized pressures or discipline to the House, it would be very chaotic.[76]

Foley's sense of a need for discipline in the House should not be confused with the extreme interparty polarization orchestrated by Gingrich. Except for rare instances, Foley would not have cast aside his conciliatory temperament to apply pressure and impose discipline on members. His support for a strong speakership had the potential for fueling party polarization by keeping members in line; even so, Foley surely would have been uncomfortable with that polarization. In her *Washington Post* obituary for Foley, Emily Langer wrote: "Mr. Foley was one of Capitol Hill's most outspoken critics of the extreme partisanship that emerged toward the end of his career, which contributed to his defeat in the 1994 election and which has since intensified so dramatically that Congress is often described as 'broken.'" Indeed, Langer reinforced the dominant image of Foley: "As he rose through the leadership ranks—from majority whip to speaker in 1989—he became known as a consensus builder."[77]

Throughout his congressional career, Foley's transformative instincts led him to focus on inclusive and bipartisan processes more than on partisan differences on policy. In contrast to the Speakers who preceded and followed him, he was more inclined to bipartisanship across the aisle in the House and across branches to the presidency. Sean Theriault saw Gingrich's transformative posture as quite different from that of Foley:

> Newt Gingrich was crucial to the transformation of the Republican Conference in the House of Representatives. When he entered the chamber in 1978 Republicans mostly cooperated with Democrats in passing legislation that they, in part, helped write. Gingrich, through both converting existing members and recruiting new members, convinced his party that the only way they were going to be a majority party was through tearing down the Democratic-led House of Representatives and rebuilding it in their own image. They succeeded in 1994 when they became a majority for the first time in 50 years. . . . Without a doubt, the Republican Conference in the House transformed from one in the image of Bob Michel to one in the image of Newt Gingrich [even though] one would be hard-pressed to argue that the Republican Conference was as conservative or confrontational *because* of Newt Gingrich's leadership.[78]

Not all observers agreed that Gingrich's particular transformative style was successful. Nearly twenty-five years after Foley's defeat, Chris Buskirk wrote in the *New York Times*, "The conservative movement of Buckley, Goldwater and Reagan was ideas-oriented, energetic, iconoclastic, and—most important—politically potent. That died sometime during the 1980s. Newt Gingrich and the Class of 1994 tried to reinvigorate the movement, but it was too late."[79]

Tom Foley also can be seen as a transitional Speaker. His institutionally focused transformational values, along with his own constituency relationships, bridged the transactional focus of his Democratic predecessors (Tip O'Neill and Jim Wright) and the transformative and partisan/ideological focus of his Republican successor (Gingrich). Thus, in his own way, Foley was transformational in his commitment to a collegial, collaborative, and bipartisan House of Representatives, without losing sight either of the importance of the individual legislator or of the majority party itself, especially in times of highly salient policy conflicts.

CHAPTER 4

MAPPING THE FIFTH DISTRICT LANDSCAPE

In 1964, the year of Tom Foley's first election, the Fifth Congressional District consisted of a large swath of the northern tier of eastern Washington State. The district swept from the forested eastern slopes of the Cascade Mountains, across the mountains and forests bordering Canada, through the Columbia River basin and the reservations of the Colville Confederated Tribes, to Spokane near the Idaho border. The Fifth District was historically Republican and moderately conservative. But in 1964, a thirty-five-year-old moderate-progressive Democrat defeated an eleven-term Republican and stayed in office thirty years.

Then, five years after he became Speaker of the House of Representatives, Tom Foley fell victim to the 1994 Republican takeover of Congress. His last campaign resulted in a narrow defeat, rivaling in its competitiveness his first election thirty years earlier and a three-way race in 1978 (table 4.1). One observer suggested that Foley's narrow defeat in 1994 could be seen as a kind of personal victory: "With a visible challenger, the term limits movement, and the shift among [Ross] Perot voters, Foley clearly was bound to lose a significant amount of ground. I think it probably was a testament to his personal popularity that he almost prevailed."[1] Because the national fortunes of the Democrats were so tilted against Foley in 1994, it would not have been surprising to see him lose by a much larger margin in this historically Republican district.[2]

Setting the stage for 1994, table 4.1 also shows the percentage of the

Table 4.1 Election Results, Fifth Congressional District, 1964 to 1994

Year	Foley Votes	Foley %	Republican Votes	Republican %	Independent Votes	Independent %	Opponent
1964	84,830	52.4	73,884	46.6			Walter Horan
1966	74,571	56.5	57,310	43.5			Dorothy Powers
1968	88,446	56.8	67,304	43.2			Richard Bond
1970	88,189	67.0	43,376	33.0			George Gamble
1972[1]	150,580	81.2	34,742	18.8			Clarice Privette
1974	87,959	64.3	48,739	35.7			Gary Gage
1976	120,415	58;0	84,262	42.0			Duane Alton
1978	77,201	48;0	68,761	42.7	14,887	9.3	Duane Alton (R)
							Mel Tonasket (I)
1980	120,530	51.9	111,705	48.1			John Sonneland
1982[2]	109,549	64.3	60,816	36.7			John Sonneland
1984	154,988	69.7	67,438	30.3			Jack Hebner
1986	121,732	74.7	41,179	25.3			Floyd Wakefield
1988	160,564	76.3	49,657	23.7			Marlyn Derby
1990	110,234	69;0	49,965	31.0			Marlyn Derby
1992	135,965	55.1	110,443	44.9			John Sonneland
1994	106,074	49.1	110,057	50.9			George Nethercutt

Note: Counties in Fifth District, 1964–1970: Chelan, Douglas, Ferry, Lincoln, Okanogan, Pend Oreille, Spokane, Stevens.

Source: Election Results and Voters' Pamphlets, 1964–1994, Washington State Secretary of State, accessed November 2, 2022, https://www.sos.wa.gov/elections/research/election-results-and-voters-pamphlets.aspx.

1. Redistricting in 1972 removed Chelan, Douglas, and part of Okanogan; added Adams, Asotin, Columbia, Franklin, Garfield, part of Grant, Walla Walla, and Whitman counties.

2. Redistricting in 1982 removed Franklin, Grant, and the remaining part of Okanogan County.

vote received by Foley in each election during his time in Congress. His totals ranged from a high of over 81 percent in 1972 to a low of 48 percent in 1978, when there was a strong independent candidate. After a relatively close two-way race in 1980, the year of Ronald Reagan's election to the presidency, Foley's vote total soared again, reaching 76.3 percent in 1988. That steady rise in support (1980 to 1986) was followed by a slide downward until 1994, when he received 49 percent of the vote in his only defeat. While navigating uneven electoral fortunes in his district, Foley nonetheless steadily moved up the House leadership ladder. In the end, his long congressional career ended five years after he reached the body's highest position, Speaker of the House of Representatives.

What accounts for Foley's varying success in Washington's Fifth District and his eventual loss in 1994? Journalists and political scientists have offered multiple explanations. Some analyses are specific to the Fifth District, while others reflect larger political and social trends in the country. This study concludes, as argued in greater detail in chapter 8, that Foley lost his seat (and the Speaker's position) as the result of a confluence of concurrent forces originating from different directions, all working against his continuation in office. In our analysis, affirmative answers to many questions intersected to create that perfect storm for Foley. While the outcome of Foley's last election was definitive, there is no single explanation for his political fate.

This chapter begins with an overview of the redistricting that produced changes in the Fifth District's boundaries. The discussion next addresses the relative support for Foley in the various counties of the district, including changes as the result of redistricting and how he fared in contrast to the Democratic presidential candidate in those elections. It then turns to an analysis of the district's political culture and policy preferences as partial explanations for his electoral successes and eventual defeat. The chapter then examines Foley's career-long positioning within the House, especially in terms of his roll call voting support for his party, for the president, and for the conservative coalition. This analysis provides a view into the polarization and change across time that affected Foley's political destiny.

Finally, the chapter looks at the national political dynamics, centered primarily on Representative Newt Gingrich (R-GA) and his sustained attacks on Congress, of which Tom Foley was the most visible leader from 1989 to 1994. We conclude that in relation to his district, Foley largely was a transactional representative, taking good care of the needs and interests of his constituents throughout his career. In the end, though, his ascension to the speakership and the expression of his personal political values while Speaker led to a more transformational orientation. The positions he took created dissonance with the values of many of his constituents and made him vulnerable to defeat at the ballot box.

District Boundaries

Congressional district boundaries serve multiple and often conflicting legal, constitutional, and political purposes. As Justin Williams has written, "The political redistricting problem can be viewed as one of dividing an area into relatively equally populated districts which are compact and contiguous, while preserving existing political and community ties and providing proportional representation for minorities."[3] At the same time, others note that "through redistricting, political parties seek to control government, incumbents seek job security, and minority groups seek representation."[4] Since the 1960s and 1970s, states have redrawn those boundaries based on the decennial census, seeking in principle to reflect "one man, one vote" as established in the landmark *Reynolds v. Simms* decision of 1964, which applied the equal protection clause of the Fourteenth Amendment to the apportionment of legislators by population in an Alabama case.[5]

When Foley first was elected to Congress, the Fifth District was clearly identified as conservative and Republican. In 1964, 158,714 voters cast ballots for the district's House seat, a figure that rose by 1976 to 207,571. That increase was a combination of at least two major forces: population growth and redistricting to equalize population among congressional districts as a result of the 1970 census. Describing why each party succeeded in the state's congressional elections, political historian Walter Nugent observed: "The easternmost District 5 appears about even on the historical record, with nineteen Republican wins and fifteen Democratic, but all of the latter [wins] were by House Speaker Tom Foley from 1964 through 1992. Since then Republicans have carried the Fifth, including (since 2004) Cathy Mc-Morris Rodgers, chair of the House Republican Conference."[6]

As shown in figure 4.1, in 1964 the district's shape was horizontal, taking in eight counties across the northern half of eastern Washington and running east to west from the Idaho border to the crest of the Cascade Mountains. The lower boundary of the district was Spokane County's southern border.[7] As longtime *Spokesman-Review* political reporter Jim Camden noted, "Essentially there was more timber country and less farm country [than the current Fifth District]. . . . Spokane has always been the largest population area in the district. But what's outside of Spokane and Spokane County has changed."[8] Foley grew up in Spokane, the district's largest city and the financial, health care, and cultural center for large sections of three states. Until 1972, the district's economy relied on farming, mining, and timber, and to a lesser extent on banking and retail commerce. As a result of redistricting after the 1970 census, the district rotated from an east-west orientation to a north-south one. The district gave up portions of the timber-oriented country in the north central part of the state (e.g., Okanogan County) and acquired largely farming counties in the south (e.g., Whitman and Walla Walla, the latter stretching to the Oregon border). With some minor adjustments after the 1980 and 1990 censuses, "over time, the basic design of the Fifth District has stayed the same."[9]

The rationale for reorienting the axes of the Fourth and Fifth Districts

1964–1970 CONGRESSIONAL DISTRICT BOUNDARIES

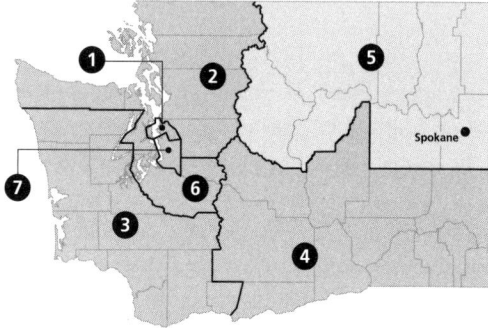

1972–1980 CONGRESSIONAL DISTRICT BOUNDARIES

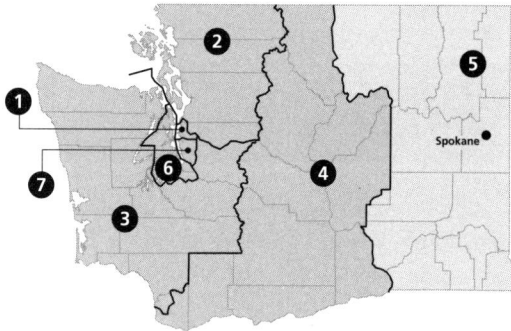

Figure 4.1. The evolution of Washington's Fifth District

Maps of Washington congressional district boundaries from 1964 to 1994 (continues on facing page).

in 1972 was not entirely clear. In 1971, after the change was first suggested, *Seattle Times* political columnist Richard Larsen, a former Foley staff member, predicted the new district would be more conservative than the previous one, in which Foley had enjoyed success in four election cycles. "Although Foley might have a personal touch with the proposed 5th district, it should be a solid Republican bastion," Larsen wrote.[10]

The largest newspaper in north central Washington, the *Wenatchee Daily World* called the shift "pure politics," arguing that the new boundaries were designed to place Republican state legislators from Walla Walla and Ellensburg in different districts, in anticipation of running for Congress. "Then they wouldn't have to compete with each other in any race for a congressional seat."[11] The *World* opposed moving the fruit-growing counties of Chelan and Douglas out of Foley's district, diluting their influence in the

1982–1990 CONGRESSIONAL DISTRICT BOUNDARIES

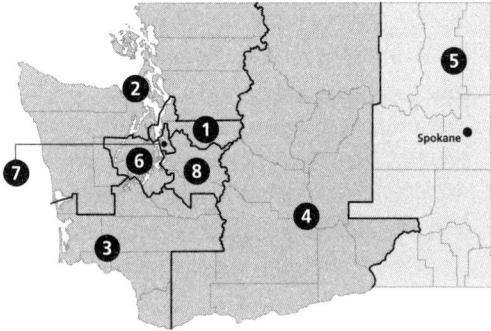

1992–1994 CONGRESSIONAL DISTRICT BOUNDARIES

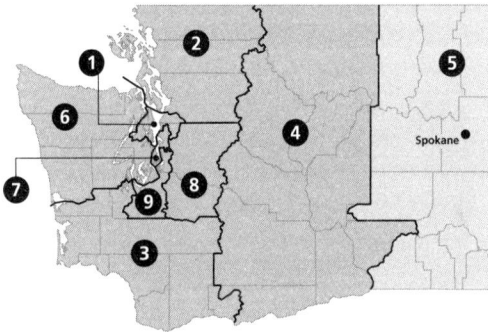

House. "As it is now, congressmen of both districts [Fourth and Fifth] must be interested in apples, cattle, fruit and timber." The map that was eventually adopted would weaken the commodity interests' influence, the editorial argued, because one representative would "need not be concerned with wheat. And the new Fifth District representative need not be concerned with apples."[12] A year later, Foley wrote to James F. Davenport of Wenatchee in an attempt to dispel fears that redistricting would shift Wenatchee and its neighboring counties out of Foley's district, "My position has been consistent throughout. . . . In all my communications with the legislature I strongly desire to continue to represent the 8 counties of North Central and Northeastern Washington."[13]

For most of Washington's first eight decades of statehood, its congressional districts were drawn by the legislature. That changed after 1983, with the creation of a bipartisan commission to study the decennial census data and divide the state into districts of approximately equal population.[14] As a result, the state enjoys what former US senator Slade Gorton called "the best model in the country" for redistricting. Each of the four legislative caucuses (House and Senate Republicans and Democrats) appoints a voting member. A nonvoting member, chosen by the other four, chairs the group. At least three commissioners must vote to approve the map. The legislature has the power to overrule the commission with a supermajority vote, but since the 1990s, lawmakers have made only minor administrative changes. "In other words, Washington State's redistricting process has earned some significant measure of bi-partisan support and deference," Marjie High wrote in her 2019 recap of redistricting history.[15]

Table 4.2 shows that apart from 1964, when Foley first won office during the landslide victory of Lyndon Johnson (and ran slightly behind Johnson), his support was usually well ahead of the presidential candidates of his own party in the district, and in 1972, 1984, and 1988, substantially so. The low vote percentages for the Democratic presidential candidates across the entire post-1964 period provides significant confirmation both of the fundamental Republican and conservative nature of the Fifth District and of the ability of Foley to overcome that counterweight. Ironically, Foley's highest vote percentage during this period came in the 1972 election when Senator George McGovern (D-SD) received the lowest percentage of any Democratic presidential candidate in the same period. Voters nationally and in the district saw McGovern's campaign platform, which included withdrawing US troops from Vietnam and providing all Americans with a guaranteed minimum income, as much too liberal.[16]

Did redistricting at the state level make any difference in Foley's electoral fortunes? The answer is hard to unravel. In 1972, the first election after the 1970 census and following the major shift in district boundaries described earlier, Foley's support skyrocketed. However, there was no difference in outcomes between the new counties added by redistricting and those counties that carried over from the previous district. In general, the new counties seemed to neither elevate nor depress Foley's support.

After much wrangling, a lawsuit, and the appointment of a geographer to draw the boundaries, the Fifth District was given its new shape and dimensions.[17] Foley decided not to challenge the plan of the court-appointed geographer. According to the *Spokane Daily Chronicle*, Foley was disappointed to lose Chelan and Douglas counties and part of Okanogan County, "but the congressman said he has many friends in southeastern Washington," now part of the new Fifth District. The same article reported that Foley hired Gary Stromier from Touchet in Walla Walla County, a former president of the Washington Wheat Growers, as a staff member

Table 4.2. Percentage Votes for Tom Foley and for Presidential Candidates in Fifth District, 1964–1992

Year	% Foley	% Democrat	% Republican	% Minor Party
1964	53.4	56.38	43.46	0.14
1968	56.8	43.48	48.38	8.20 (Wallace)
1972	81.2	34.50	60.07	5.18
1976	58	43.03	53.41	3.57
1980	51.9	41.8	53.54	4.67
1984	69.7	38.69	60.10	1.20
1988	76.3	47.74	50.60	1.45
1992	55.1	40.05	36.30	22.34 (Perot, +0.94 other)

Note: Totals may not equal 100 percent due to rounding error. The figures include results for the counties represented in the Fifth District; there is some change in those counties as a result of redistricting produced by the decennial census.

Source: Election Results and Voters' Pamphlets, 1964–1992, Washington State Secretary of State, accessed November 2, 2022, https://www.sos .wa.gov/elections/research/election -results-and-voters-pamphlets.aspx.

to help him become acquainted with the southern counties of his new district.[18]

The percentages for Foley increased across the board in 1972 but then decreased in 1974. Table 4.2 shows support for Foley tended to move parallel to support for Democratic presidential candidates but after 1964 always stayed at a much higher level than the candidate at the top of the ticket, even among those counties with the highest levels of Democratic presidential candidate support. After the 1980 census, the 1983 redistricting, the last done by the legislature, made only minor changes to the Fifth District's boundaries in order to equalize population. Foley's percentages in the 1984, 1986, and 1988 elections were substantially larger than those preceding or following that period. Table 4.3 shows the percentage of the vote received by Foley in those counties in Foley's district across his service and by all counties, regardless of when they were part of the Fifth District. The inclusion of the southeastern Washington counties clearly had little effect on Foley's overall electoral support. While there was significant variation across time in terms of specific county-level support for him, there was also substantial common distance between counties from one time period to the next, even though the counties themselves moved up and down in support.

Table 4.3 Percentage of Foley Vote in Fifth District by County and Election Year

County	1964	1966	1968	1970	1972	1974	1976	1978[1]	1980	1982	1984	1986	1988	1990	1992	1994
Adams	—	—	—	—	81.1	62.3	60.1	44.6	47	59.6	67.7	77.1	75.5	66.7	50.4	41
Asotin	—	—	55.2	—	82.5	63.4	70.9	53.1	56.2	70.7	71.2	78.4	76.9	71.9	51.1	47.9
Chelan	50.2	55.9	—	68.8	—	—	—	—	—	—	—	—	—	—	—	—
Columbia	—	—	—	—	76.9	61.4	62.4	40.9	46.7	59.5	66.1	73.3	73.7	65.8	47.5	40
Douglas	53.8	59.4	62.4	73.7	80	76.7	63.4	42.8	55.9	—	—	—	—	—	—	—
Ferry	61.1	58.2	59.8	71	82.1	69	72.8	56.1	51.9	64.2	69.9	79.1	73.4	66.2	49	45.1
Franklin[2]	—	—	—	—	82.1	69	72.8	56.1	51.9	—	—	—	—	—	—	—
Garfield	—	—	—	—	82.1	56.4	62.1	51.3	55.9	67.9	71.9	79.6	78.8	61.8	48.7	44.2
Grant	—	—	—	—	80.9	68.1	63.9	38.7	41	—	—	—	—	—	—	—
Lincoln	44.5	47.2	54.8	71.2	82.3	66.4	58.6	50.9	55.5	65.8	68.7	78.5	75.7	65.1	50.3	41.2
Okanogan	52.9	58.9	60.8	70.8	83.8	73.6	67	48.8	53.6	—	—	—	—	—	—	—
Pend Oreille	59.7	60.7	61.9	71.3	81.2	70.2	63.6	49.3	53	64.1	65.6	76.3	75.6	69.8	51.3	44.5
Spokane	54.4	56.8	55.4	65.8	81.6	63.1	55.5	48.6	52.3	65	70.6	75.1	77.3	69.3	56.8	51.1
Stevens	49.3	51.2	54.2	64.4	78.5	64.4	61.4	36.3	45.1	57	60.2	65.9	67.7	62.2	44.6	44.4
Walla Walla	—	—	—	—	77.7	64.2	67.7	42.3	45.9	59.9	55.5	71.7	75.3	71.4	55.5	47.1
Whitman	—	—	—	—	82.1	64.5	61.3	50	57	67.4	54.9	76.5	76.4	67.5	54.9	50.4
All Counties	52.4	56.5	56.8	67	81.2	64.3	58	48	51.9	64.3	69.7	74.7	76.3	69	44.1	49.1

Source: Election Results and Voters' Pamphlets, Washington Secretary of State's Office, 1964–1994, accessed November 2, 2022, https://www.sos.wa.gov/elections/research/election-results-and-voters-pamphlets.aspx.

1. Duane Alton (Republican) received 40.59 percent, and Mel Tonasket (Independent) received 9.26 percent of the total votes in 1978.

2. Only portions of Grant and Franklin Counties were included in the Fifth District to achieve population balances (1972–1980).

In the three elections in the 1990s, Foley's support in Pend Oreille County dropped from 69.8 percent to 44.5 percent, while decreasing from 69.3 percent to 51.1 percent in Spokane County. Consistent with that drop, his Whitman County support fell from 67.5 percent to 50.4 percent. The gaps between the counties remained pretty much the same, suggesting much broader national electoral and political forces were also at work. In addition, the values of voters in the urban areas of Spokane County and the rural areas of Whitman County may have changed.

How can one explain both the persistence of Foley's support across that thirty-year period and then his defeat in 1994? In the remainder of this chapter, we suggest two explanations: a combination of his observed role orientations in regard to both his district constituency and his leadership in the House (transactional vs. transformational) and the relative preponderance of national over local forces that engaged electoral alternatives in the context of political culture.

Political Culture

Perhaps the most important work on American political culture has been that of Daniel Elazar, who positions political culture in the context of "path dependence." Path dependence suggests that at any point in time, a community's political culture can be traced to its particular history, which creates momentum that persists through time and structures subsequent outcomes.[19] Political culture reflects the characteristic distribution of path-dependent behaviors and values (those that persist over time) distinctive to a political or geographic area, such as a congressional district or counties within it. Consequently, the question is whether Washington's Fifth District has or had identifiable beliefs and behaviors that can structure and explain voting patterns across the thirty years of Foley's incumbency.

According to Elazar and others, the historical foundation of political culture is rooted in sociocultural differences among the peoples who came to the United States over the years, differences that date back to their home countries and the beginnings of settlement in the American colonies and, later, the United States.[20] Because the various ethnic and religious groups that came to these shores tended to congregate in their own settlements (or were forced to by dominant groups) and because they continued to settle together as they and their descendants moved westward, the political patterns they bore with them are distributed geographically today.[21]

Elazar identified three major types of political culture found in American communities: individualistic, moralistic, and traditionalistic. *Individualistic* political cultures see government "as a marketplace (means to respond efficiently to demands)." *Moralistic* political cultures view government "as a commonwealth (means to achieve the good community although nongovernmental action is preferred)." *Traditionalistic* political cultures focus on politics "as a means of maintaining the established order."[22]

The question then becomes how the historic political culture of the Fifth District affected the fortunes of Tom Foley at the beginning and end of his thirty-year career. The political culture composition of the Fifth District, disaggregated to the county level, is shown in table 4.4, along with the distributions for Washington State and the United States. Given the path-dependent nature of political culture, as defined by Elazar, we assume that within any particular county there is little or no change across time periods. Instead, the changes in the county distributions of culture may stem from replacement sorting or be externally produced by redistricting, perhaps bringing different county cultures into the district and displacing other cultures.

Table 4.4 shows that the relative number of dominant moralistic culture counties in the Fifth District remained nearly the same from 1964 to 1994 (79 percent vs. 75 percent), even with the change in many of the particular counties, but that the moderate moralistic counties were replaced by minor moralistic counties. On the other hand, the minor individualistic counties in 1964 (Chelan and Douglas) were replaced by a moderate individualistic county (Adams). There was no change in the percentage of traditionalistic counties. Overall, then, the Fifth District was marginally less moralistic in 1994 than in 1964 and marginally more individualistic in 1994 than in 1964. On the surface, this may suggest a partial explanation for the loss of support for Foley in 1994, especially in the wake of independent presidential candidate Ross Perot's strength in and the nationalization of the House election in 1994 through Newt Gingrich's Contract with America. Table 4.5 shows the percentage of support for Foley in the county cultural categories in 1964 compared with 1994. To be sure, we do not assume county-level change in the cultures but rather the change in the counties within the Fifth District. We look at whether the counties that replaced other counties with a different political culture had different levels of support for Foley. We include only information for the moralistic and the individualistic cultures, since Elazar identified no traditionalistic culture in any county of Washington.

There seems to be no clear difference in the political culture distinctiveness of support for Foley, partly because the moralistic culture dominated

Table 4.4. Political Culture in Fifth District, Washington State, and the United States

	1964	1994		
Moralistic	Fifth District	Fifth District	Washington	United States
None	0%	0%	0%	58%
Minor	0%	21%	15%	14%
Moderate	25%	0%	23%	12%
Dominant	75%	79%	62%	17%
TOTAL	100%	100%	100%	101%
N	(8)	(14)	(39)	3066
Mean	2.75	2.57	2.46	.89
Individualistic				
None	75%	91%	62%	48%
Minor	25%	0%	23%	24%
Moderate	0%	9%	15%	5%
Dominant	0%	0%	0%	12%
TOTAL	100%	100%	100%	99%
N	(8)	(11)	(39)	(3066)
Mean	.25	.21	.54	.91
Traditionalist				
None	100%	100%	100%	100%
Minor	0%	0%	0%	8%
Moderate	0%	0%	0%	19%
Dominant	0%	0%	0%	25%
TOTAL	100%	100%	100%	100%
N	(8)	(14)	(39)	(30,266)
Mean	.00	.00	.00	1.28

Source: Nicholas P. Lovrich, Jr., county-level recoding of map of "The Regional Distribution of Political Cultures within the States," in Daniel J. Elazar, *The American Mosaic: The Impact of Space, Time, and Culture on American Politics* (Boulder, CO: Westview Press, 1994), 242–243.

most counties in the district, regardless of the change in the particular county composition of the district. The two largest declines in Foley's support across his thirty years in Congress emerged in Ferry and Pend Oreille Counties, which were (and are) dependent on logging and mining. The Fifth District overwhelmingly comprises counties with moralistic political cultures. Yet until the 1990s, Foley's issue and policy positioning seemed transactional in character, responding to the dominant economic makeup of the district rather than the moralistic communitarian values.

Table 4.5. County Political Cultures and Vote for Foley: 1964 versus 1994

| County | Level of Political Culture Present[1] | | | | | | | | Foley % | |
| | 0 | | 1 | | 2 | | 3 | | | |
	M[2]	I	M	I	M	I	M	I	1964	1994
Chelan	—	—	—	x	x	—	—	—	50.2	—
Douglas	—	—	—	x	x	—	—	—	53.8	—
Ferry	—	—	—	—	—	—	x	—	61.1	45.0
Lincoln	—	—	—	—	—	—	x	—	44.5	41.0
Okanogan	—	—	—	—	—	—	x	—	52.9	—
Pend Oreille	—	—	—	—	—	—	x	—	59.7	44.5
Spokane	—	—	—	—	—	—	x	—	54.4	51.1
Stevens	—	—	—	—	—	—	x	—	49.3	44.4
Adams	—	—	x	—	—	x	—	—	—	41.0
Asotin	—	—	—	—	—	—	x	—	—	47.9
Columbia	—	—	—	—	—	—	x	—	—	40.6
Garfield	—	—	—	—	—	—	x	—	—	44.0
Walla Walla	—	—	—	—	—	—	x	—	—	53.0
Whitman	—	—	—	—	—	—	x	—	—	50.0

Note: An x in a cell means that for that county the particular political culture is present at that level. Thus, Ferry County has been identified as having a "dominant presence" of the moralistic political culture. Recall that the political cultures of the counties are assumed to be constant across time, but their effect on political outcomes may vary from election to election depending on a variety of forces, including the larger political environment and changes in the particular candidate(s). Thus, in the 1964 election (during the LBJ/Goldwater presidential election), Foley received slightly over 61 percent of the vote in Ferry County, but in the 1994 election he received only 45 percent of the vote, even though the political culture had not changed. This may suggest that there was some change in the nature of the electorate (sorting resulting in more Republicans) or in the political environment, or in the attractiveness of the Republican opponent (Nethercutt).

1. 0 = no presence of that culture; 1 = minor presence of that culture; 2 = moderate presence of that culture; 3 = dominant presence of that culture.
2. Type of political cultures present where M = moralistic, I = individualistic; T = traditionalistic. As noted in chapter 4, this table includes only information for the moralistic and the individualistic cultures, since Daniel Elazar identified no traditionalistic culture in any county of Washington.

Given the district's economic base, Foley clearly exhibited transactional leadership, providing economic incentives from his positions on the Agriculture Committee and later in House leadership. At the same time, he often expressed transformational values in his posture toward the House itself, with his emphases on civility and bipartisanship. Later in his career, additional transformational issues emerged in the form of constitutional, value-based national policy conflicts. These included opposition to a proposed constitutional amendment to forbid burning of the American flag, opposition to term limits for members of Congress, and support for a ban on so-called assault weapons. These issues combined to provide Foley with the leverage to rise in the House leadership. First, the district reelected him term after term because of his benefits to the district. Second, with that apparently secure base (along with his strong relationships in the Democratic Caucus), Foley built and sustained the institutional support to become Speaker. Comparing himself to the rest the country, "he said he was proud to be a lifelong Democrat, and would probably be classified as a liberal because of his support for civil liberties, civil rights and the belief that government can solve some of the country's problems."[23]

Yet Foley's political downfall may be attributed to a mix of transformational issues, such as the reputation of the House of Representatives itself (expressed in the backlash to the House bank and post office scandals) and the potentially transactional issue of the North American Free Trade Agreement (NAFTA). Foley was a strong supporter of NAFTA, but the legislation was opposed by a majority of his fellow Democrats in the House, members of his leadership cadre, and labor unions in his district. We address those particular issues in subsequent chapters.

Issues of Public Policy

Tom Foley was ultimately defeated when the transformational national dialogue (inspired by Newt Gingrich and influenced by conservative media) overpowered the local transactional interests and when the clarity of the impact of the transactional issues became muddied by the multidimensional content of NAFTA and the barrage of critical talk-radio messages. In this context, Lee Drutman has identified three trends: "The first is the nationalization of American politics. The second is the sorting of Democrats and Republicans along urban/rural and culturally liberal/culturally conservative lines, and the third is the increasingly narrow margins in national elections."[24] To some extent, Tom Foley suffered from all three, but one seems more important than the others: the nationalization of American politics.

This nationalization trend affected Foley's ability to survive the 1994 election on several fronts. First, Gingrich's repeated attacks on Congress, and the House of Representatives in particular, could not help but reflect negatively on the Speaker of the House, even in his own district, and especially in the face of Foley's nonconfrontational mode. Second, Ross Perot's 1992 presidential bid (and the significant support he received in the Fifth District) damaged Foley's popularity and foreshadowed his 1994 defeat. The Perot movement eroded Foley's traditional base of support by tapping into voters' resentment of the federal government and the frustration with the two-party system. Third, several issues in the campaign attracted such national-interest groups as the National Rifle Association, the National Federation of Independent Business, and the Freedom Leadership Political Action Committee, a group opposed to statehood for the District of Columbia, into the Fifth District.[25]

What made eastern Washington voters receptive to the barrage of criticism of Foley, especially by those from outside the district? A recent analysis of the Washington State electorate has shown the presence of two Washingtons, at least in the culturally derived values of its people.[26] The two Washingtons were identified through cluster analysis, a statistical technique based on the degree to which units of analysis (e.g., counties or individuals) share, in this case, levels of support for cultural public policy measures, as expressed in aggregate patterns of voting for multiple initiatives and culturally distinct candidates.

The results show that one Washington cluster is concentrated around Puget Sound and contains ten counties, dominated by King, Pierce, Skagit, Snohomish, and Thurston. The "Other Washington" cluster contains the state's remaining twenty-nine counties, encompassing the western Washington counties outside the Puget Sound cluster as well as all of the counties in eastern Washington, including all of the Fifth Congressional District. Table 4.6 compares the results for the Puget Sound cluster with various sets of the counties in the Fifth District (which changed across time with redistricting). The results are based on votes for two specific 2012 statewide initiatives with direct relevance for trade-offs between transactional and transformational politics: I-502, which legalized recreational marijuana, and I-74, which legalized same-sex marriages.

The distinctions among the sets of "Other Washington" counties are based on periods during which the particular counties were part of the Fifth

Table 4.6. Average Percent "Yes" Aggregate Votes on Two Initiatives by
Puget Sound Cluster and Disaggregated "Other Washington" Cluster

	I-502: Legalize Marijuana	I-74: Legalize Same-Sex Marriages
Puget Sound Cluster	58.8%	57.0%
District 5: Other Washington Cluster		
1964–1994 (5)	48.2%	35.0%
1964–1970 (2)	50.5%	39.0%
1964–1980 (1)	51.0%	40.0%
1972–1980 (2)	45.0%	31.0%
1972–1994 (6)	44.7%	36.0%

Note: The "Other Washington" clusters reflect those counties in the Fifth District for that particular period: 1964–1994: Ferry, Lincoln, Pend Oreille, Spokane, Stevens; 1964–1970: Chelan, Douglas; 1964–1980: Okanogan; 1972–1980: Franklin, Grant; 1972–1994: Adams, Asotin, Columbia, Garfield, Walla Walla, Whitman.

District during Foley's terms, namely, the entire period from 1964 to 1994; only the period from 1964 to 1970; only the period from 1964 to 1980; only the period from 1972 to 1980; and only the period from 1972 to 1994. These Fifth District boundary differences are the result of redistricting over Foley's thirty years in Congress.

Table 4.6 illustrates that regardless of the particular set of counties in the Fifth District within the thirty-year period, those counties are clearly different from the Puget Sound cluster. To be sure, there is some difference among those five sets of Fifth District counties. Thus, those counties that were in the district in 1964 exhibited slightly more support for the two cultural initiatives than those that did not enter until after the redistricting based on the 1970 census. Based on this analysis, the 1972 redistricting shifted the district in a slightly more conservative direction than it otherwise might have taken.

Table 4.7 reinforces the picture of the cultural environment in which the Fifth District counties reside. From the statewide poll data, many of the "Other Washington" counties are in the Fifth District.[27] There is a clear difference between the two groups. The "Other Washington" group (including the Fifth District) is less Democratic, angrier with the federal government, more likely to see government as a threat to rights, more likely to identify as conservative, less likely to be liberal on social issues, more

Table 4.7. Political Orientations of Puget Sound and Other Washington Clusters, 2015

Political Orientation	County Cluster	
	Puget Sound	Other Washington (Including Fifth District)
Democrat	36%	28%
Angry with Federal Government	73%	86%
Government Threat to Rights	40%	50%
Conservative	40%	50%
Liberal on Social Issues	49%	43%
Conservative on Fiscal Issues	53%	62%
Government Controls Too Much	34%	41%
	N = (339)	N = (162)

Note: Fifth Congressional District counties subsumed in the Other Washington cluster.
Source: Elway Research.

likely to be conservative on fiscal issues, and more likely to believe that government controls too much. When national politics overwhelmed the transactional concerns of the respective economies in the district, then the differences in the policy questions noted here surely worked against Foley.

Our goal in this chapter has been to unravel the reasons for the anomaly of Tom Foley's twin achievements: a thirty-year career of election and reelection in which he was significantly more progressive or liberal than the majority of his constituents and a historically unparalleled rise for someone from a largely rural district in a West Coast state to the speakership of the House of Representatives. Both distinctions ended abruptly in 1994. While the outcomes occurred on both sides of the country, many of the reasons were related. The explanation for Foley's defeat, if simple in individual causes, was more complex in how the causes interacted.

First, of course, is the political culture of Foley's Fifth District in eastern Washington. Foley had overcome the constraints produced by his moderate-to-progressive political ideology and style. But the moderate conservatism of much of his district rested as a crucible in which significant opposition to his ideology and style could be cultivated, given the right combination of forces all pointing in the same direction. Political culture is a condition that persists through time and does not need to be re-created to be lasting. It did not require a large change, a significant polarization, or a greatly heightened salience to move enough voters to produce the small margin that led to his defeat in 1994. But the culture was there, providing the latent conditions for the loss of support for Foley in response to other, more temporal, forces.

Second, Foley and his staff did not commit as much effort to continuing to nurture his support in his district as they should have. The responsibilities of the speakership surely shaved time from Foley's days that might otherwise have underpinned a historically unstable foundation of support. Years later, Garfield farmer Judy Olson, a statewide leader of the Washington Association of Wheat Growers and later president of the national association, recalled that Foley spent less time in the district because "he had both hands really full being Speaker." Foley may have misjudged his constituents' familiarity with his accomplishments, Olson said. "He was of the mindset that, 'If my district doesn't know what I have done, can do, and am doing, they've just got to have confidence. And I've been doing this for thirty years. They know me, they've seen what I do.'"[28]

Third, recall how wildly Foley's victory margins fluctuated across time, ranging from a high of 81 percent in 1972 to a low of 48 percent in 1978. Many reasons accounted for those swings, but one cannot ignore the role the political abilities (or lack thereof) of Foley's opponents played in his victories. If one takes the votes for president as an indication of core partisan support, how else can one account for 1972, when Foley received 81 percent, but the head of his ticket, presidential candidate George McGovern, obtained only 34.5 percent in his district? To be sure, McGovern was perhaps the most liberal candidate that Democrats nominated for president in the second half of the twentieth century.[29] Even so, the gap of nearly 50 percentage points between Foley and McGovern attested to Foley's capacity to appeal to voters in his district independent of his national party's platform, along with the failure of Fifth District Republicans to nominate a strong challenger.[30]

Fourth, as the leader of the Democratic Party in the House, Foley suffered collateral damage from the constant barrage of criticism leveled at Congress by Republicans, most notably Newt Gingrich. Foley ascended to the Speaker's position in the wake of Jim Wright's 1989 resignation after attacks by Gingrich and others. In recounting the consequences of Wright's decision to resign, political historian Julian Zelizer observed:

> Speaker-elect Foley promised the nation that his number one goal would be to end the toxic environment on Capitol Hill. . . . "I think we need to work very seriously at restoring a sense of comity and confidence between members of the two parties," he said. Hoping

to declare a truce, Foley promised to begin his term by reaching out to Republican leaders and avoiding the ugly tactics that had caused a backlash against Speaker Wright. He acknowledged that there were Democrats who were "very bitter about what they regard as the crucifixion of Jim Wright," but he would not let them take over.[31]

Gingrich's attacks on the Democrats in the House seemed to soften after Wright's resignation, but as the Republican whip, he continued to confront the Democratic leadership over scandals and controversies during the next three years of Foley's speakership. After Bill Clinton's election in 1992, "the challenge to the new president from the Newt Gingrich–led Republicans was the most significant headache he [Clinton] acquired."[32] Political scientist Martin Wattenberg has suggested that Ross Perot's relative success in the 1992 presidential election opened the way for Republican congressional candidates and their leaders to "identify which of their legislative proposals would play well with the Perot constituency." By embracing Gingrich's Contract with America, Republican candidates for the House attracted many of the voters who had backed Perot two years earlier. In Wattenberg's analysis: "Independent voters propelled Ross Perot in 1992 to the best performance in eighty years by a presidential candidate from outside the two major parties, and in 1994 they were responsible for breaking the longest continuous partisan hold of the House in American electoral history."[33]

Indeed, in the Fifth District, Foley's support dropped from 68.8 percent in 1990 to 55.2 percent in 1992, the election in which Perot obtained more than 21 percent of the presidential vote. Foley's vote dropped another 6 percentage points to 49.08 percent in 1994, when Republican challenger George Nethercutt no doubt benefited from Perot's endorsement during a visit to Spokane four days before the 1994 election.[34] Fifth District Republicans continued to enjoy that advantage in subsequent congressional elections.

Policy Effects

The debate over term limits for members of Congress and other officials pulled Foley into a political quagmire. The term-limits movement arose in response to public perceptions of too many entrenched officeholders at all levels. Washington State was one location where that debate twice reached statewide ballots. Thus, in 1991, Initiative 553, asked: "Shall there be limitations on terms of office for Governor, Lieutenant Governor, state legislators, and Washington State Members of Congress?" Foley opposed that measure, arguing that voters had the opportunity in every election to limit the terms of incumbents.

Figures 4.2 and 4.3 show the relationship between county-level support for term limits and county-level support for Foley. In both cases there is a fairly strong negative relationship. Generally speaking, the greater the support for terms limits, the less the support for Foley. It is tempting to suggest that Foley's electoral support levels were tied to his position on term limits, but the direction of the causal relationship could be in the other direction. In other words, it is possible voters who opposed Foley for a variety of reasons extrapolated that opposition to his position on terms limits simply because he opposed them.

Foley's 1994 opponent, George Nethercutt, asserted that while Foley had served the district well and deserved voters' respect and gratitude, it was time for him to retire. "He's a nice man, but he's been serving the region for 30 years and it's time for a change," Nethercutt said.[35]

The transactional nature of Foley's relationship with his constituents was reinforced soon after his death in 2013. Nearly twenty years after Foley left office, the *Newport Miner* in Pend Oreille County presented a long list of benefits Foley had brought to the county. The *Miner* quoted a former Public Utility District commissioner, John Middleton, as saying: "I have nothing but respect for Tom Foley, both as a man and as a legislator." Middleton described a trip to Washington, DC, in the late 1980s or early 1990s to oppose the possible sale of the Bonneville Power Administration, which markets wholesale electrical power from thirty-one federal hydroelectric projects in the Northwest. Foley agreed with the commissioner's position, Middleton recalled. "He said, 'If that's what you want, that's what you'll get.'" The *Miner* described Foley's support for a tax bill to benefit a newsprint mill in Usk (near Newport) and efforts on behalf of the Kalispel tribe.[36] Foley's ability to serve his district's economic interests became a liability by 1994, however. "His ability as speaker to bring home federal benefits was a point Nethercutt used against him, accusing him of pork-barrel politics," the *Miner* lamented."[37]

Polarization in the House of Representatives

Along with the challenges of running for reelection in 1994 and the path-dependent character of Washington's Fifth District, Foley's defeat might be

Figure 4.2. Relationship of 1992 term limits support (I-573) by county in Fifth District

I-573 ballot question: "Shall candidates for certain offices, who have already served for specific time periods in these offices be denied ballot access?" This double line graph shows the relationship between the percentages of support for term limits and support for Tom Foley by county. *Source*: Washington Secretary of State.

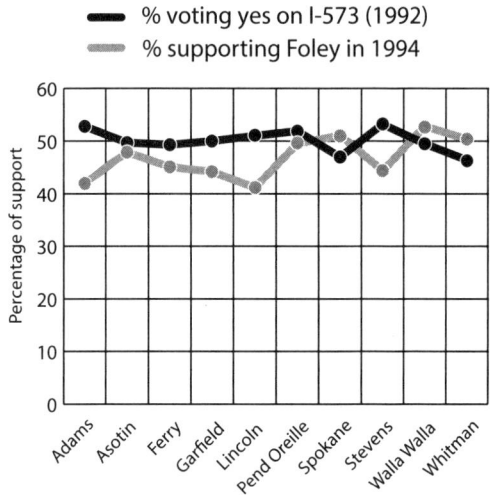

Figure 4.3. Relationship of 1991 term limits support (I-553) by county in Fifth District

I-553 ballot question: "Shall there be limitations on terms of office for Governor, Lieutenant Governor, State Legislators and Washington State members of Congress?" This double-line graph shows the relationship between the percentage voting for Foley and the percentage supporting I-553 in each of county in the Fifth District. *Source*: Washington Secretary of State.

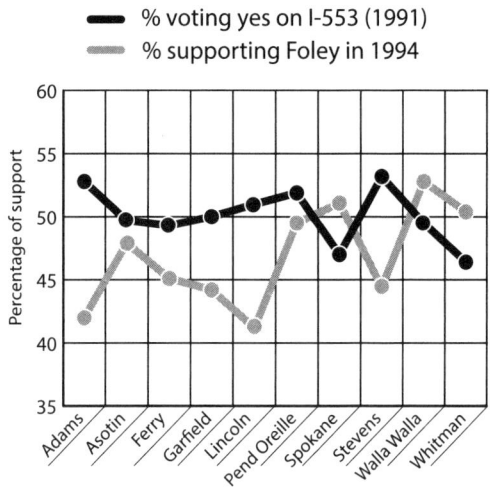

linked to changes in the culture and politics of the House of Representatives and, more broadly, to the divisive politics and culture of the country. Foley rose to the speakership after three decades of changes in the US political environment. Political scientists Thomas Mann and Norm Ornstein have suggested that widely observed contemporary problems with the House emerged, at least in part, because "the parties have become ideologically polarized, tribalized, and strategically partisan. . . . Our Madisonian system

is predicated on the willingness of elected officials representing highly diverse interests to engage in good-faith negotiations and compromise."[38]

Other observers have documented the increased partisan polarization
in Congress. Sean Theriault wrote in 2008, "The parties in Congress have
been polarizing for around 35 years."[39] He concluded that "the divide between the political parties in Congress can increasingly be characterized
as a disagreement about procedures."[40] In an era of increased polarization,
how did Foley manage the cross-pressures between being seen as too liberal by his constituents and too conservative by many of his liberal fellow
congressional partisans, especially late in his leadership career? Theriault's
theory about the nature of party polarization in Congress identifies two
sources: procedural votes and policy votes. He suggests the major source
of polarization came from procedural votes. During his time in Congress,
but especially when he was in leadership, Foley often focused on process
and procedures as well as policy. His efforts to build consensus and engage Republicans in policy making created an unusual mix of challenges
for him and for Democrats. Theriault quotes John Aldrich, who suggests
"the parties in Congress are strong today because members want them
that way."[41]

Figure 4.4 shows the growth of polarization across the twenty years
(1976 to 1994) of Foley's experience in leadership positions. Several patterns emerge. First, Foley always voted with the majority of the Democrats
more than his caucus did as a whole. Second, the distance was greater in
the early part of his leadership career than in other years, save for the very
last prespeakership period. Third, the average unity score of both parties
increased significantly across the twenty years, supporting the polarization
hypothesis. Fourth, by the end of the period, the two parties were very similar in their absolute levels of unity/cohesion and at the highest level for that
period, reflecting substantial polarization.

Holding the center became a more significant challenge for the Speaker;
indeed, the average Democratic Party unity score by the early 1990s was not
much higher than it was in the mid-1980s. But the growth in Democratic
Party unity in the 1970s to mid-1980s was significant, reflecting the "sorting" of partisan affiliation among outlier House members from the South,
many of whose districts were now represented by Republicans. As majority
leader, Foley's party unity score was substantially higher than that for the
party as a whole, and his allegiance to the Democratic Party may have led to
his electoral vulnerability after he became Speaker in 1989.

The increased power of the speakership combined with the increased

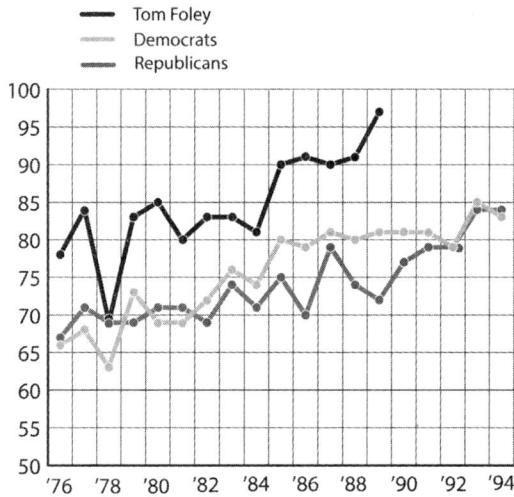

Figure 4.4. Party unity, roll call votes, House of Representatives
After becoming Speaker, Foley rarely voted. *Source: Congressional Quarterly Almanacs* (1967–1995).

polarization of the congressional parties, as Democrats moved to the left and Republicans to the right. By 1994, political scientist James Campbell wrote, "The parties were now quite evenly and intensely competitive in both presidential and congressional elections."[42] Campbell also observed: "The greater ideological change of congressional Democrats also makes sense in terms of the changing coalitions of the parties. The subtraction of the southern conservatives from the otherwise fairly liberal Democratic Party made a bigger difference to the ideological balance within the Democratic party than the addition of those southern conservatives made to an otherwise already fairly conservative Republican party."[43]

In 1994 generally, and in Foley's district in particular, voters were less inclined to vote for a Democrat for Congress. His defeat reflected increasing polarization in the electorate both nationally and locally. Theriault argues, though, that "the lion's share of polarization in both chambers is brought about by the ideological voting of members above and beyond their constituencies' growing partisanship."[44]

Despite his support for a strong speakership, which contributed to party polarization by imposing party discipline on members, Foley surely would have been uncomfortable with the degree of party polarization that emerged in the late 1980s and continues to the present. In their analysis of the 1994 election, *Washington Post* reporters Dan Balz and Ronald Brownstein wrote: "As conservative Republicans replace moderate Democrats across the South, the center of the House is being systematically obliterated."[45] As someone who was comfortable in that center, Foley found that his home base had grown considerably smaller. His obituary in the *Washington Post* described him as "one of Capitol Hill's most outspoken critics of the extreme partisanship that emerged toward the end of his career, which contributed to his defeat in the 1994 election."[46]

Theriault attributes the rise of party polarization in Congress (which, as we noted, can "increasingly be characterized as a disagreement about procedures") to three major forces, producing an electorate that has become "increasingly balkanized."[47] First, there has been a "geographic sorting" of the adherents of the two major parties within the southern districts represented by Republicans rather than conservative Democrats. Second, Theriault argues that the electorate has become increasingly ideological, with fewer moderates and more liberals and conservatives. Third, he contends that citizens have aligned their voting preferences, their partisan identification, and their political ideology. That is, conservative voters are more likely to identify as Republican and to vote for Republican candidates. At the same time, liberals are more likely to identify as Democrats and to vote for Democratic candidates.[48]

It is important to note that while Foley lost both his congressional seat and the speakership in 1994, the outcome was only partially a result of what he did or did not do personally. Rather, major changes in the political landscape of the country and in Congress produced an earthquake of shifting partisan plates. To be sure, there was an increase in partisan polarization in the House, but that change was in a reciprocal relationship with the electorate itself. The sorting of the electorate created a political terrain that enabled Gingrich-led Republicans to move through electoral pathways around the country into the majority. Given his role as head of the Democratic Party in Congress, Foley was tethered in his own district by a knot of intertwined dilemmas. On the one hand, being Speaker surely took his time, attention, and strategy away from the district. In 1992, the success of Ross Perot revealed a weakness in the partisan ties of the Fifth District. At the same time, though, Foley might well have won reelection if he had committed more resources and time to campaigning at home. Yet even if he had clung to his own seat, the larger dynamics across the country still would have cost him the speakership.

CHAPTER 5

HOLDING THE CENTER

In his landmark study, *Home Style: House Members in Their Districts*, political scientist Richard Fenno examined the ways in which members of the House of Representatives interact with their constituents. Focusing on how they view their home districts, Fenno wrote: "In talking about their geographical constituencies . . . members of Congress focus on prepolitical description." By that, he meant that they did not describe their districts in political terms, such as "partisan" or "safe" (for the incumbent). "Neither does this broadest perception have much emphasis on specific issues," he continued. "Interests, yes; ideology, yes; but issues, not much."[1]

Yet in the district that Tom Foley represented for thirty years, a number of region-specific domestic issues were at play—in possible contradiction of Fenno's assertion. Among those issues were controversy over Snake River dams and their impact on anadromous fisheries (salmon and steelhead) in the context of massive hydroelectric energy production, flood control, and irrigation;[2] federal policy in regard to the creation of wilderness areas and national forest management in the context of preservation versus logging;[3] struggles over the continued funding of Fairchild Air Force Base west of Spokane; potential negative economic consequences of proposed threats to the aluminum industry;[4] support for veterans hospitals in Walla Walla and Spokane;[5] and support for a national ban on assault weapons after a former airman's rampage at Fairchild Air Force Base left four dead and twenty-three wounded. Compared with the prominent place of those particular issues, though, in terms of land mass and in long-term economic and political centrality, rural agricultural interests were persistent and preeminent. The importance of agricultural issues prevailed for the district even though the district's largest urban center was Spokane (population 181,608 in 1960, the census before Foley's first election).

To illustrate "the man in the middle" position held by Foley, this chapter focuses first on Foley's long-standing support for agriculture's central importance in the Fifth District. We then turn to a discussion of the controversy over the issue question of the North American Free Trade Agreement (NAFTA) with Mexico and Canada, a policy with potential great positive effects for agricultural interests in Foley's district, as well as hypothesized negative impact on labor employment, especially in the Spokane area.

The central role of agriculture in Washington's Fifth District and Foley's support for its interests were crucial to providing him with an uninterrupted thirty-year stint in the House of Representatives. This persistent and unbroken electoral success for Foley, a moderate liberal, emerged despite his eastern Washington constituents' general conservatism.[6]

Foley's three-decade-long career in Congress also persisted in the face of other more value-based issues that may not have worked in his favor. His public positions on such valence issues as a constitutional amendment to prohibit burning of the American flag, attempts to restrict certain categories of guns, and term limits for members of Congress did not seem to meld well with those of the majority of his constituents. In a study of Speakers of the House, Ronald Peters described Foley as a "moderate Democrat from a Republican-leaning district in eastern Washington State."[7] But the debate over NAFTA in the early 1990s placed Foley truly "in the middle" on an issue important to many in his district. That middle position was not a policy orientation, since he clearly was strongly in support of NAFTA, in both principle and practice. Rather, Foley's political position reflected his role as Speaker of the same party as a president who pushed for NAFTA, his own ideological support for free trade, and his position as representative of an agricultural district that many contended would benefit from expanded international markets. In contrast, several members of his own party leadership in the House opposed NAFTA, seeing it as a threat to the American economy, especially to manufacturing jobs.[8] This position was shared by many nonagricultural labor interests in Foley's district, as well as by Democratic House members who represented districts in other parts of the country with significant labor constituencies.

As previously noted, agriculture not only was important to Foley's district but also played a key role in his rise in the House leadership. His chairmanship of the Agriculture Committee (1975–1981) became one of his power bases on which he built his climb to the highest position in the House. Fenno described the importance of the House member's "presentation of self" to her or his constituency. That presentation of self is calculated to win the voters' trust.[9] Given the importance of agriculture to the district's economy and given his own image as a lawyer from Spokane, Foley surely must have wanted to establish an image of himself that would generate trust of him in the small towns and rural areas of his district. In his coauthored memoir, published after he left Congress, Foley ruefully described some of his own "presentations of self" that seem designed to win that trust from portions of his rural and agricultural constituency that may not have been naturally comfortable for him. An example took place in 1967, in the third year he was a member of Congress. Foley was invited to be grand marshal of the Omak Stampede in north central Washington, often called "one of the premier rodeos in the West." Here is how Foley recounted that experience:

> So there was a parade. . . . Then they brought up fifty riders representing the Omak-Okanogan Sheriff's Posse, all carrying American flags, and I thought "this has got to be slow." I was told that we were going to go around the ring a couple of more times with this very large cavalry. Instead, they all went off again at full gallop. I got caught up in the group. Suddenly I found my horse going counter-clockwise to a general clockwise direction of the posse. . . . And suddenly I am out there all alone. The posse had disappeared through the chute. I'm struggling to get control of one rein that's been lost and a stirrup that's somehow disappeared under the horse's belly. . . . There was a general guffawing, and hooting, and applauding, and so on. . . . Dick Larsen, who was my administrative assistant, told me, "That was wonderful." "What do you mean wonderful? I made a fool of myself." "Exactly," he said. "That's exactly what you did, and it's just terrific." . . . He said, "You proved that you were from Spokane, that you couldn't ride worth a damn, but you got out there and made them feel good about the fact that they could. You'll win this county, I predict it." And I did.[10]

Larsen, later a *Seattle Times* columnist, offered this additional detail: "The rodeo announcer, suppressing a laugh, declared over the public address system, 'Looks like Congressman Tom ain't been spending a lot of time taking riding lessons.'"[11] The episode was embarrassing at the moment, but Foley took pleasure in retelling the story in later years. Even so, he told his district staff: "No more horses." The 1967 Omak Stampede also may have been the last time Foley wore a cowboy hat in public. While Foley preferred tailored suits and crisp white shirts in Washington, DC, and for public appearances in his home district, his advisers convinced him to wear a plaid shirt and blue jeans for campaign photos in 1994.

When it came to gun control, Foley's position had long been at odds with a majority of Democrats in Congress. But Foley's opposition to restrictions on gun ownership weakened after an incident in his home district. On June 20, 1994, a recently discharged airman went on a rampage at the hospital of Fairchild Air Force Base, about eight miles west of Spokane. The man killed four people and wounded twenty-three others before military police killed him. The gunman used a MAK-90 semiautomatic rifle, a version of the Soviet-designed AK-47. Touring the base a few days after the shooting, Foley said that he supported a ban on assault weapons such as the one used in the shooting.[12] Referring to a bill banning certain assault weapons the House had narrowly passed the previous month, Foley told reporters he would have voted in favor of the legislation if there had been a tie.[13] The National Rifle Association, which interpreted Foley's support for the assault weapons ban as a reversal of his longtime opposition to gun control, poured thousands of dollars into the district and also sent several members of its staff and board to Spokane to campaign against Foley. The most prominent anti-Foley spokesperson was actor and pro-gun activist Charlton Heston, who spoke at a fundraising dinner in Seattle for George Nethercutt, Foley's Republican opponent in 1994. Heston also appeared in two anti-Foley commercials that were broadcast repeatedly during the last two weeks of the campaign. "Shame on you, Tom Foley," Heston scolded in the commercials.[14]

Agriculture and the Fifth District

Foley's career-long advocacy for his district's agricultural interests was also reinforced over time, especially with the political and interest-based benefits derived from his early ascension to chair of the House Agriculture Committee. But while that trust served Foley well in the long run of thirty years, it could not survive the country's changing times, energized by Newt Gingrich's repeated assaults on the Foley-led Democratic House. Nor could it overcome the effect of distance, both geographic and political, presented by Foley's movement up the leadership ladder of the House to the top rung, that of Speaker. Indeed, three decades after his initial election victory, a preelection survey of Fifth District voters produced the following headline: "Speaker Foley Faces Uphill Battle, Nethercutt Holds Lead."[15] The accompanying story reported that while 77 percent of Foley supporters called his position as Speaker an important factor in their preference, "only 31 percent of Nethercutt supporters said that Foley being speaker was important." In addition, only 50 percent of Foley supporters called his role as Speaker of the House very important, compared with 11 percent for supporters of George Nethercutt, Foley's opponent.[16] As a result, Foley's opponent found fertile ground for the seeds of discontent fed by national political figures such as Gingrich, Ross Perot, and talk-radio host Rush Limbaugh.

Throughout his career, agriculture was a dominant force in the economy of Foley's district, and he scored points with many constituents with his knowledge of federal farm programs, policies, and price supports. After just two years in the House, Foley aptly navigated a complicated discussion of wheat prices and production costs in Waterville, in Douglas County. Afterward, farmer Dave Dorsey thanked him: "We appreciate your knowledge of the farm program and your aggressiveness in this. We didn't have to explain it to you when you went back there two years ago."[17] At the same time, though, the 1966 campaign divided two members of a prominent Lincoln County farming family. Gene Moos, president of Western Wheat Associates, a group promoting wheat exports, agreed to be chair of Wheat Growers for Foley. His cousin Donald Moos endorsed Foley's opponent, Dorothy Powers, a columnist for the *Spokesman-Review* in Spokane.[18]

Agricultural policy also gave Foley an opportunity to advance in the House leadership much sooner than he expected. In 1966, North Carolina voters ousted Harold Cooley, chair of the Agriculture Committee. Representative William R. "Bob" Poage (D-TX), who replaced Cooley, appointed Foley, then in his second term, to chair the Domestic Marketing and Consumer Relations Subcommittee. Foley was one of the first members of the House cohort elected in 1964 to chair a subcommittee. "The appointment had nothing to do with skill or ability—it was strictly seniority," Foley said. Nonetheless, that position gave him increased visibility and a larger staff. In addition to setting federal farm policy, the Agriculture Committee assumed a major role in President Lyndon B. Johnson's anti-poverty program through its jurisdiction over food stamps and commodity distribution.[19]

As a subcommittee chair, Foley discovered the importance of building a constituency for farm legislation among urban members of Congress. Foreshadowing Foley's capacity to bridge gaps across potentially contending policy positions, he thought the Agriculture Committee should also address conservation, nutrition, and consumer protection issues. In 1967, Foley joined Representative Neal Smith (D-IA) to introduce the most sweeping changes in federal meat inspection laws in sixty years. Smith had been trying since 1960 to toughen federal meatpacking laws. In Foley, he found a helpful ally. Under then-existing law, meat was exempt from federal inspection unless it was produced for interstate commerce. The Smith-Foley amendment required federal inspection of all meatpacking plants, regardless of where the meat was sold. Although Poage and other House members argued before the committee that state meat inspection laws were adequate, the bill passed 403–1 after it reached the House floor. The Senate followed suit, and President Johnson signed the bill into law.[20] After leaving office, Foley called his work to improve the safety of America's food supply one of his proudest accomplishments.

Early in his career, Foley stayed abreast of constituent concerns by engaging in extensive tours of the district during congressional recesses. While Spokane was the district's largest city and home to print and broadcast media, many stops on those tours were in the small towns with heavy agricultural bases in the western part of the Fifth District. The level of wheat production in that district's counties dominated the agricultural sector of the district. In 1964, counties in the Fifth District produced 11.3 million bushels of wheat. The 1972 redistricting moved two counties (Chelan and Douglas) out of the district, taking with them 4.2 million bushels of wheat production (by the 1964 count), but eight counties replaced them: Adams, Asotin, Columbia, Franklin, Garfield, Grant, Walla Walla, and Whitman. The new counties brought with them 1964 levels of nearly 51 million bushels of wheat. By 1992, shortly before the end of Foley's time in office, the counties of the Fifth District produced an annual total of more than 73 million bushels of wheat.[21]

Reflecting his interest in agriculture, and its importance to his constituents, Foley spent considerable time in the district's farm counties. Typical was a week in January 1970, documented by Art Hanson, manager of Foley's Spokane office, which took him in a nearly five-hundred-mile loop from Spokane to Wilbur, Waterville, Chelan, Okanogan, Tonasket, Republic, and Kettle Falls, then back to Spokane (figure 5.1).[22] Accounts of this and other district trips illustrate the hectic pace of Foley's visits to eastern Washington, especially early in his time in Congress, but also the diverse interests of his sprawling district and the importance to him of staying in touch with those interests.

Tom Foley tours the Fifth District

Tom Foley stayed abreast of constituent concerns with extensive tours of the Fifth District during congressional recesses. Typical of the pattern was a week in January of 1970, documented by Art Hanson, manager of Foley's Spokane office:

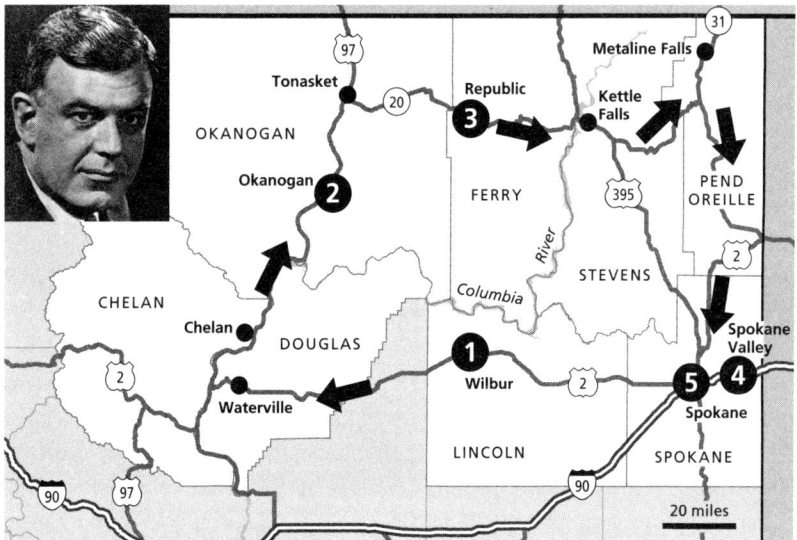

1 **Jan. 13:** Breakfast at Ma's Cafe at Wilbur, meeting with the publisher of the *Wilbur Register,* meeting with Douglas County commissioners in Waterville, dinner with leading citizens in Chelan.

2 **Jan. 14:** Breakfast with Okanogan County commissioners and the county Democratic chairman, meeting with representatives of the Fruit Growers Association, lunch with the Women's Democratic Club, visit to offices of Forest Service and Washington Department of Public Assistance, interview with two radio stations, dinner in Tonasket, drive to Republic.

3 **Jan. 15:** Breakfast with Stevens County commissioners in Republic, tour of Boise-Cascade lumber mill in Kettle Falls,

radio interview, tour of Metaline Falls City Hall, dinner and informal discussion, drive to Spokane.

4 **Jan. 16:** Demonstration of a butane-operated automobile by Dick Bond (Foley's 1968 opponent), talk to student-body officers at West Valley High School, lunch at the Spokane Club with officers of the Spokane County Medical Society, two television interviews, discussion with Joe Drumheller (a prominent Spokane Democrat), meeting with Spokane Mayor David Rogers.

5 **Jan. 18:** Meeting with Bud Quackenbush, Jim Gillespie, Hank Higgins and Jack Geraghty (all heavily involved in Foley's re-election campaigns), flew to Seattle.

Figure 5.1. Tom Foley tours the Fifth District

Source: Foley Papers, Washington State University Library.

Photo courtesy of Gonzaga University; map by Emmett Mayer III

Concurrent with Foley's rise in the agricultural policy-making arena was his growing capacity to economically benefit his district in other arenas as well. The 1970 election reflected the domestic conflict over the war in Southeast Asia, including protests against the war by university and college students across the United States. Foley's Republican challenger, George Gamble, demanded the expulsion of students and the dismissal of faculty members "who advocate, promote and participate in violence and destruction on our college campuses." Foley responded that college administrators could handle the problem without federal interference.[23]

Regardless of their views on campus demonstrations, eastern Washington residents benefited from their congressional delegation's ability to bring federal spending to the state. In October 1970, Foley joined Senator Henry Jackson (who also was up for reelection that year) at the Grand Coulee Dam, where construction crews poured the first concrete for the third powerhouse, a $350 million project.[24] The National Park Service describes the dam's central role in the agricultural development of eastern Washington in this way:

> With the end of World War II, the economy in the Northwest continued to boom. Water pumped from Grand Coulee began reaching Columbia Basin lands in 1948 and today irrigates about 670,000 acres, although the project was designed to deliver a full water supply to 1.1 million acres. In a region once used only for dry land farming and livestock grazing, crops grown today range from forage and cereal grains to fruit, vegetables, and specialty crops such as mint and wine grapes.[25]

Foley's support for the dam and other regional irrigation projects on the Columbia and Snake Rivers meshed tightly with the support he showed for agricultural commodities. Years later, Foley reflected on the change in the public's attitude toward federal spending. "In the late Fifties and early Sixties, nationally there was this sense that the government was well motivated and tried hard," he recalled. "If that was true nationally, it was even more true in the Pacific Northwest," where federal money funded the building of dams on the Snake and Columbia Rivers, as well as supported nuclear weapons research at Hanford. At the time Foley left office in 1994, however, many Americans distrusted the federal government, believing it was too big, too intrusive, and too inefficient.[26]

In the 1974 election, Foley faced Gary Gage, a member of the John Birch Society. Gage raised issues similar to those of previous Republican candidates: deficit spending, high taxes, and excessive government regulation. He also questioned Foley's effectiveness as a senior member of the House Agriculture Committee. "The farmers I talked to are asking [about] and are more concerned about their own businesses than they are [about] his career, and they are asking, 'What is he doing for us?' and it's more 'What's he doing to us?'" Gage blamed Foley for not pushing to exempt farmers from the Occupational Safety and Health Act.[27] Gage's complaints failed to gain traction, though, as Foley comfortably won reelection to a sixth term that year, receiving 64.3 percent of the vote to Gage's 35.7 percent.

The 1974 election, three months after Richard Nixon resigned, swept Democrats into office across the United States. Democrats picked up forty-nine seats in the House of Representatives and three in the Senate. Perhaps more significant for Foley's political future was the number of new Democrats, the so-called Class of '74, who ran against politics as usual and advocated for changes in campaign finance laws. As noted in chapter 2, the infusion of reform-minded Democrats boosted the stature of the Democratic Study Group (DSG). The DSG, founded in the 1950s by a handful of moderate and liberal members, had grown by 1970 to include nearly half of the House Democrats.[28]

The DSG indirectly opened the path for Foley's leadership ascent, including in the agricultural policy domain. In 1976, former Georgia governor Jimmy Carter ousted Gerald Ford from the White House after less than three years in office. After their big gains in 1974, Democrats actually picked up one additional House seat, boosting their margin over Republicans to 292 to 193. One of the new Democrats that year was Leon Panetta (D-CA), who joined the House Agriculture Committee, chaired by Foley. Panetta offered this view of Foley's leadership style: "He represented the kind of honor and integrity that made a freshman member look up to a senior member of Congress." Panetta recalled the respect Foley showed for Representative William R. "Bob" Poage (D-TX) after replacing him as chair of the committee.

> To the distinction of Tom Foley and who he is, he placed Poage next to him, as you know. I think he referred to him as "cochair" as well and always gave him a great deal of deference. Because he respected Poage and respected the seniority system and for the sake of everyone getting along, he established a great relationship

that worked when I was a member of the Agriculture Committee. Even though Tom Foley was chair, all of us paid respect to Poage as the person next in line.[29]

Panetta's characterization of Foley was shared by Representative Dan Glickman (D-KS), elected to the House in 1976 and later secretary of agriculture. He described Foley as "extremely bipartisan. He was extremely deferential to the Republicans on the committee. He was not a polarizing figure at all; he was an anti-polarizing figure." Glickman noted that agriculture committees in both the House and Senate always have been more bipartisan than most other committees in Congress.[30]

Foley's 1978 reelection bid was complicated by several issues, including farmers' growing discontent with US farm programs. But in September 1977 the *Wall Street Journal* published a glowing profile of Foley, praising his role in shaping a compromise in passing a major farm bill.[31] President Jimmy Carter sought to limit the cost of farm programs because he had pledged to balance the federal budget by 1981. But his budget goals collided head-on with the demand of senators and representatives from farm states to raise supports for wheat and corn to a level that Carter called unacceptable. Through a series of parliamentary maneuvers, Foley found common ground between the Senate's already-passed legislation and the White House proposal.[32] After the House passed the bill by a 294–111 vote on July 28, Foley's colleagues gave him a standing ovation. The episode illustrated Foley's mastery of the legislative process; as Karen House, the author of the *Journal* article, wrote, "His nature is to avoid confrontations; he rarely twists arms. Instead, he builds coalitions, but he does so by finding common interests rather than wheeling and dealing to balance opposing interests. And he eagerly includes Republicans in his coalitions."[33] Ironically, more than a decade later, after Foley became Speaker, some Democrats complained about his tendency to compromise with Republicans.

The good feelings over passage of the 1977 farm bill were short-lived. In December, farmers' frustrations at low crop prices reached a boiling point. More than twelve hundred farmers from four states crowded into the basketball coliseum at Washington State University in Pullman for a hearing by the House Subcommittee on Grains and Livestock. Foley, as Agriculture Committee chair, arranged the meeting and was one of five House members who attended. But his credentials and expertise failed to impress the audience in the heart of wheat country. Roy Cochran, a seventy-three-year-old Colfax farmer, chastised Foley before being cut off by the subcommittee's chair, William Poage of Texas, who had been replaced by Foley as chair of the full committee two years earlier. "I am ashamed to be connected with agriculture under present conditions," Cochran declared to applause. "If I were a congressman, supposedly representing agriculture, I would also be ashamed." A reporter described the congressman's reaction: "Foley, as he did most of the day-long hearing, looked sullen."[34]

Foley played a major role on the farm bills of 1981 and 1985, much to the benefit of his constituents. In shepherding that legislation, Foley signaled his adept use of transactional values. Notwithstanding the occasional attacks from agriculture-based constituents (such as the angry crowd in Pullman in 1977), his chairmanship of the Agriculture Committee demonstrated to the major interests in his constituency that he could "deliver" in a way that served their interests. Throughout his time in the House, Foley could count on developments in agricultural commodity research to buttress his claim of being a friend of agriculture. The regular appearance of new strains of wheat, by far the dominant commodity in the Fifth District, provided continuing testament to Foley's support for his district's constituency.

Representative Jim McDermott, who represented an urban district in Seattle from 1989 to 2017, described Foley's approach to dealing with his rural constituents: "He would come out [to the district] at the end of his two years, and he would say to the wheat farmers, 'Hey, look, you guys, WSU [Washington State University] has produced another strain of wheat. It'll be the best!'" The farmers appreciated Foley's support for wheat research at the university and, indirectly for them, McDermott said.[35] He recalled that Foley once expressed surprise that he was appointed to the Agricultural Committee in his first term. "I didn't know anything about wheat crops. I was a lawyer. I didn't know farmers in my family, nothing," Foley told McDermott. "By the end of those first two years, I knew more about wheat rust than anybody on the face of the earth because I was the guy who was running [the] subcommittee in the Agriculture Committee, and I did my job."[36]

NAFTA

In November 1993, the first year of President Bill Clinton's first term, Congress took up the North American Free Trade Agreement among the United States, Canada, and Mexico. The accord was described as "a sweeping trilateral agreement to eliminate, over time, most barriers to trade and investment in North America and to strengthen intellectual property rights."[37]

According to some critics, though, approval of NAFTA resulted in "policies that could have been undertaken anyway . . . simply the culmination of a process of dramatic economic and social restructuring that had occurred, or was occurring, to a greater or lesser degree in each country."[38] Those policies were negotiated and argued over at two different levels. The first level was national, where the agreements were fought out among representatives of the countries. The second level was domestic, particularly in the United States, where approval required action by both the House and the Senate.[39] This level provides insight into Tom Foley's leadership style and principles. Clinton had made passage of the trade agreement a top priority for his first term, and he succeeded. In the analysis of Maxwell A. Cameron and Brian W. Tomlin:

> Clinton was able to convince the U.S. Congress to pass the North American Free Trade Agreement through his persuasive and bargaining skills. His efforts, which were concentrated on undecided lawmakers, were complemented by efforts from allies that included economists, Nobel Prize winners, governors and foreign policy experts. Together, they were able to stem massive opposition to the bill from organized labor, consumer groups, environmentalists and African-American leaders. He was also able to modify the bill to be acceptable to more lawmakers.[40]

The congressional votes on NAFTA reflected divisions in the country and within each party. In the House, the vote was 234 to 200. Significantly, more Republicans (132) voted in favor than Democrats (100).[41] Minority whip Newt Gingrich (R-GA) urged House Republicans to support NAFTA. "This is a vote for history, larger than politics, larger than reelection, larger than personal ego," said Gingrich, who usually relished confrontations with the majority Democrats.[42] The Senate's approval, on a 61–38 vote, followed a week later. As in the House, Republicans provided the margin of victory, with 34 Republican senators joining 27 Democrats in favor.[43] On December 8, 1993, Clinton signed the enabling legislation, ending "the lengthy political process that produced it. NAFTA, which lowers trade barriers over a period of 15 years across a broad spectrum of goods between the U.S., Canada and Mexico, was the subject of one of the most heated political contests of recent times."[44]

For Americans other than those working in agriculture or members of labor unions, NAFTA was an esoteric issue whose impacts and technicalities were not on their minds. Yet certain sectors of the economy, including in Foley's Fifth District, saw significant implications, both positive and negative, housed in NAFTA's details. Advocates said NAFTA would benefit many agricultural interests, opening Canadian and Mexican markets to grain commodities while boosting Mexico's struggling economy. In their 2000 analysis, Maxwell Cameron and Brian Tomlin suggested that "opening agriculture across the board was probably the single most important concession made by Mexico" at a September 19, 1991, trilateral meeting in Dallas, where "negotiations on agriculture really got under way."[45]

Ken Casavant, a longtime agricultural economist at Washington State University in Foley's district, recalled that the state's wheat growers didn't fully appreciate Foley's support for them. Casavant observed that agricultural groups were divided on this legislation: "Each group looked at NAFTA based on their commodity. NAFTA was a collision of competing interests." He summed up the split in this way: "If you worry about yourself, you're against NAFTA; if you think of all commodities, then trade matters."[46] Nationally, there was disagreement among farm groups over details of the trade agreement. "Support for NAFTA among agricultural groups was mixed throughout the negotiations, reflecting the great diversity of interests in American agriculture," political scientist William Avery wrote. He identified grain producers, of which there were many in Foley's district, as among the greatest potential beneficiaries, explaining, "In virtually every grain commodity, American farmers already had a commanding lead in trade with Mexico. Lowering trade barriers was expected to produce even more opportunities for grain exports."[47]

At the same time, though, President Clinton, Foley, and other congressional advocates of NAFTA had to overcome considerable opposition from labor interests, including the AFL-CIO. At the labor group's convention in San Francisco in October, the union's president, Lane Kirkland, blamed former president George H. W. Bush for leaving behind a flawed and unratified trade pact. At the time, the AFL-CIO represented 13.3 million members of ninety-five unions. Kirkland said the federation would not relent in its opposition to the trade agreement, in spite of a personal appeal from Clinton. "By and large, his agenda is our agenda," Kirkland said of Clinton before the president spoke. "But we do have one major difference of opinion. Among the poison pills left behind by George Bush is a lethal one called NAFTA."[48]

Reflecting labor's opposition to the trade agreement, David Bonior, the House Democratic whip in 1993 and a member who represented a district near Detroit, was firmly opposed to NAFTA. "Every fiber in my body reacted against the unfairness of a trade regime that protected capital, intellectual property, and physical property at the expense of labor," Bonior wrote in his 2018 memoir. "I foresaw this trade deal as a lose-lose for workers in all three signatories to the deal: Canada, Mexico, and the United States."[49] In Foley's home state, the Washington State Labor Council (AFL-CIO) strongly opposed NAFTA. In a newsletter issued a day after the House vote on the enabling legislation, the council's president, Rick S. Bender, wrote: "We are all deeply disappointed and angered by the lack of support we received from our congressional delegation. We devoted literally thousands of hours of work and our members' hard-earned dues to these representatives who abandoned us when the tough vote stared them in the face." Bender singled out for praise Jolene Unsoeld, the only Washington State representative who voted against the agreement, stating, "She has proven herself to be an honorable and loyal friend of labor and we must assure her reelection."[50] In a speech on the House floor, Unsoeld justified her opposition to NAFTA for two overlapping reasons: "sustainable use of resources and the advancement of basic labor rights. . . . They would both be part of a NAFTA worthy of support. They are absent in this NAFTA and I urge my colleagues to vote no."[51]

However, Unsoeld's opposition to NAFTA did not save her seat in 1994. The five other Democrats in the delegation supported the agreement, perhaps in deference to Foley. Four of them lost their seats in the next election, and one, Al Swift, chose not to run again and was replaced by a Republican.

Fourteen months after Clinton signed NAFTA into law, the US Department of Commerce issued a glowing report titled "NAFTA: The First Nine Months." The report used economic formulas to assert that NAFTA had created 127,000 US jobs because of increased exports to Mexico. Unstated in the Commerce Department report, according to the Congressional Joint Economic Committee, was that Mexican imports to the United States had increased even more, creating a theoretical job loss of 137,000 jobs, a negative job balance of about 10,000 US jobs. As of January 9, 1995, the US Labor Department had certified 17,374 workers as eligible for NAFTA-related benefits. The congressional report also noted that some US exports to Mexico were transshipments from other countries by companies that used US ports as a point of departure into Mexico to avoid higher Mexican tariffs on European goods.[52]

In a 1998 analysis, Frederick Mayer pointed out the contradiction between Republican support for NAFTA and Democratic opposition.[53] But in the House, the opposition did not include Foley. Support for the agreement—and for President Clinton's agenda—put Foley at odds with Bonior and Richard Gephardt, the majority leader, both from industrial states (Michigan and Missouri). Representative Norm Dicks (D-WA), a Foley ally who voted for NAFTA, explained the split this way: "Gephardt and Bonior would have been more sympathetic to the labor unions, and probably not as trade oriented. Foley was supporting the president, a Democratic president. And he had a lot of trade opportunities in his district."[54]

The policy disagreement between Foley and his deputies remained low-key and never affected their ability to work together. "Foley and Majority Leader Gephardt kept their own participation low-key and carefully refrained from the sort of heated rhetoric that would make reconciliation after the fight difficult," congressional scholar Barbara Sinclair observed.[55] Consistent with Sinclair's analysis, Andrew J. Taylor pointed out the role of the Republican minority of the House in passage of the trade package. "It might not be an understatement to say that, without [minority leader Robert] Michel, NAFTA would have been defeated," Taylor wrote.[56] Supporting this perception of the Michel-Foley relationship, Douglas Harris quoted from an oral history of the two leaders: "Michel characterized their closeness even as he lamented the decline of such comity; he said to Foley . . . 'Even though we'd get involved in very vigorous debates on key issues, we never let it degenerate to a fight between personalities.'"[57] Of course, Foley and Michel did not disagree on NAFTA, enabling Foley to deliver a victory for President Clinton. "Ultimately, NAFTA needed GOP votes to pass, with 132 Republicans among the 234 House members who supported it," Taylor wrote.[58]

Reflecting on the 1994 election and NAFTA's effect on Foley's political fate, Leon Panetta, White House budget director and chief of staff under Clinton, observed: "The Republicans had a lot of meat to throw at members in the election in terms of ads that went after those votes." He speculated that Foley might have kept his seat "if he had gone the other direction on some of those proposals. . . . But that would have been against every fiber of his being in terms of what was right." Now, members of Congress are less inclined to take principled stands, Panetta said. "When you look at a dysfunctional Congress, it would be great to have more Tom Foleys who had the guts and courage to vote for what was right, regardless of the political impact that it might have."[59]

Foley's role and position in regard to NAFTA, which would weaken barriers to imports to and exports from Canada and Mexico, placed him in the middle of a web of NAFTA's supporters and detractors, including his own leadership group and members of his own party in the House. NAFTA was strongly supported by Foley, many of his constituents, some Republicans in Congress, and President Clinton. In that context, the *Baltimore Sun*'s Karen Hosler wrote:

> House Speaker Thomas S. Foley of Washington, who supports the treaty but who seems unlikely to take a vigorous role in the debate, said there is simply no point in trying to invoke party discipline on an issue over which even Mr. Clinton's top advisers are at odds. . . . Too many people have divided opinions on it. In those circumstances, it is extremely difficult and rather useless to try to declare an official position because members are going to follow their judgments and take the position they determine to be in the interest of their constituents.[60]

On the other hand, many Democratic House members with strong labor interests opposed NAFTA, fearing job losses to competition from Mexico and Canada and the movement of production facilities to those countries. Several prominent national political figures, including Ross Perot, did not support NAFTA. And perhaps most troubling to Foley was the division within his own party leadership cadre about the issue. When the final vote came in November, "NAFTA split the House Democratic leadership. Speaker Thomas S. Foley (Wash.), caucus Chairman Steny H. Hoyer (Md.) and Vice Chairman Vic Fazio (Calif.) backed the agreement, while Bonior and Majority Leader Richard A. Gephardt (Mo.) opposed Clinton on the issue."[61]

When Foley spoke on the floor of the House, he reflected on the divisions within his party and in Congress: "This has been a long debate. Not only a long debate today, but a long debate over recent weeks and months. And it has been a difficult debate, difficult in so many ways, for so many of us. We find our parties divided, not one against the other, but internally divided. Our leadership's divided, our members divided." In addition, members found themselves at odds with friends and allies in their home districts, "with whom we have had so many years of association, and respectful cooperation.[62] Foley's support for NAFTA and free trade was shared by Robert Michel, the Republican House minority leader. Andrew Taylor noted, "It was on the North American Free Trade Agreement (NAFTA) negotiated by Bush but requiring congressional approval under Clinton that Michel struck the biggest blow for international liberal economic principles."[63]

On NAFTA, Foley faced opposition from within his own party, including members of his leadership team. There was also anti-NAFTA sentiment among prominent political figures on the right, Ross Perot, Pat Buchanan, and Ralph Nader (whom Michel called "the Groucho, Chico and Harpo of NAFTA politics"), and prominent House Republicans such as Dan Burton (R-IN), Duncan Hunter (R-CA), Ralph Regula (R-OH), Gerald Solomon (R-NY), and Dan Young (R-AK)."[64] Congressional scholar Matthew Green analyzed Foley's position on NAFTA from several perspectives, concluding:

> Foley's decision to support NAFTA is therefore not adequately explained by a desire to support the congressional party's policy preferences. Furthermore, given that many opinion polls showed a plurality, if not a majority, of the public opposed NAFTA, its passage was unlikely to help the immediate election chances of House Democrats. But Foley could possibly achieve other leadership goals by helping pass the trade agreement. First, although deference to the institutional presidency on foreign affairs matters had arguably declined since the 1970s and the Vietnam War, it had not vanished entirely. Second . . . support for the agreement by Foley and others reflected the belief that party leaders should stand behind the initiatives of their party's president. . . . Foley may have hoped to satisfy a third goal—re-election to Congress—by backing NAFTA because the economic interests of Foley's export-oriented state . . . would likely benefit from the trade agreement.[65]

For most of his time in Congress, Foley identified as a defender of free trade. His press secretary, Jeff Biggs, wrote: "His was a position that came with a political price, particularly with organized labor. . . . Foley's free trade advocacy also put him at odds with the rest of his leadership team during the congressional debate over the North American Free Trade Agreement (NAFTA) and was a factor in his 1994 congressional defeat." Foley agreed that supporting NAFTA hurt his final reelection bid: "It wasn't so much that it produced active resistance, but more that it led to a disenthralling reaction. . . . I think the long ties I had with labor were put under strain by such things as the WTO [World Trade Organization] issues embodied in the agreement."[66] The tensions between Foley and organized labor were reflected in this assessment from David Groves, the Washington State Labor

Council's communications director: "When the Democrats from our state [with the exception of Jolene Unsoeld] voted for NAFTA, we had a significant drop in union household turnout in the 1994 election and that was a factor in a dramatic shift in representation."[67]

Two years before Foley's final campaign, a poll of Washington State voters assessed NAFTA's impact on the Northwest economy. Of the respondents, 35 percent had no opinion, and only 14 percent thought it would have no impact. The poll results showed that "the most positive response came from the counties between Everett and the Canadian border (43%) and from Eastern Washington (40%)," while the least favorable response came from residents west of Puget Sound, where only 22 percent anticipated a positive impact from NAFTA. While Foley speculated after leaving office that the trade agreement strained his ties with labor, union members were positive by a two-to-one margin. The perceived negative impacts of NAFTA in the statewide sample were the following: jobs going to Mexico (23 percent), job loss (13 percent), countries will overtake the United States (12 percent), too much trade (9 percent), and other countries wouldn't participate (6 percent). While none of those negative percentage figures seem overwhelming, given the relatively small margin by which Foley lost the 1994 election and when combined with other issues such as his opposition to term limits, they certainly could have swayed the election outcome.[68]

Many of the agricultural constituencies that supported NAFTA probably saw an economic self-interest in its provisions, particularly the opening of commodity exports to Canada and Mexico. Eric Uslaner's 1998 study (published five years after the agreement's passage) notes that "NAFTA also promised greater market access for many agricultural products . . . to the Mexican market." He also wrote that "members who have either many farmers or many white-collar residents are more supportive of NAFTA . . . a member whose district has 10% farmers is 24% more likely to back the pact than one with no farmers."[69] Washington State University agricultural economist Ken Casavant reflected that NAFTA was good for agriculture, with one exception. "What we didn't do was move enough money and support to industries that bore the brunt of negative impacts. We could have and should have done more, and we could have followed up if Foley had stayed in office" after 1994, he said.[70]

Congressional scholar Barbara Sinclair concluded that NAFTA "tested the leadership's ability to cope with a deep policy split." She described the conflicting expectations that Foley and others faced: "The expectation that they would advance the legislative preferences of the majority of their members clashed with the expectation that they would support the policy priorities of a president of their own party."[71] But another important factor not considered explicitly by Sinclair was the centrality of NAFTA to one of Foley's major constituencies: agricultural interests. Growers of wheat, barley, peas, and lentils were poised to benefit from greater export opportunities.

To be sure, Foley's position on NAFTA also reflected his supportive opinions on free trade and his belief that the Speaker of the House should support a president of his own party. Two weeks before the House vote, President Clinton wrote to Speaker Foley: "Rejecting NAFTA would, quite simply, put us on the wrong side of history. That is not our destiny. I ask the House of Representatives to join me in choosing the path of expanded trade, to make the decision to compete in the world, rather than to retreat behind our borders."[72]

Despite their disagreement, members of the Democratic leadership worked hard to maintain postures to minimize long-term negative effects on the party. Sinclair notes that Bonior refrained from using the Democratic whip organization to oppose NAFTA, while Foley and Gephardt "kept their own participation low-key and carefully refrained from the sort of heated rhetoric that would make reconciliation difficult."[73] The responses of Gephardt and Bonior surely derived from respect for Foley, not from fear of retribution. Twenty-five years after NAFTA, Bonior lavished praise on Foley, calling him "one of the most respected individuals in not only Congress but all of Washington. . . . Tom was widely considered to be one of the most competent public servants of his time."[74] Bonior's regard and respect not only smoothed relations among the members of the Democratic leadership but also made it possible to take conflicting positions on important issues of public policy without long-term damage to the party itself. George Kundanis, a key Foley staff member, said the personal relationships among the three leaders overrode their differences over NAFTA. "Foley, Gephardt and Bonior were very close personally," Kundanis said. "With the division in the ranks, Foley was hands off, so there was no reason for conflict among the three. Bonior's dissatisfaction was more directed at Clinton."[75]

After the NAFTA vote, the *Washington Post* reported that Ross Perot, the 1992 independent presidential candidate, accused the White House of "buying votes" to secure passage. "No votes were changing until the pork started flowing," said Perot, who called the White House's use of enticements "absolutely corrupt." Perot made two predictions: NAFTA would hurt both parties in the 1994 congressional elections, and "the anger of working Americans could lead to cancellation of NAFTA in 1995."[76] Perot's first prediction was partially accurate: Democrats lost their majority in the House in the 1994 election. But the second prediction, that NAFTA would be repealed, did not come to pass.

The probable NAFTA-related losses were not confined to Washington State. Martin Wattenberg wrote four years later: "The effect of the dramatic swing by Perot voters toward House Republicans can also be clearly identified through an analysis of the election returns by congressional district. . . . There was a strong relationship in Democratic-held seats between the percentage of the vote Perot received in the district and the share of the two-party vote gained by Republican House candidates in 1994."[77] Whether that shift was caused by NAFTA (and Perot's opposition to it) is unclear, but Perot made an issue of it in 1994 congressional races, including Foley's reelection bid.

While Foley speculated his support for NAFTA may have cost him votes in 1994, a statewide poll showed strong support for the agreement from areas close to the Canadian border and in eastern Washington. Even so, only 40 percent of respondents in eastern Washington favored NAFTA.[78] But the question still can be raised as to whether the NAFTA agreement was sufficiently salient to Washington voters to make a difference in their decision to vote for or against Foley, especially if mobilized by union opponents. It is also possible that NAFTA could have had an effect on support for Foley, independent of the previous support of Perot voters. Foley received 55 percent of the vote against Republican challenger John Sonneland in 1992, the year that Perot ran for president. In the Fifth District, Perot received over 22 percent of the vote for president while Bill Clinton received a plurality of only 40 percent. Then, in 1994, Foley's support fell off to where he received 49 percent of the vote, a decline in support that can be attributed to a number of issues, of which NAFTA was only one.

While other domestic issues were important to Foley and to his district, agricultural policy was consistent and powerful. Exports of grains, fruits, and vegetables, encouraged by NAFTA, also had implications for US relations with Mexico, Canada, and other countries. Foley's representational role emphasized transactional values in his district, but he also held and expressed transformational policy values at the national level. His transactional political actions were sufficient to keep him in office for fifteen terms, especially when the positive effects for his district, particularly those for farmers and other agricultural interests, were widely seen and accepted.

Another insight into Foley's leadership style can be found in the Democratic leadership's split over NAFTA. While Foley strongly supported the passage of the agreement, siding with President Clinton, the other members of his inner circle did not. Given the 58 percent opposition to NAFTA among the Democratic House members, Richard Gephardt and David Bonior, the majority leader and whip, clearly represented the position of the caucus on that particular issue to a greater degree than did Foley. All three men played down the division. Foley wrote, "It was an act of some forbearance on Dick Gephardt and David Bonior's part that they didn't demand a caucus" vote on the agreement.[79] In their memoirs, neither Bonior nor Gephardt raised the issue of their disagreement with Foley over NAFTA. To the contrary, both men acknowledged Foley had a more "free market" ideology that downplayed the importance of tariffs. Reflecting on his relationship with the Speaker, Gephardt said:

> I sat through innumerable meetings with him where he was the best I've ever seen at relating to people, listening to people, politely disagreeing with people. I remember the one phrase he always used when he would start into some discussion where it wasn't going to be very pleasant. . . . He started by saying, "With respect, blah, blah, blah . . ." And that kind of threw people off. Even though they knew they were going to disagree, it kind of backs people down a little bit and makes them more willing to listen and find a way through the issue, even though you have broad disagreement.[80]

Foley's support for agricultural interests and free trade failed to assure his reelection in 1994. Perhaps part of this vulnerability came from a generational change among farmers. Robert "Mac" Crow of Garfield, who had organized a group called Farmers for Foley in the late 1970s, speculated that by 1994, many of Foley's early supporters had retired, moved off the farm, or died. The younger farmers who replaced them did not have a personal relationship with Foley or were unfamiliar with his accomplishments. "I can go down the list [of farmers] and check off the dads who were Foley, the kids who were not," Crow said. "The young farmers were getting their information from different sources, including talk radio, and forming different opinions of Foley from their parents."[81] Loss of support from farmers was only one weak spot in Foley's 1994 reelection campaign, but it may have been the one that hurt the most.

THE PINNACLE OF POWER

During the months after Jim Wright's resignation as Speaker, Tom Foley did what he did best: mediate, conciliate, and work out compromises. His tact, wit, and sense of fair play soothed the animosity that the ethics investigation of Wright had generated in the House. In contrast to his image in the press as a perpetual critic of the Democrats, Republican whip Newt Gingrich, who had agitated for Wright's ouster, acknowledged that under Foley's leadership, the House was a more congenial place to work.

Foley's constituents in eastern Washington recognized his visibility and power. They received him warmly during his visits to the district and reelected him by a comfortable margin in 1990. But in Washington, DC, Foley's honeymoon with the House of Representatives was short-lived. Republican House members, chafing at their seemingly perpetual minority status, resumed their rhetorical attacks on the Democrats after a truce of only a few months. At the same time, some Democrats, especially those from the party's liberal wing, grumbled that Foley was not aggressive enough in challenging the White House agenda. Thereafter, Capitol Hill reporters periodically detected hints of a revolt in the Democratic ranks. Representative Nancy Pelosi (D-CA), a future Speaker, said she was asked by fellow Democrats in 1994 to run against Foley out of concern that the party would lose its House majority. "There was no way I was going to run against the Speaker, no way in a million years," Pelosi, then in her fourth term in the House, told a biographer.[1] In spite of the grumbling, no other Democrat ever stepped forward to formally challenge Foley.

As Speaker, Foley got along well with George H. W. Bush, elected president in 1988, succeeding Ronald Reagan. On some issues, Foley extended to the White House the model of bipartisan compromise he had perfected in the House. On others, though, they disagreed. In the summer of 1990, for example, Foley opposed a Bush-backed constitutional amendment to prohibit burning of the American flag, and six months later, he argued against Bush's request for authority to wage war on Iraq. In sum, Foley's first three years as Speaker of the House, although not free of difficulties, confirmed his place as one of the nation's most influential elected officials. By nearly all accounts, he led the House with style, grace, and a commitment to make government work. By focusing on the national interest, Foley demonstrated transformational values in what political scientists Sarah Binder and Thomas Mann described as "a fusing of purpose among previously disconnected or conflicting individuals that produces a mutual and continuing pursuit of a higher purpose."[2] At the same time, the hardball politics of the 1990s tested Foley's statesmanlike approach. Increasingly, he found it difficult to balance his conciliatory nature with the demands of some Democratic colleagues to stand up to the president.

After the partisan sniping that marked the last six months of Jim Wright's term as Speaker, Foley's first task was to restore civility and fairness to what he described as a "very divided and surly House of Representatives."[3] To do so, he had to assure Republican members that their voices—and votes—counted. "My overwhelming desire is to return the House to an atmosphere of collegiality, comity and respect," Foley said shortly after becoming Speaker.[4] Wright, who remained in the House for several months after resigning as Speaker, had nothing but compliments for his successor, calling him "uniquely well-suited" to the speakership.[5] His comments echoed praise for Foley eleven years earlier by another Texan, William R. "Bob" Poage, after Foley had succeeded him as chairman of the Agriculture Committee.[6]

Under Wright and his predecessors, because of their substantial majority, the Democrats always won voice votes, regardless of the number of members who actually voiced "yes" or "no" to the question. But on one occasion in 1989, with Foley in the chair, the Republicans prevailed in a voice vote. "On this day right after Foley became speaker, there was a voice vote," Representative Mickey Edwards (R-OK) recalled. "The few Democrats on the floor at the time shouted 'yes' and the Republicans, in much greater number, shouted 'no,' and we were all poised to demand a [recorded] vote."

After Foley ruled that the negative votes had prevailed, "every Republican on the floor rose spontaneously and gave Tom Foley a standing ovation."[7]

Republicans appreciated Foley's respect for them and the rules of the House. "Even the most vicious Republican operative would have to give Foley credit for changing the tenor of business in Congress," John Buckley of the National Republican Congressional Committee said.[8] Representative Newt Gingrich (R-GA), the author of the 1989 ethics complaints against Wright, called Foley "a partisan [Speaker], but a pleasurable one." Foley and House Republican leader Robert Michel of Illinois "have found a much more reasonable and fairer method of cooperation than we had under Jim Wright," Gingrich said.[9]

This cooperative spirit was apparent in the fall of 1989 when leaders of both parties hammered out a plan to raise House members' pay by coupling it with a ban on outside speaking fees or honoraria. The leadership argued that pay for members of Congress, last raised in 1987, had failed to keep pace with salaries for business and law. Remembering the public's outrage over a pay-raise attempt the previous year, leaders wrapped the 39 percent salary increase in what they called an "ethics package." The measure required House members to donate speaking fees to charity, starting in 1991. It also required additional financial disclosures and limited gifts to members.[10]

In an attempt to prevent the pay raise from becoming a partisan issue in the following year's election, leaders of both parties said they would discourage challengers from attacking incumbents who voted for the salary increase. Democratic national chairman Ronald Brown, his Republican counterpart, Lee Atwater, and the chairs of the parties' congressional campaign committees wrote that the raise was "not an appropriate point of criticism in the coming campaigns. Further, we will publicly oppose the use of this issue in any campaign in the 1990 cycle."[11] Distributed to House members before the vote, the letter was intended to dispel their fears of retaliation. On November 16, the House approved the bill by a 252–174 vote, and the Senate concurred a day later. As a result, House members' pay rose from $89,500 in 1989 to $96,600 in 1990 and to $125,000 in 1991.[12] The compromise, linking the pay raise to the speaking-fee ban, "was handled artfully, in typical Foley style," said Representative Sid Morrison (R-WA).[13]

Critics of Congress protested, however, that the ethics provisions did not justify the raise. "Foley and Michel are dreaming if they think they'll get away with this," activist Ralph Nader asserted. David Worley, a Georgia

Democrat who had lost to Representative Newt Gingrich in 1988, charged that members of Congress were "putting a gun to the American taxpayers' head, saying, 'Pay me more or I'll take bribes from special interests.'"[14] Worley recalled that soon after his comments were published in the *Washington Post,* he received a telephone call from the executive director of the Democratic Congressional Campaign Committee, advising him that his criticism was politically unwise. According to Worley, "It was made clear to me that the national party wouldn't be giving me any help" in his planned 1990 campaign against Gingrich. Worley also resented his party's attempt to muzzle dissenting opinions by threatening to withhold campaign aid. "The agreement typified the kind of 'You scratch my back, I'll scratch yours' culture of Washington at the time," he complained.[15]

After the tense atmosphere that marked the last months of Wright's speakership, reporters on Capitol Hill welcomed Foley's low-key approach. "The speaker's news conferences are characterized by the light banter and frequent laughter of a casual chat rather than the thinly veiled acrimony of an interrogation," a *Baltimore Sun* reporter wrote.[16] For the first time, a stenographer attended the daily press conferences and produced transcripts of the questions and answers, a great convenience to reporters covering the House.[17]

One of Foley's challenges as Speaker was to deal simultaneously with a variety of issues, some routine, many controversial. In 1981, he had given up the chairmanship of the House Agriculture Committee, partly out of a desire to broaden his policy expertise. Foley's ability to recall names, numbers, and details helped him stay on top of legislation and constituent concerns. But after he became Speaker, the demands on his time made it harder to monitor issues firsthand. As a result, he relied more on his staff to develop positions and strategy. Referring to Foley's management style as Speaker, a reporter wrote, "He has surrounded himself with bright people, gives them wide latitude and expects them to take responsibility."[18]

Foley's inner circle included three longtime aides: Werner Brandt, his executive assistant, later sergeant at arms of the House; George Kundanis, director of the Democratic Steering and Policy Committee; and Jeff Biggs, press secretary. Before joining Foley's staff, Brandt, Kundanis, and Biggs had been American Political Science Association congressional fellows in his office. Foley's wife, Heather, an attorney and former staff member for Senator Henry Jackson, served as his unpaid chief of staff, overseeing DC and district offices. A reporter described her as "his intimate confidant, policy adviser and political antenna."[19] In eastern Washington, staff members in Spokane and Walla Walla regularly sent news clippings and other political intelligence via mail and facsimile machines. The staff's importance grew after Foley became Speaker, with key aides serving as gatekeepers to Foley. Brandt explained: "As he advanced, the breadth of individuals and groups wanting access grew. That's natural."[20]

Foley's constituents basked in the glow of his newfound celebrity status. A visit to Walla Walla in August 1989 attracted a handful of national reporters, curious to see whether Fifth District residents responded any differently to their congressman. After a drive from Spokane through the rolling hills of the Palouse, Foley attended a watermelon feed at the home of farmer Don Schwerin. "The populist tradition of the mountain West is that we want to see the guy come around," Schwerin said, referring to Foley's need to stay abreast of his constituents' concerns.[21] The next day, addressing 250 people at a Rotary Club luncheon, Foley received a standing ovation after declaring: "It has been the greatest honor of my life to be the representative from the Fifth Congressional District in the state of Washington."[22] The statement became his verbal signature at the end of most speeches in the district.

Meeting with the editorial board of the *Walla Walla Union Bulletin*, Foley reaffirmed his support for two important local projects: a new building for the US Army Corps of Engineers and the Department of Veterans Affairs Medical Center, which had been threatened with closure.[23] Recounting a conversation with Edward Derwinski, secretary of veterans affairs, Foley said: "We have a little joke. Every time he sees me, he says to me, with careful enunciation: 'W-A-L-L-A W-A-L-L-A.' . . . He knows I have some concern here. . . . I think the secretary knows where [Walla Walla] is."[24] At a Democratic Party reception later that day, Foley supporter Eleanor Kane told a reporter, "It's really kind of unbelievable for those of us who have known him for so long. We watch C-Span and say: 'That's our congressman.'"[25] Kane's comment typified the pride of many eastern Washington residents who had watched Foley rise through the leadership ranks.

Foley quickly demonstrated he could use his position to the benefit of the entire state, not just his district. The day that he became Speaker, he was invited to lunch with President George H. W. Bush. Representative Norm Dicks of Tacoma asked Foley to speak to the president about a $77 million land claim settlement with the Puyallup Indians. "Foley raised it over lunch, and Bush said he was going to sign the bill as long as he didn't have to pronounce the name of the tribe," Dicks said.[26] The House responded to Foley's gentle persuasion on several occasions in 1989, setting aside money for cleaning up nuclear waste sites at Hanford. Asked how he did this, Foley explained: "Any speaker has an opportunity to convey to members his interests in his district, state and region, and usually that's persuasive if it doesn't involve impossible requests."[27] Foley's response appeared to downplay the real power and influence that he exerted to influence legislation as Speaker.

Foley's cooperative spirit extended the length of Pennsylvania Avenue, too. George H. W. Bush had campaigned for the White House in 1988 offering a "kinder, gentler America"—in effect, repudiating the Reagan administration's two-term agenda to reduce the size of government by cutting social programs. Foley resisted frequent appeals from liberal House Democrats to be more aggressive in dealing with the White House. On several occasions during his first year as Speaker, Foley insisted that his job description did not include finding ways to annoy the president. "I keep having people say to me, 'You ought to be the constant daily scourge of George Bush,' that I ought to get up in the morning and figure out what I can say or do to embarrass the president or obstruct the president or whatever," he said. "That's not my concept of the job. . . . There are some places where you have to take a stand even if you fail, but for the most part, I would rather have a successful and important achievement in cooperation with the executive branch than just have a political issue."[28]

His desire for good relations with the president was personal as well as institutional: "I had known President [George H. W.] Bush for many years as a man of great decency and civility." Foley wrote later that Bush "had come into office promising cooperation and not conflict, and I believed the Democrats in Congress, consistent with principle, should reciprocate."[29] Similarly, President Bush had kind words for the House Speaker. "I would describe my relationship with Tom Foley as friendly, respectful, and pleasant even when we disagreed," Bush said six years after leaving the White House. "We did not see eye to eye on issues, but he was always cordial, and he treated me with respect when I was president."[30]

At Foley's invitation, Bush visited Spokane in September 1989 to commemorate Washington's one hundred years of statehood. The president spoke in Riverfront Park, which fifteen years earlier had been the scene of Expo '74, an environmentally themed world's fair. With Foley's help, Bush, who claimed during the 1988 campaign that he would be the environmental president, planted a twelve-foot American elm sapling grown from seeds from a tree planted by John Quincy Adams in the 1820s.[31] That evening, Bush, Tom and Heather Foley, and Environmental Protection

Agency administrator William Reilly dined at Patsy Clark's restaurant, the restored mansion of a turn-of-the-twentieth-century mining millionaire. Bush picked up the tab for dinner.[32] During the next three years, however, events would often test the friendship of the president and the Speaker.

US Policy in Central America

Two months after that friendly dinner in Spokane, a horrible crime in Central America set the stage for a confrontation between Congress and the White House. The murders of six Jesuit professors and two members of their household reopened the debate over a decades-long policy of providing military aid to El Salvador's government.

In the 1980s, as part of President Ronald Reagan's campaign to suppress leftist struggles for independence in Central America, the United States had poured nearly $5 billion into El Salvador in the form of military aid to the right-wing government. Democrats in Congress challenged the policy, but their attempts to cut off US support always fell short. That situation changed after the November 16, 1989, assassination of the six Jesuits, their cook, and her daughter at Central America University in San Salvador. Evidence later showed that the massacre was carried out under orders from military officials.[33] Although the Bush administration decried the killings, the White House resisted changing the policy that bankrolled the killers. Instead, at the Salvadoran government's request, Bush agreed to send additional weapons to the military.[34]

Foley's initial response to the El Salvador killings was restrained and carefully phrased, consistent with his moderate philosophy. But perhaps influenced by his Jesuit education in Spokane and the horrific nature of the crime, within days he was moved to speak out more forcefully. A week after the killings, he condemned the violence and called for renewed efforts to negotiate a cease-fire in El Salvador. Rather than proposing his own peace plan, as Jim Wright had done two years earlier for Nicaragua, Foley preferred a bipartisan approach. "I would prefer to do it with the administration, rather than in contest with them," he said.[35] Foley appointed Representative Joseph Moakley (D-MA), chair of the House Rules Committee, to lead a task force to investigate the murders and recommend ways for Congress to respond. After waiting months for Congress to act, peace activists in eastern Washington chose a bold stroke to get the Speaker's attention: a full-page advertisement in the national edition of the *New York Times*. Bearing the signatures of more than 650 Fifth District residents, the advertisement appealed directly to Foley, using the headline "Stop U.S. Military Aid to El Salvador."[36]

The Coalition for Central America, a group of activists based in Pullman and nearby Moscow, Idaho, collected more than three thousand signatures opposing US aid to El Salvador. One of the petition drive's architects, Laird Hastay of Pullman, said the ad was not intended to embarrass Foley. Instead, the objective was "to back him up, to show him he has . . . broad constituent support" to change US policy, much as former Speaker Jim Wright had negotiated an end to US aid to the Nicaraguan Contras two years earlier. Referring to Foley's reputation as a compromise builder, Hastay said, "He's much more than that. He's a very forceful leader when he chooses to be."[37] Another Pullman activist, Carol Budi Smith, said, "We don't have a particular dislike for Mr. Foley. We feel he needs to be nudged."[38] Organizers chose the national publication rather than a district newspaper because they wanted Foley and his Capitol Hill colleagues to see the message. Nonetheless, the ad received widespread newspaper and television coverage throughout the Fifth District and prompted an editorial in the *Seattle Post-Intelligencer* that called on Foley to heed his constituents' message.[39]

Foley's press secretary, Jeff Biggs, attempted to defuse the ad's implied criticism of his boss, suggesting the appeal might be better directed at the White House. Foley already was working to cut off the aid, Biggs insisted: "He [Foley] would likely see this as Eastern Washington evidence of a national groundswell of concern over the administration's policy in El Salvador."[40] Lobbyists in Washington, DC, who worked on foreign policy issues said the newspaper ad may have convinced Foley to press more vigorously for a change in policy. The report from Moakley's task force, issued on April 30, 1990, gave Foley another reason to act decisively. The report concluded that "the murders of the Jesuits reflect problems within the Salvadoran armed forces that go far beyond the actions of a particular unit on a particular night."[41]

In late May, a little more than a month after the *Times* ad, a large majority of the House endorsed an amendment to a foreign aid bill requiring the Salvadoran government to engage in peace negotiations to receive any more US military assistance. It was the first time a House majority, including many Republicans, voted to put conditions on US aid to El Salvador.[42] Foley called the measure "a watershed" in US policy. As a result of the vote, "almost certainly, in some form, military aid will be curtailed in the future," Foley said. "There's increasingly a greater number of members who believe that we should modify military assistance to El Salvador and condition it in a way that would encourage both sides to bring the war to a close."[43] The murders in San Salvador were the catalyst for a major reversal of US policy in Latin America. But without his constituents' demand for a stronger US response, it was unlikely that Foley would have moved quickly or forcefully to pressure his colleagues to curtail the aid.

Flag Burning and the Constitution

Less than a month after the El Salvador vote, a Supreme Court decision set the stage for another policy dispute between Bush and Foley, this one over a proposed constitutional amendment to prohibit desecration of the American flag. In 1988, Bush had criticized his Democratic opponent, Massachusetts governor Michael Dukakis, for vetoing a bill that would have required teachers in his state to lead the Pledge of Allegiance to the flag. Bush also attacked Dukakis's membership in the American Civil Liberties Union, which also opposed the bill. The court's ruling in a flag desecration case less than a year after the election gave Bush another opportunity to make the American flag a political issue. Ruling on June 11, 1989, on the appeal of a Texas case, the court struck down a federal law making it a crime to burn the American flag.

Bush immediately asked Congress to pass a constitutional amendment to permit anti-flag desecration laws—in effect, modifying the First Amendment's right of free expression. "What the flag encapsules is too sacred to be abused," Bush said the day after the court's ruling. "I am for free speech, but I am for protecting the flag against desecration."[44]

Foley, who opposed any attempt to amend the Bill of Rights, said that he would not stand in the way of the House's consideration of the measure. "I deplore flag burning, as do all members of the House," Foley explained, "and I hoped that a statute [forbidding flag burning] would be sustained by the court as a method of responding to this problem." But Foley also declared his opposition to changing the First Amendment: "Flag burning isn't worth tampering with the most important repository of personal liberty that any country has ever established in its history," he insisted.[45] Foley perhaps thought back to his 1965 vote to make it a crime to burn a draft card, a position he later regretted.[46]

When the anti-flag-burning amendment came up for a vote in the House of Representatives, Foley went to the floor to speak for only the second time since becoming Speaker a year earlier. "We should not amend the

Constitution of the United States to reach the sparse and scattered and despicable conduct of a few who would dishonor the flag and defile it," he said. He also voted against the amendment, one of the few occasions as Speaker when he cast a recorded vote. Although the measure received a majority in favor, 254–177, it fell 34 votes short of the two-thirds needed for passage.[47] A week later, the Senate likewise failed to give the amendment a two-thirds majority.[48] But after the House vote, the Senate debate was anticlimactic.[49]

Foley's Democratic colleagues praised him for his forceful opposition to amending the Constitution and for his refusal to make the vote a test of party loyalty. After the amendment reached the floor, he declared that members were free to vote their conscience on the issue, adding, however, "I'm going to give advice to any member that is willing to take it, that I think this is a mistake."[50] In the week preceding the vote, at least thirty undecided members received low-key phone calls from Foley. His approach paid off when most of the wavering members voted against the proposal. "Regardless of whether Foley's handling of the issue is eventually deemed brilliant or stupid, his view that the Bill of Rights should remain unblemished had a stunning impact on members," columnist Richard E. Cohen wrote.[51] In October, at a press conference to sum up accomplishments of the session, House majority leader Richard Gephardt praised Foley's leadership on the flag issue. Gephardt said that Foley "got people to think both in the Congress and in the country, and I attribute it to Tom Foley, that we protected our Constitution and protected our flag at the same time."[52]

Although the National Republican Congressional Committee threatened to make Democrats' opposition to the amendment an election issue, the effect was negligible. Foley and others who opposed the amendment faced little criticism when campaigning for reelection that fall. By November, events in the Middle East had eclipsed the debate over flag burning.

War in the Persian Gulf

A long-standing border dispute between Iraq and its tiny neighbor, Kuwait, became the catalyst for massive US military involvement in the Persian Gulf region and led to a historic debate in Congress over giving the president the authority to wage war. Initially, however, policy makers in Washington paid little attention to the Iraq-Kuwait quarrel. The border dispute came against a background of a contradictory US policy toward Iraq. The United States had quietly sided with Iraq during its war with Iran in the

1980s, sharing military intelligence and providing credits for purchase of US agricultural commodities. By 1989, the United States had become one of the largest purchasers of Iraqi oil. In early 1990, the Bush administration resisted efforts in Congress to impose economic sanctions on Iraq for its human rights violations.[53]

In what proved to be a strategic miscalculation, April Glaspie, the US ambassador to Iraq, assured Iraqi president Saddam Hussein on July 25, 1990, that the United States did not take sides on his nation's dispute with Kuwait. The US government has "no opinion on the Arab-Arab conflicts, like your border disagreement with Kuwait," Glaspie said.[54] On July 31, the assistant secretary of state for Near Eastern affairs, John Kelly, told a congressional committee that no treaty obligated the United States to come to Kuwait's defense.[55] Two days later, Iraqi tanks rolled over the border into Kuwait. As Iraqi troops occupied the country, the Kuwaiti royal family fled to Saudi Arabia.

When first asked about the invasion, President George H. W. Bush did not initially appear concerned. In the words of one historian, the president was "flummoxed. His instincts to resist aggression were aroused but there appeared no urgency to intervene."[56] After a National Security Council meeting on August 2, Bush responded to a reporter's question about Kuwait: "We're not discussing intervention."[57] Some historians subsequently gave British prime minister Margaret Thatcher credit for shaking Bush out of his apparent ambivalence. The two leaders met on August 2–3 in Aspen, Colorado, for a previously scheduled conference about the end of the Cold War. Thatcher urged Bush to take whatever steps were necessary to expel Iraqi forces from Kuwait and pledged British participation in any military action. In subsequent public statements, Bush took a harder line against Iraq. Returning to Washington, DC, from a weekend meeting with his senior military and foreign policy advisers, Bush stepped off a helicopter on the White House lawn and declared: "This will not stand. This will not stand, this aggression against Kuwait."[58]

Foley's first public statement about the invasion came at his August 2 press conference. "Obviously [the invasion] is a reckless action by Saddam Hussein. It is not something that apparently he was going to be dissuaded from doing by any respect for international law or reason or relationship with other countries," Foley said. While calling the invasion "a matter of the gravest concern for the American government," he said it was too early to speculate about a possible US military response. Foley declined to criticize the Bush administration for its previous opposition to economic sanctions against Iraq, saying that such sanctions would not have deterred Iraq's invasion of Kuwait.[59]

Bush initially justified his decision to send US troops to the Persian Gulf not because of the invasion of Kuwait, which the United States had no obligation to defend under any treaty, but because of the perceived Iraqi threat to Saudi Arabia. On August 3, a reporter asked Foley how the United States should respond if Iraqi forces moved into Saudi Arabia. "Oh, I think it would raise the most serious security questions for the United States," he responded. "It would be a decision, of course, for the president, but I would support concerted military action to support Saudi Arabia in that event, meaning with other countries." Foley observed, however, that US policy makers did not know Iraq's intentions. Referring to the size of the occupying force in Kuwait, he said, "We don't have the answers to that, [or] at least I don't." The situation in the Persian Gulf had not yet reached crisis proportions. Foley spent the rest of that press conference responding to questions about a civil rights bill, campaign finance reform, and the legislative calendar.[60]

In the next week, the White House struggled to define the diplomatic standoff in terms that would justify a US military response. The request by King Fahd of Saudi Arabia for US military assistance came only after repeated telephone calls to him from Bush, along with a visit to that country by defense secretary Dick Cheney. Members of the Saudi royal family were reluctant to allow US soldiers on Saudi soil and did not consider Saddam Hussein's threat to invade Saudi Arabia to be serious. Cheney's persistence ultimately persuaded the king to agree to the US position.[61] That shift enabled Bush to go on national television August 8, 1990, and assert: "The Saudi government requested our help, and I have responded to that request by ordering U.S. ground and air forces to deploy in the kingdom of Saudi Arabia." By the time the American people heard those words, units of the Eighty-Second Airborne Division were already in Saudi Arabia.[62] Foley said he supported the president's decision to send troops, but he put more faith in the economic embargo as a strategy to force Iraq's withdrawal. "Military action to eliminate Iraqi presence from Kuwait would be extremely difficult," he said in Boise, Idaho, where he was campaigning for Representative Richard Stallings (D-ID), who was seeking reelection in a conservative district.[63]

Bush justified the deployment, calling Operation Desert Shield a purely defensive mission. "A line has been drawn in the sand," he said at a press conference following his speech. "My military objective is to see Saudi Arabia defended."[64] Congressional leaders were generally supportive of the president's decision. "Democrats and Republicans, House and Senate . . . are very strongly of the opinion that the president had to act," said Foley, who had been briefed by the White House before Bush's speech.[65] George Mitchell, the Senate's Democratic leader, agreed with the president's action. Neither raised questions in public about the open-ended nature of the commitment or whether Bush could order such a large military response without first consulting Congress.

Later, President Bush wrote to Foley and Senator Robert Byrd (D-WV), president pro tem of the Senate, to inform them of the deployment, similar to his action in 1989 when he ordered US troops to invade Panama. But the White House did not consider this letter a formal notification under the War Powers Resolution of 1973 because Bush did not believe that hostilities were imminent.[66] It was not until late November, when the number of US military personnel in the region doubled, that leaders of Congress began trying to probe Bush's intentions. Former US attorney general Ramsey Clark believed Congress had failed to assert its constitutional authority early enough to deter Bush. "As President Bush pushed the country toward war, Congress was paralyzed and acted as if the prospect of a major military venture was not its concern," Clark wrote.[67]

Throughout the fall, a series of United Nations resolutions condemned Iraq's actions and called for a complete withdrawal from Kuwait. Saddam Hussein refused, and the State Department pursued a diplomatic strategy while the Pentagon began developing plans to expel Iraq from Kuwait by military means. The growing US presence in the Middle East aroused little scrutiny from Congress or the public. At an October 27 press conference to summarize the accomplishments of the 101st Congress, Foley and other Democratic leaders did not mention the Persian Gulf crisis at all. Instead, they celebrated the passage of a bill to reduce the federal deficit, opening what Foley called "a new era of fiscal responsibility for our federal government." He also listed childcare legislation, the Americans with Disabilities Act, and the reauthorization of the Clean Air Act as examples of what he termed an "extraordinarily productive" session. Foley predicted the public's appreciation for Congress would be reflected in the success of Democratic candidates in the following week's election.[68]

That prediction proved true for many Democrats, who in 1990 gained 8 seats in the House, bringing their ranks to 267, their largest majority since 1983. They also picked up an additional seat in the Senate, bringing their margin there to 56 to 44. But in Foley's case, his victory also reflected the failure of the Republicans to recruit a credible challenger. He comfortably defeated Marlyn Derby, his 1988 opponent, who ran as a write-in candidate after no Republican candidate filed before the primary election. Foley carried every county in the district, winning 110,234 votes to Derby's 49,965. Significantly, though, Foley's vote total fell 50,000 from 1988, when turnout was inflated by the presidential election, while support for Derby remained constant.[69]

One measure of Fifth District voters' discontent was how Foley's support declined in some rural areas. In the tiny Whitman County precinct of Dusty, Derby outpolled Foley 45–13. Derby also beat Foley in two other rural precincts, St. John and Wilcox. Voters interviewed by the *Spokesman-Review* blamed Foley for failing to provide relief to farmers pinched by low wheat prices. "We feel like we're being hit from all sides at once, so quite frankly what you're seeing in the vote is a knee-jerk reaction to that," said Steve Appel, vice president of the Washington State Farm Bureau, who lived in Wilcox. "It seems that Mr. Foley has forgotten where he has come from." Of the rural discontent, a reporter wrote: "Let the record reflect that if and when Tom Foley is voted out of office, his ouster began in this struggling farm town [Dusty] on the western edge of the Palouse."[70]

To keep his Middle East policy from becoming a campaign issue, Bush waited until two days after the election to divulge that a major escalation of US forces was imminent. At a November 8 news conference, Bush announced: "I have today directed the Secretary of Defense to increase the size of U.S. forces committed to Desert Shield to insure that the coalition has an adequate offensive military action to achieve its common goals."[71] Bush was vague about the number of additional personnel who would be deployed, but within weeks, the number of military personnel in the region had doubled to more than 440,000, the largest overseas concentration of US forces since the Vietnam War.

The president neither requested nor received legislative approval for what was a major shift in US policy. Some members of Congress complained that they had learned of Bush's plan only an hour before the announcement.[72] Foley and other congressional leaders had no advance notice of Bush's plan to shift US forces from a defensive to an offensive capability. "There was," according to Foley, "a call from Secretary [of Defense Dick] Cheney in the morning—not very elaborate, just an announcement—the Administration was doubling the forces. This, of course, had never been discussed with the congressional leadership group that had been visiting the White House in recent weeks."[73]

A week later, on November 15, in an attempt to win their support, Bush invited two dozen key members of Congress to the White House. After the meeting, Foley said that Bush had insisted that the US troops in Saudi Arabia were there only "for defensive purposes," contrary to the president's statement of a week earlier. The US military buildup, intended to force Iraq to withdraw from Kuwait, had "very, very strong bipartisan support," Foley said. Bush knew that he was coming perilously close to the point at which he would need to consult formally with Congress, as the War Powers Resolution required. At the meeting, the president showed a copy of the Constitution and referred to language giving Congress the sole power to declare war.[74]

Afterward, Foley continued to insist that any decision by the White House to "go from defense and deterrent to something more aggressive" would require Bush to involve Congress.[75] Perhaps in recognition of that sentiment, Bush invited Foley and three other congressional leaders to accompany him to Saudi Arabia to spend Thanksgiving Day with US military personnel. "Regardless of the questions raised about overall policy, there is no question this represents bipartisan support for men and women in the field in Saudi Arabia," said Jeff Biggs, Foley's press secretary.[76]

One justification for US military intervention was Iraq's alleged nuclear weapons capability. In August 1990, New York Times columnist William Safire had written about the specter of a nuclear armed Iraq.[77] But the Bush administration did not raise this theme publicly until November, after a New York Times–CBS poll found that the only rationale for war that a majority of respondents supported was to prevent Iraq from building a nuclear bomb. When Bush visited US troops in Saudi Arabia at Thanksgiving, he emphasized the nuclear risk: "Every day that passes brings Saddam one step closer to realizing his goal of a nuclear weapons arsenal. And that's why, more and more, your mission is marked by a real sense of urgency."[78] This argument foreshadowed that used in 2005 by his son, President George W. Bush, who raised the threat of "weapons of mass destruction" as a justification for invading Iraq.

That weekend, Secretary Cheney and national security adviser Brent Scowcroft made the rounds of the Sunday morning television interview programs to reinforce the need to block a suspected Iraqi nuclear weapons program. Foley, though, was skeptical of this assertion. "I'm a bit puzzled," he said. "Until recently, the reports were [Saddam] was years away" from having nuclear weapons.[79]

On November 30, at the urging of the United States, the UN Security Council adopted a resolution giving an ultimatum to Saddam Hussein: Withdraw all Iraqi forces from Kuwait by January 15, 1991, or face a military attack by the US-led coalition.[80] Bush now had the authority he believed he needed to order US forces into action. In his opinion, attacking Iraq did not require congressional endorsement. Foley disagreed, telling Bush at a White House meeting, "If you decide to go to war, you'll have to come to Congress."[81]

By a margin of 177 to 37, the House Democratic Caucus on December 4, 1990, adopted a resolution urging Bush not to take any offensive military action without the formal approval of Congress.[82] Clearly, though, Bush had a political advantage: the forces needed to attack Iraq were already in the Middle East, preparing for combat. By the end of 1990, war seemed inevitable. Meanwhile, in Foley's home district, a new peace group, Citizens against War in the Middle East, called on Foley to block Bush's preparations for war. "Give the embargo more time to work," the group wrote. "Bring the U.S. troops home and replace them with a genuine U.N. peace-keeping force."[83]

When the new Congress arrived in Washington, DC, on January 3, 1991, the prospect of war in the Persian Gulf was the talk of the capital. At his first press conference of the year, Foley announced that the House would remain in session three days a week after members were sworn in, rather than recessing until after the president's State of the Union address. He also insisted that Congress must act before Bush ordered any US forces into combat. "I think it is constitutionally . . . required of the president to get authority from the Congress before moving from a standing start into an offensive action in the absence of any attack on the troops with a military engagement of this size and circumstances," he said. "And that's been made very clear to the president by any number of us."[84]

Days later, on January 7, Foley announced that a debate on authorizing US military force to carry out UN resolutions would begin soon. "We hope that diplomacy will succeed in avoiding war . . . but in any event, I think the time has come for the House to speak," he said.[85] The next day, Bush wrote to Congress asking for a resolution endorsing "use of all necessary means to implement U.N. Security Council Resolution 678," which called for Iraqi troops to leave Kuwait by January 15, 1991. "Such action would send the clearest possible message to Saddam Hussein that he must withdraw without condition or delay from Kuwait," Bush declared.[86]

The House debate began on January 10 and continued for two days. More than half of the House's 435 members participated. The rhetoric was restrained as members recognized the gravity of their decision. Around one o'clock on the afternoon of January 12, Foley relinquished the gavel and went to the floor of the House to close the debate. Foley declared his support for an amendment proposed by majority leader Gephardt and Lee Hamilton (D-IN), a senior member of the House Foreign Affairs Committee, asking Bush to give the UN economic sanctions more time to work. He challenged the White House's assertion that a resolution authorizing military force was merely a diplomatic tool to enhance Bush's leverage with Iraq. Bush "has said again and again that, if given the power, he may well use it, perhaps sooner than we realize," Foley said. He urged his colleagues to avoid second-guessing or partisanship once the decision was reached:

> However you vote . . . let us come together after the vote with the notion that we are Americans here, not Democrats and not Republicans, all anxious to do the best for our country, without recrimination as to motive, without anything but the solemn pride that on this great decision day we voted as our conscience and judgment told us we should. And though our opinion may change over the years, we will not then bear the burden of a harsh judgment on our honor and our actions at this moment.[87]

Foley obviously worried that members who opposed the war might be targeted in the next election—especially if the war turned out to be a glorious success. His concern was legitimate. The following week, Clayton Yeutter, President Bush's choice to become chairman of the Republican National Committee, said that Democrats who opposed giving the president war authority would regret it at the polls. Asked about Yeutter's implied threat to target members who voted no, Foley retorted: "I think any effort to make the decision on war authority for the president a political issue is unwise. . . . I have great respect for Clayton Yeutter, and I think he is an able man. But I think his judgment has deserted him on this particular statement."[88]

The House voted 250–183 against the Gephardt-Hamilton resolution. By the same margin, it adopted an amendment from minority leader Robert

CHAPTER 6

Michel (R-IL) and Stephen Solarz (D-NY) authorizing the Bush administration to use all force necessary to expel Iraq from Kuwait. The Senate's vote in favor of a similar resolution was much closer, 52–47, but Bush needed only a simple majority to move ahead. The Monday following the vote, Foley was asked whether any chance for peace remained. "I don't see, in an intellectual sense, much that one can [cling] to," he said, referring to the failure of UN Secretary-General Javier Perez de Cuellar's attempt to find a diplomatic solution.[89]

Even on the eve of the congressional debate, the American public remained skeptical that war was necessary to achieve the stated US objective. On January 9, according to an ABC–*Washington Post* poll, only 39 percent of Americans agreed the United States should go to war "immediately" if Iraq did not withdraw from Kuwait by the January 15 United Nations deadline.[90] Five days later, after the congressional vote but before the war began, a *New York Times*–CBS poll found that 56 percent of Americans preferred a Middle East peace conference as the best way to force Iraq to leave Kuwait. Only 33 percent favored war.[91]

The war began on January 16 at 5:30 p.m. Washington, DC, time when a US Navy cruiser fired a cruise missile at a target inside Iraq. Within hours, bombs were falling on Baghdad. Once US forces were under fire, Congress closed ranks behind Bush. To constituents who had written in opposition to the war, Foley wrote: "Now that hostilities between the United States and Iraq have begun, it is incumbent upon us to stand united in support for the American men and women in the Gulf who have embraced the duty and burden of conducting the war."[92]

Two weeks after the air war began, Bush basked in the admiration of Congress when he went to Capitol Hill for his State of the Union address. Interviewed after the speech, Foley described the supportive atmosphere in the House chamber but lamented, "Too bad it takes a war to bring the country so closely together." Referring to such national problems as drugs, crime, and health care, Foley said, "If we could only have the same sense of common purpose and determination for these things, we would likely be crowned with success." Foley largely supported the domestic agenda that Bush laid out in his speech, with the exception of the president's request to cut the capital gains tax.[93]

On February 24, the ground war began when US Marine units crossed from Saudi Arabia into Iraq. Four days later, after exactly one hundred hours of ground combat, Iraqi troops began retreating from Kuwait. At Bush's urging, US commanders declared a cease-fire to begin at 8:00 a.m.

(local time) on February 28.[94] The war caused remarkably few American casualties; 148 US service personnel were killed in action, according to the Pentagon.[95] Estimates of the number of Iraqi casualties varied widely. The US Central Command put the number of Iraqi deaths at 100,000, a figure independent military analysts called greatly inflated. Those experts suggested a death toll of 8,000 to 25,000 Iraqis was more accurate.[96]

After the cease-fire was announced, Foley expressed pride in the American forces and relief at the outcome of the war. "The president's announcement last night that the military phase of Operation [Desert] Storm is over is wonderful news," he told reporters. "The relatively low loss of [American] life is something, I think, for which all of us are deeply grateful. . . . The speed with which the ground war was concluded and the apparent willingness of Iraq to accept all of the U.N. resolutions is very, very good news indeed."[97]

Perhaps sensitive to complaints that he had not returned to eastern Washington over the Christmas holidays, Foley spent part of the Easter congressional recess in the Fifth District. In Othello and Walla Walla, he spoke primarily about the domestic postwar agenda: the economy, education, and transportation. No one asked him to explain his opposition to Bush's request to use military force in the Persian Gulf.[98] But at a town meeting in Pullman, several constituents grilled Foley about his absence from the district before the Gulf War debate in Congress.

In November, after Bush announced the troop buildup in the Persian Gulf, Whitman County peace activists had called on Foley to conduct a town meeting to hear their opposition to the war. Throughout the winter, Foley's staff insisted that the crisis would keep him in Washington, DC, precluding any district visits.[99] In late March 1991, after the conclusion of the war, Foley's constituents finally had their say. More than three hundred of them crowded into the Pullman High School theater to express their dissatisfaction with the war and with Foley's failure to hear their protests earlier. "Your absence in the district in December looms a little large," said Tom Savage of Garfield, Washington, a member of Citizens against War in the Middle East. Foley responded that other than six days with his wife in Barbados between Christmas and New Year's Day, he had remained in Washington, DC, to be available to consult with President Bush.[100] Foley stayed well beyond the scheduled closing time of the Pullman meeting, insisting that Congress had done all that it was empowered to do under the Constitution. An out-of-town reporter later wrote, "The exchange [was] friendly, intelligent, logical, intense—Tom Foley's idea of a good time."[101]

And as much as Foley appeared to enjoy such discussions, he did not linger in eastern Washington. After three days in the district, he returned to Washington, DC, and from there flew to Barbados to resume the vacation that had been cut short by impending hostilities in January.

In April, the Republican National Committee's Yeutter renewed his attack on Democrats who had voted against the war resolution, accusing the party of retreating into isolationism. In an interview with the *Washington Times*, Foley called the charge "absolute nonsense" and gave this explanation of the position that he and many of his fellow Democrats had taken: "The moment the president sent in the troops in August, I said . . . and everybody else said, 'He's done the right thing.' There was no argument about it, no argument that we were getting involved in a quagmire [as] in Vietnam." Democrats supported strict enforcement of the UN sanctions, Foley said, but they broke with the president over how much time to give the sanctions before commencing military action. And, he asserted, the decision of timing belonged to Congress, not to the president alone, stating, "This is the highest constitutional responsibility of the Congress to make this judgment."[102] In asserting the prerogative of Congress to determine when and how the nation would go to war, Foley was being true to the constitutional principles he cherished. Given Bush's belief that the president had the authority to act—irrespective of Congress's opinion—Foley's arguments might have been more influential in October, before Bush doubled the size of the US military presence in the Middle East.

Americans rejoiced at the war's outcome: US casualties were light, Iraq withdrew from Kuwait, and the United States emerged as the dominant nation in a post–Cold War world. As a result of the low American casualties and the enthusiasm with which the US news media, especially cable television networks (including CNN), covered the war, Bush's popularity soared. In one poll, he received a 92 percent approval rating, the highest figure ever recorded.[103] But Bush failed to convert his high poll ratings into victory the following November. Democratic candidate Bill Clinton, governor of Arkansas, capitalized on Americans' insecurities about the economy. Third-party candidate Ross Perot peeled votes away from Bush. Clinton received less than 50 percent of the popular vote, but he easily won the Electoral College. While eastern Washington voters reelected Foley with 55 percent of the vote, the margin of victory was down sharply from his 69 percent margin two years earlier.[104]

A final measure of Foley's relationship with George H. W. Bush came less than a month before the president left office. On Christmas Eve 1992, Bush granted full pardons to former defense secretary Caspar Weinberger and five other officials implicated in the Iran-Contra scandal, which Congress had investigated five years earlier. As a member of the joint congressional committee, Foley had expressed skepticism that President Reagan did not know about the scandal.[105] The pardon cleared Weinberger of charges he had lied to Congress about aid to the Nicaraguan Contras and arms sales to Iran.[106] Two days later, the *Los Angeles Times* reported that Foley and Representative Les Aspin (D-WI) had given tacit support to the pardon for Weinberger, who was scheduled to go on trial in January.[107] The newspaper's report placed Foley at odds with House majority leader Richard Gephardt, who denounced the president's action. "The pardon maintains the appearance of an Iran-contra cover-up, suggests presidential approval of violations of law, and condones ill-founded foreign policy decisions that never would have been made in the light of day," Gephardt complained.[108]

The *New York Times* took Foley to task for what it called "congressional complicity" in the pardons. "By making it politically easier for President Bush to issue the pardons, Mr. Foley and Mr. Aspin indicated that the truth of the charges [against Weinberger] mattered little," the paper said in an editorial.[109] Lawrence Walsh, the independent counsel who prosecuted the Iran-Contra defendants, was outraged, later calling the pardons "the last card in the cover-up."[110]

Foley, on vacation in Barbados when Bush announced the pardons, did not publicly comment on the press reports. But a spokeswoman said Foley told White House officials he would neither support nor oppose the pardon for Weinberger. "He said that was purely within the president's prerogative," said Robin Webb, Foley's deputy press secretary. "If the president ultimately decided to pardon Weinberger, (Foley) would not criticize it."[111] By not voicing disapproval of the president's plan, however, Foley may have unintentionally given Bush a signal to proceed—pardoning not just Weinberger but the five others as well. And Foley's reliance on a legal justification (the separation of powers) may have reflected his inclination to sometimes put process ahead of substance, in this case the Reagan administration's defiance of Congress. More than seven years after the US arms-for-hostages shipments to Iran, the pardons brought the Iran-Contra affair to a close.

As 1993 began, Foley looked forward to working with a Democratic president for the first time in a dozen years. But simmering administrative problems that predated Foley's election as Speaker were about to boil over.

Congressional reforms of the 1970s, which toppled the seniority system, had left untouched the House bank, post office, and restaurants. Sloppy management and lax oversight of those units were to reflect unfavorably, and perhaps unfairly, on Foley. At the same time, Tom Foley and other long-term incumbents were about to collide with a new political phenomenon: the movement to limit terms of members of Congress.

CHAPTER 7

DEFENDING THE REPUTATION OF THE HOUSE

Just as no single event put Tom Foley on the path to become Speaker of the House in 1989, no single issue caused his defeat five years later. As the most prominent Democrat in Congress, Foley became associated with positions that did not always play well in his conservative home district. He also faced challenges in reconciling his former role as a House reformer with his new role as the institution's chief defender. Strong voter discontent arose in response to his stand on management of the House of Representatives and term limits for members of Congress. In both cases, Foley surely took positions on principle rather than for personal gain or political expediency. Ultimately, however, his approach failed to withstand the attacks on the institution that had begun five years earlier but intensified in the months leading up to the 1994 election. As political reporters Dan Balz and Ronald Brownstein wrote in their postmortem of that election: "Republicans led by Newt Gingrich had done much to amplify those scandals and as a result to undermine public confidence in the institution, confident that the fallout would harm Democrats much more than themselves."[1] In retrospect, Foley's defenses of Congress were inadequate to the forces such as those that were unleashed in the late 1980s and early 1990s.

For more than 150 years, the House of Representatives had operated a small bank (in reality, a check-cashing agency) as a convenience to its members. The revelation in the fall of 1991 that dozens of representatives routinely overdrew their accounts between paychecks sparked public outcry at what appeared to be an abuse of privileges. Foley closed the bank in the spring of 1992, but the damage to Congress's reputation had been done. On the heels of the bank scandal came a grand jury investigation of corruption in the House post office. Press reports of lavish redecoration of the Speaker's office and other parts of the Capitol contributed to the image of an imperial Congress with Foley at its head—a perception that some Republicans encouraged.

Meanwhile, a well-funded national movement to impose term limits on Congress emerged in the 1990s, fueled in part by criticism of congressional pay and perquisites. To be sure, Washington State voters defeated a term-limits initiative in 1991, possibly because voters did not want to lose Foley's clout. But term-limits backers in Washington tried again in 1992 and turned the public's animosity toward Congress into support for their initiative, which narrowly passed. The following year, Foley joined in a widely publicized legal challenge to that initiative, prompting critics to accuse him of suing his constituents. His involvement in the lawsuit, however principled, added to the impression of an entrenched incumbent protecting his privileges. These two issues intertwined against a backdrop of public hostility toward government and an increasingly militant Republican Party determined to take control of the House of Representatives.

The House bank was founded in about 1830 as part of the paymaster function of the sergeant at arms office. It served as a payroll disbursement office, allowing members to draw advances against their next paycheck.[2] Eight months after becoming Speaker of the House, Foley learned about some of the bank's problems, though he had little hint of the scandal that was to erupt two years later. The General Accounting Office (GAO), the investigative arm of Congress (now the Government Accountability Office), alerted Foley in December 1989 that Jack Russ, the House sergeant at arms, had written more than $100,000 in personal checks at the House bank without having funds to cover them at the time. Foley, in turn, notified Representatives Robert Michel of Illinois and Richard Gephardt of Missouri, the Republican and Democratic floor leaders, respectively, of the problem. He also directed Russ—under whose jurisdiction the bank fell—to stop doing personal banking there, and Russ agreed.[3]

Almost as an afterthought, the GAO's report mentioned that a number of House members (the only people authorized to have bank accounts) had written checks without sufficient funds in their accounts. Technically, no checks "bounced." The bank spared the writers embarrassment by covering the checks with money on deposit from other members, and the offenders paid no penalty or interest for this privilege. In response to the audit, Russ told Foley in a January 1990 letter that he would tighten the rules to discourage overdrafts by House members. When the GAO audit was made public in February, most of the attention focused on Russ's own overdrafts. But without mentioning names, the auditors again expressed concern about the number of checks House members had written without sufficient funds. It was at this point, perhaps, that Foley might have acted more decisively to halt the abuses. A *Washington Post* reporter later observed: "Throughout the affair, Foley never chose a bold stroke," such as firing Russ as sergeant at arms. "The series of small steps that he took were unsuccessful, and it is still not clear how Foley expected his tactics to achieve the desired objective of cleaning up the bank's shoddy accounting practices and reforming its generous overdraft policies."[4]

At the time, though, Foley's options were limited. He could not unilaterally fire Russ because the sergeant at arms then served at the pleasure of the entire Democratic Caucus, not the Speaker. In the fall of 1990, Foley proposed that the Speaker nominate the sergeant at arms and four other officers. But the caucus's committee on organization balked. Some members were friends of Russ, and others feared giving too much power to the Speaker. No one in the caucus seemed to grasp the implications of the continuing bank problems. Still, it seems puzzling that someone with as much knowledge of House procedures as Foley did not find a way to check the abuses, fix the bank, and deflect the critics. In February 1991, he did ask a Washington, DC, commercial bank to examine House bank procedures. The report showed that dozens of House members had written hundreds of bad checks totaling thousands of dollars.[5]

Other problems arose when, on September 18, 1991, the GAO published a second report, covering the year ending June 30, 1990. During that period, House members wrote 8,331 checks without sufficient money in their accounts to cover them. Two dozen congressmen had written bad checks in excess of $1,000, yet the bank had failed to penalize the violators. Foley and his staff were furious that the problems had not been taken care of and that Russ seemed unwilling to take responsibility for them.[6]

The following week, Foley announced that the House bank no longer would cover overdrafts of members unless they first obtained a line of credit on which they would pay interest. "Members of Congress will have the same—no better, no worse—provisions in this bank as they would have in an individual banking institution," he declared. "Any other practices will cease immediately." Frustrated by the bank's failure to curb the check-writing abuses, Foley declared: "It was a matter that had been raised before, and I thought had been corrected, and it's going to be." Asked by a reporter whether he had written any bad checks, Foley replied that he did all his banking at a commercial bank in Spokane. His cash for everyday purchases came from his wife, "such as she chooses to give me."[7] A few days later, though, Foley acknowledged that on December 27, 1990 (after the period of the GAO audit), he had written a $540 check on a House bank account without sufficient funds to cover it.[8]

Foley bristled at what he considered distorted news coverage of the uproar. At an October 3 news conference, he explained the bank's financial basis:

> The operations of the House bank do not involve appropriated funds on deposit. They involve the members' personal funds on deposit. No taxpayers' money is involved in any question of unsufficient [sic] funds or in any operations of deposit or transactions in the bank. There has never been any loss of funds, either of members or taxpayers, but no taxpayers' money is involved in any way.[9]

He went on to draw other distinctions between a commercial bank and the House bank: "This bank makes no loans, earns no income and consequently pays no interest"—points he was to repeat often over the next year. The Federal Deposit Insurance Corporation did not guarantee deposits. If a member wrote a check without sufficient funds, "the person who was carrying that check was the other person who had a deposited balance, not the taxpayer," Foley said.[10]

With the support of Michel and Gephardt, Foley also asked the House Ethics Committee to examine the GAO audits and determine whether any rules of the House had been broken. Foley did not consider writing a few overdrafts to be an ethical violation. Instead, he was concerned about "significant, substantial, repeated abuses of the privileges of the bank."[11] The GAO reports did not identify bad-check writers, and neither Foley nor the bank would release the list. But many members asked the sergeant at arms office to issue a letter absolving them of any overdrafts.[12] House members went public with declarations that their records were clean, trying to put distance between themselves and the offenders. Among those was Representative Larry LaRocco (D-ID), a former banker, who criticized his colleagues' sloppy financial practices. "Members of Congress are supposed to be the protectors of the public money," he said. "No wonder the public loses confidence in Congress."[13]

On the heels of the House bank disclosures came a report that House members owed more than $250,000 to the company that operated restaurants in the Capitol and adjoining congressional office buildings. Private groups had run up many of the bills by sponsoring receptions, but the House members who reserved the rooms were responsible for the debts.[14] The two news reports—on the overdrafts and the restaurant bills—opened the door for a critical examination of members' other privileges. At his October 3 press conference, reporters peppered Foley with questions about free congressional parking at Washington area airports, free prescription drugs from the Capitol physician's office, and allegations that the sergeant at arms interceded when members received District of Columbia parking tickets.[15] A *Time* magazine story asked: "Wonder why Congress is so arrogant about bounced checks? Perhaps because its members are so used to the freebie life."[16]

Foley hoped that cracking down on bank procedures and referring the problem to the Ethics Committee would halt the controversy. "This is now a matter that is over and done with," he declared in a speech on the House floor.[17] His pronouncement proved to be premature. The House bank story refused to die. The critical GAO report generated a flurry of negative headlines; columnists and cartoonists nicknamed the affair "Rubbergate." *New York Times* columnist William Safire suggested that the bad checks might be covering more serious offenses: "At large are officials who willfully and frequently abused their privilege. All should be exposed; some should be made to pay substantial taxes with penalties; a few deserve censure."[18] The conservative *Washington Times* intoned: "Everywhere except on Capitol Hill, 'rubbergate' will be remembered as an integrity test for House Speaker Tom Foley. He failed that test with a cynical flair not seen in these parts since former House Speaker Jim Wright bleated his way back to Texas declaring himself a sacrificial lamb," a reference to Wright's 1989 resignation.[19]

One of the few newspapers that came to Foley's defense was the *Albany Democrat-Herald* in Oregon, which pointed out in an editorial that no check by a member of Congress ever "bounced"—that is, was sent back to the payee. "The continued use of this term gives people entirely the wrong impression and shows how lazy the national press can be," the paper complained.[20] David Broder of the *Washington Post* acknowledged that the public easily could misinterpret details of the bank's operation. Nonetheless, the bank was in the Capitol, Broder wrote in early 1992, and "The clowns who ran it were on the federal payroll." Broder argued that the scandal represented everything that Americans disliked about Congress. "Like the $640 toilet seat that came to symbolize Pentagon waste, the check-bouncing story seems certain to become a shorthand symbol of a Congress that is relentlessly undisciplined in far larger fiscal matters."[21] When Broder's column appeared in the *Oregonian* (Portland, OR), it was accompanied by a Pat Oliphant editorial cartoon depicting Foley as a maid in a frumpy dress and headscarf, watching television while garbage piled up under the rug behind him. The caption read: "The 1992 bad housekeeping award."[22]

For a few months, the bank scandal disappeared from the headlines as the Ethics Committee quietly looked into the matter. In February 1992, a new issue called attention to another aspect of Foley's management of the House: renovations and redecorating of the Capitol. An Associated Press dispatch from Washington, printed in several papers in Foley's district, reported that Foley had moved the House Documents Room out of the Capitol to make more space for the Speaker's staff. Another project divided the public House dining room to create a second Speaker's dining room. The story also called attention to the purchase of a $72,500 Oriental rug for the Rayburn Room, a reception area in the Capitol, and installation of marble floors in Capitol elevators. Foley's press secretary, Jeff Biggs, defended the expenditures. Foley's "view of the Capitol . . . is that this is not an office building," Biggs said. "It amounts to a national monument, and he thinks it ought to reflect that trust." The privately funded Capitol Preservation Society purchased the rug and donated it to the government, he said. And the marble in the elevators was more durable than the carpet it replaced.[23] Although Biggs's arguments were rational, coming so soon after the bad-check scandal, the redecorating story resonated with a public already skeptical of congressional privileges.

A federal grand jury investigation that surfaced in March 1992 revealed a more sinister side of the House's internal operations. Initially, the grand jury looked into allegations of theft, embezzlement, and the sale of illegal drugs at the House post office, which was not part of the US Postal Service. Later, the inquiry broadened to address allegations that members of the House obtained cash from the post office disguised by phony stamp purchases.[24]

A cloud of suspicion moved over the Speaker's office when Heather Foley voluntarily testified before the grand jury. Tom Foley declared that his wife was not a suspect in the investigation; his staff later distributed a March 26 letter from the US attorney confirming that she was not suspected of any wrongdoing. The letter from John M. Campbell, chief of the Justice Department's public corruption section, said that Heather Foley "was neither a subject nor a target of this office's ongoing investigation into allegations concerning the operation of the House . . . post office."[25] Even so, the allegations prompted several news articles questioning the propriety of her role in running the House.[26] Foley adamantly rejected suggestions that his wife leave her unpaid job in his office. "My wife has done nothing wrong," he insisted. "There's no reason for her to step aside as my chief of staff."[27]

On March 12, Jack Russ, sergeant at arms of the House since 1983, resigned, saying that he hoped his departure would "put this matter [the bank scandal] to rest and allow the House of Representatives to move forward and address the important issues of the day without further distraction."[28] Foley nominated his longtime administrative assistant, Werner Brandt, as interim sergeant at arms. That prompted Newt Gingrich, the leader of a group of insurgent Republicans, to suggest on the House floor that Brandt somehow had helped cover up the post office scandal. Complaining that Foley had not consulted the Republicans about replacing Russ, Gingrich said, "If we had been asked, we would have objected to the appointment of a man who may have been involved in actions stopping the Capitol Police from investigating cocaine selling in the post office."[29] In a demonstration of loyalty to Brandt, Foley went to the floor ten minutes later to denounce Gingrich's remarks. "To suggest some misbehavior without proof, without validation, and without cause by a man of sterling reputation is a despicable act," Foley stormed, in a departure from his usual temperate manner. "There is a point at which the patience of decent people ought to say: 'Enough.'"[30]

Foley may not have recognized that Gingrich was using the problems with the bank and the post office, along with his complaint about Brandt's appointment, to attack the integrity of Democratic House members and undermine the credibility of the Democratic leadership. In his 2020 account of Gingrich's rise to power and the resignation of Speaker Jim Wright, historian Julian E. Zelizer asserts that the Democrats' failure to vigorously defend Wright in 1989 laid the groundwork for the subsequent attacks. "The shock had been not just that Gingrich and the Republicans had been willing to engage in a full-throated effort to bring down the Speaker of the House before he was proven guilty of any infraction but that the Democrats let it happen," Zelizer wrote.[31]

Had Foley recognized earlier the threat that Gingrich presented to Democratic control of the House—and to Foley's speakership—the Republican might never have become a thorn in the Speaker's side in 1992. Columnists Jack Anderson and Michael Einstein suggested in April of that year that Foley had missed an opportunity by failing to campaign against Gingrich in 1990. Criticized for his role in the 1989 bipartisan agreement to give members of Congress a pay raise, Gingrich won reelection by fewer than one thousand votes in his Georgia district. In Anderson and Einstein's opinion, Foley should have raised money for Gingrich's Democratic opponent, David Worley, and rallied Georgia Democrats behind him. "Had this been done, according to some party strategists, Gingrich could have been pinned down in his own district this year fighting for his life at the polls instead of roiling the waters closer to the Potomac," Anderson and Einstein wrote.[32] Yet Foley declined to get directly involved in the campaign to oust Gingrich, perhaps believing such behavior incompatible with being Speaker—at least as Foley defined the job. Such outright partisanship was not his style.

Similarly, Foley's reluctance to act decisively against Russ stemmed in part from his desire to avoid confrontation. Reflecting in a 1992 interview about the sergeant at arms' troubles, he said: "I had no authority to fire Russ. I could have asked him to resign, I suppose, but I couldn't dismiss him. And what I was seeking to do in the early months of my speakership, was to restore a sense of calmness and comity to the House."[33]

A week after Russ's resignation, three post office staff members pleaded guilty to embezzling postal funds, and House postmaster Robert Rota quit. In April, Heather Foley gave a rare interview to explain her interest in the post office investigation. "I was only peripherally involved in the House post office to make sure the three employees who said they had stolen money did not stay here [on the congressional payroll]," she said. Recalling her testimony before the grand jury, which she said lasted about twenty minutes, she insisted, "I've done nothing wrong—quite the contrary." She blamed criticism of her on a campaign by the *Washington Times* to discredit her husband.[34]

On April 1, the House Ethics Committee completed its investigation of the bank, identifying the twenty-two worst offenders, who collectively wrote some eleven thousand insufficient-funds checks. Two weeks later, responding to public pressure, the committee released a list of an additional 303 current and former House members who also had overdrawn their accounts: 187 Democrats, 115 Republicans, and 1 independent (Bernie Sanders of Vermont). According to the report, Foley had 2 overdrafts during the period, majority leader Richard Gephardt had 28, and Republican whip Newt Gingrich had 22. The report also revealed that 4 members of President Bush's cabinet and 5 Republican senators had written bad checks while they were in the House. Foley told reporters that the members on the list broke no House rules and violated no laws. Disclosure of the names, he said, "brings to a close this whole matter"—another statement that proved overly optimistic.[35] As a *New York Times* reporter observed, the scandal seemed "to have a resonance that extends far beyond its inherent facts." For example, a *New York Times*–CBS poll reported that nearly half the public believed, incorrectly, that taxpayer money was used to cover the shortfalls in House members' checking accounts.[36] That and other misperceptions prompted Foley to repeat an observation of Will Rogers that was often quoted by his mentor, the late senator Henry Jackson: "It isn't what the people don't know that's the problem, it's what they know for sure that ain't so."[37]

In mid-April 1992, Alan Secrest, a Democratic political consultant, said it was too soon to assess the damage to the members who wrote checks without sufficient funds. "There's a very strong political undertow at work here," Secrest explained. "What we don't know yet is whether you're talking about a tidal wave."[38] Yet Foley's usually acute political radar failed to alert him to the potential hazards that lay ahead. Representative Al Swift (D-WA) recalled walking to a floor vote with two Democratic colleagues, both critical of Foley's handling of the bank affair. Swift asked them what they would have Foley do. "One said, 'Well, you'd close the God-damned thing,' and the other said, "Absolutely not! You'd tell those . . . members of the press to go shove it . . . and not take away our bank.'" Their comments illustrated Foley's predicament. At a meeting of the Democratic leadership and whip organization, a House member complained that Foley was caving in to outside demands to close the bank. Swift remembered Foley looking sternly at the member and demanding: "Will you please tell me why it is you want to save a bank that pays you no interest, from which you cannot get a loan, from which you cannot do any other banking business and, at any time, by a simple majority vote of the House, can make any of your private business public?" According to Swift, the congressman had no reply.[39]

Even though dozens of Republicans—including Gingrich—were on the list of bad-check writers, Republican members of the House and their allies painted the scandal as a Democratic one, the product of too many years of control of the House of Representatives.[40] Republicans ran a radio advertisement in Spokane that purported to be a meeting of House members.

In the commercial, the unnamed leader told the congressmen not to worry about their overdrafts. The ad asserted that the bank scandal resulted from the Democrats being in power too long: "When the Democrats took over the House of Representatives, the Dodgers were still in Brooklyn, and no one had heard of Elvis."[41] A Republican TV commercial included an excerpt of Foley's statement: "I regret that I wasn't more energetic" in cracking down on abuses at the bank. The commercial then urged voters to "bounce the Democrats!"[42] In response, Democrats ran commercials of their own, naming the most prominent bad-check writers among the Republicans. Foley pointed out that the executive branch enjoyed more privileges than did members of Congress. "The president [George H. W. Bush] is the king of perks," Foley declared in early April. "The vice president [Dan Quayle] is the crown prince of perks."[43]

After the list of bad-check writers was made public, grumbling among House Democrats increased. Representative John Bryant of Texas, who had written fifty-five checks without sufficient funds, demanded that Foley resign as Speaker at the end of year.[44] On the House floor, Bryant called on Foley to step down because "he refuses to be a political leader."[45] Buttons appeared on Capitol Hill promoting "Stenholm for Speaker" (Representative Charles Stenholm, another Texas Democrat). Representative Charlie Rose (D-NC) also expressed an interest in replacing Foley as Speaker. But another Texan, Representative Charles Wilson, defended Foley. "People are looking for somebody to be mad at," Wilson said. "What could he [Foley] have done?"[46] Jeff Biggs, Foley's press secretary, believed that the same House members then criticizing Foley for inaction "would have laughed in his face" if he had acted on his own to curb members' perquisites.[47] Former Republican representative Bill Frenzel of Minnesota, who left the House in 1991, agreed: "The members are eager to blame Tom Foley, but they would have revolted if he had tried to close the bank down when he was first warned."[48] Foley curtly brushed aside suggestions that he resign. Asked whether he felt any pressure to step down as Speaker, Foley declared: "Absolutely not; absolutely not."[49] Reflecting years later on the challenge to his leadership from disgruntled members of the House Democratic Caucus, Foley wrote: "I took them at about ten cents on the dollar." Losing the speakership was "a remote possibility, but unlikely in my judgment."[50]

During the congressional Easter recess of 1992, Foley returned to eastern Washington for a series of town meetings. There, the bank scandal attracted only a handful of questions, to the surprise of the regional and national reporters who covered the trip. "Folks in the southeast corner of . . . Foley's sprawling district seem to care more about drawdowns than overdrafts," Peter Callaghan of the *Morning News Tribune* (Tacoma, WA) wrote, referring to a controversial proposal to assist migrating salmon by increasing the flow of water from Snake River dams. But constituents appeared puzzled, Callaghan wrote, when Foley explained that the House bank was a payroll-disbursing office, not a real bank.[51]

The district tour included a stop in Walla Walla, where 360 people attended a town meeting at Whitman College. As at other meetings, citizens appeared satisfied with Foley's commitment to improve management of the House or were unwilling to challenge his explanation. No one asked him directly about the bank scandal or the ongoing investigation of the House post office. A retired teacher, Raymond Jones, said afterward that the House bank scandal was not as serious as the Iran-Contra affair or the savings and loan problems of the late 1980s.[52] Joel Connelly of the *Seattle Post-Intelligencer* observed that Foley, accompanied by five staff members from three of his offices, "was notably sharper on regional issues . . . than on an Eastern Washington visit a year ago."[53]

In April, the *Spokesman-Review* of Spokane published the results of a poll showing Foley with a high approval rating among voters in Spokane County. Two-thirds of the respondents thought he was doing a good job as their congressman; a slightly smaller number, about 60 percent, approved of his performance as Speaker of the House. The poll results seemed to negate the criticisms of a potential Republican challenger, state representative Duane Somers of Spokane. "Haven't they been reading the papers? Maybe they don't realize who has responsibility for the problems" in Congress, Somers grumbled.[54] Because the favorable poll results were based only on Spokane County, they may not have accurately measured support for Foley in the district's outlying counties. Bill Hall, editorial page editor of the *Lewiston Morning Tribune* in neighboring northern Idaho, later recalled that Foley seemed perplexed by the national outcry over the bank scandal. Referring to Foley's argument that no tax dollars were lost, Hall said, "He didn't realize that out in America, that [distinction] didn't matter. He just didn't understand why people would be upset over this."[55] Foley never undertook the aggressive public relations campaign that would have been necessary to correct public misunderstanding of how the bank operated. Reflecting after leaving office on the public outrage toward Congress during those years, Foley wrote:

The bank issue . . . touched a public raw nerve about several things. One, the public's cynical view of the low ethical standards of Congress, and resentment about what they considered the excessive privileges and perquisites members of Congress received which distanced them from ordinary citizens. It was as if somebody alleged that members of Congress didn't have to pay gasoline tax when they went to a gas station. . . . With the House bank, people knew that if they had an overdraft at their bank they'd have to pay for it. It made them angry.[56]

Foley nevertheless weathered this storm on Capitol Hill. By late summer of 1992, newspaper headlines proclaimed: "Tom Foley Quiets His Critics" and "Foley, Pummeled Last Spring, Again Paramount in the House."[57] He emerged from the scandal in a stronger position within the Democratic Caucus. "I think members have seen that I have tried to represent the interests of the House and want to continue to do that," he said.[58] In August, Foley won the endorsement of two heavyweight committee chairmen: Dan Rostenkowski of Ways and Means and John Dingell of Energy and Commerce.[59] Two potential candidates for Speaker, Charlie Rose of North Carolina and Dave McCurdy of Oklahoma, retreated from suggestions they take on Foley. But another would-be challenger, Charles Stenholm of Texas, chided his colleagues for agreeing to vote for Foley without first obtaining any assurances of changes in the House. "They're already pledged [to support the Speaker] and it's business as usual. It's not comforting," Stenholm complained.[60] With no opposition within his own caucus, Foley's reelection as Speaker was all but certain. But subsequent events showed he underestimated the negative fallout of the bank scandal in his home state. In November, he would confront for a second time a statewide campaign to impose a legal limit on his tenure in Congress.

Sheryl "Sherry" Bockwinkel was an unlikely figure to lead a charge to retire the Speaker of the House. A Democrat from Tacoma, Washington, she was among a group of peace activists who opposed US funding for the military government of El Salvador in 1990. She participated in a sit-in at the Tacoma office of Representative Norm Dicks (D-WA). When Dicks telephoned from Washington, DC, to scold the protesters and defend his position, "we got really mad and decided to run someone else," she said. They settled on Mike Collier, who challenged Dicks in the Democratic primary. Dicks, first elected to the House in 1974, refused to debate Collier and outspent him

16 to 1. Collier drew only 16 percent of the primary vote, and Dicks cruised to an easy victory in November. "We realized that you can't beat an incumbent," Bockwinkel lamented. "How do you beat someone like [Dicks]?" she asked.[61]

Bockwinkel next worked on a state legislative race in which Democrat Helen Myrich ran for an open House seat. Unable to match the Republican candidate's spending, Myrich fell 439 votes short of winning. The House Democratic Caucus in Olympia gave only $650 to Myrich's campaign, while pouring thousands of dollars into incumbents' reelection treasuries, a practice that Bockwinkel called unfair.[62] The unsuccessful campaigns of Collier and Myrich convinced Bockwinkel the deck was stacked in favor of incumbents at both state and federal levels. "There's only two parties left: the incumbents and the rest of us," she said in 1991.[63]

Coincidentally, Oklahoma voters approved a term-limits initiative the same day in 1990 that Dicks won the primary. Bockwinkel and Gene Morain, who also worked on Collier's campaign, requested a copy of the Oklahoma initiative. In December 1990, they attended a conference of term-limit advocates organized by two national groups. After returning to Tacoma, they formed LIMIT: Legislative Initiative Mandating Incumbent Terms. Bockwinkel became the chair and Morain the treasurer. In January 1991, they submitted to the secretary of state's office a term-limit initiative, which was given the number I-553.[64] "The next thing you know, we had a bunch of people—many from the Collier campaign—getting signatures," Bockwinkel said. "We were such babes in the woods—we didn't know how hard it is" to get an initiative on the ballot.[65]

The Republican Party's 1988 platform had endorsed limits on congressional terms, but neither presidential candidate George Bush nor candidates for Congress made it an issue. The first national term-limits group formed in 1989 and two more organized in 1990, all with connections to the Republican Party or the Libertarian Party. In 1990, Oklahoma and California voters approved measures to limit terms of state legislators, while a Colorado initiative set limits for members of Congress as well as state officials.[66] The term-limits movement was yet another expression of public discontent with Congress in the 1990s. But with the exception of Bockwinkel's early efforts, it was hardly the grassroots movement its proponents claimed. Instead, it was part of the antigovernment agenda of several well-funded conservative groups. "This is not a spontaneous uprising by the public," political scientist Thomas Mann of the Brookings Institution in Washington, DC, explained to a newspaper in Tacoma. "It is a powerful combination of activist fund raising and organizing with a somewhat hidden agenda combined with a public distaste for Congress."[67]

The 1991 proposal of Bockwinkel's group called for a six-year limit for state representatives, an eight-year limit for state senators, three two-year terms for US representatives, and two six-year terms for US senators. It also limited the governor and other state officials to two four-year terms. The law would have applied to sitting officeholders, requiring any incumbent already over the limit to step down after finishing one more term. If the initiative had passed, it would have required Foley and the state's seven other House members to leave office in 1994. The measure also would have barred Governor Booth Gardner from seeking a third term in 1992.[68]

Washington law required initiative backers to obtain the signatures of 150,001 registered voters (8 percent of the votes cast for governor in the last election) to place their proposal on the general election ballot. By the end of February, four months before the July 5 deadline, sponsors had gathered only about 12,000 signatures. A month later, LIMIT was $10,000 in debt. But in April, the Washington group received a check for $100 from a national term-limits group, Citizens for Congressional Reform (CCR). That $100 was the first installment of what would eventually be nearly half a million dollars in contributions from the group. Separately, CCR contracted with a California company that hired professional signature collectors, paying them sixty cents per name—a tactic that violated Washington State law and was widely criticized in newspaper columns and editorials. State election officials took no action against the initiative backers, believing the ban on paid signature collectors to be unenforceable. By the July deadline, the company had provided 121,000 of the 254,000 signatures on the initiative, far more than needed to place it on the general election ballot.[69]

In October, the *News Tribune* of Tacoma reported that the money for CCR came primarily from a libertarian group, Citizens for a Sound Economy. Its major supporters were billionaire brothers David and Charles Koch, executives of Koch Industries, a Kansas-based cattle, real estate, and oil and gas conglomerate. In addition to term limits, Citizens for a Sound Economy favored a smaller federal government, abolition of the income tax, and privatization of the US Postal Service. David Koch was the Libertarian Party's vice presidential candidate in 1980; many of the term-limit movement's national leaders had Libertarian connections. The initiative's conservative backers did not bother Bockwinkel. "I think that points to the broad spectrum of support this movement speaks to," she said.[70] Bockwinkel said she discovered David Koch's broader political agenda by reading the Tacoma newspaper. "I woke up one morning, read the paper, and said 'Who is this guy?'"[71]

The political alliances on the other side were just as odd. Opposition came from major corporations, unions, the Washington State Grange, and such good-government groups as the League of Women Voters and Common Cause.[72] They coalesced in a group called "No on 553," led by Mark Brown, deputy director of the Washington Federation of State Employees. Bockwinkel dismissed her opponents as "the establishment," saying they were "concerned about keeping the people in power who they've worked on for 30 years."[73]

The National Rifle Association (NRA), an ally of Foley for most of his time in Congress, contributed $10,000 to the "No on 553" campaign. Neal Knox, a former director of the NRA's Institute for Legislative Action, said Foley asked for the group's help. "Tom had been a good friend to the NRA, and truth is, you don't want to see your friends term-limited out," he said. In fact, the NRA had presented Foley with its Defender of Individual Rights Award in 1978 after he opposed gun registration rules proposed by the US Bureau of Alcohol, Tobacco and Firearms.[74] The group's 1991 contribution "caused a bit of a flap among NRA members in the state, who didn't think [opposition to term limits] was appropriate," Knox acknowledged. Although Knox personally opposed term limits, believing they would give too much power to congressional staff members, the NRA at other times and in other states had supported them.[75]

In August 1991, the opponents commissioned a statewide survey of voter attitudes. The results disappointed the sponsors. After hearing only the ballot title, 73 percent of prospective voters supported the initiative and only 23 percent opposed it. However, the consulting firm that conducted the survey, the Analysis Group, discovered that initiative supporters were receptive to arguments that passage of the initiative would hurt the state's economy. "We can beat term limits at the ballot," the consultants wrote, "but only if we control the terms of the debate—moving it from a discussion of term limits to a debate about the economic impact of limits."[76]

The poll queried voter attitudes about state officials and the congressional delegation. Two-thirds of those surveyed had a "warm" feeling toward Foley, just a percentage point less than those who felt warmly about the late senator Henry Jackson (who at the time of the survey had been dead for eight years). Foley, the pollsters determined, was "the one leader most of these voters do not want to lose." Respondents were not thrilled with the congressional delegation as a whole, which they judged deficient when compared with the state's historical legacy. Accordingly, the consulting firm recommended that the anti-term-limits campaign should not focus on "saving the entire delegation, but individual leadership represented by people like Foley" and Governor Booth Gardner.[77]

Bockwinkel acknowledged that "a few good politicians" such as Foley and Gardner might be lost to term limits, but she argued that other qualified officeholders would come forward to take their place. A poll taken by initiative proponents showed only a slight decline in support when respondents learned that passage of the measure would force Foley's exit from office after one more term. Foley initially hesitated to speak out against the initiative because he did not want his comments to seem self-serving. In an interview, though, Foley called the initiative flawed in method and substance. "Any individual member of Congress is always subject to the voters telling us whether they want to dismiss us or not," he said. As he insisted, "The basic problem with the initiative, aside from procedural defects that are fundamental and constitutional problems that are even more fundamental, is that it would deprive voters in our state of the opportunity to make their own choices."[78] Ralph Munro, the Republican secretary of state in Olympia, was more blunt, calling the initiative "stupid, absolutely insane. It would be doomsday for the Pacific Northwest"—referring to the possibility that other states would take advantage of Washington's loss of seniority.[79] That summer, Foley, Gardner, and other officials went to court in an attempt to keep the initiative off the ballot. The Washington Supreme Court ruled in August that their claim was premature because any constitutional questions could be addressed after the election.[80]

After Labor Day, the "No on 553" campaign kicked into gear. Heeding the advice of the August poll, the opponents emphasized economic arguments. In a brochure headlined "There's Too Much to Lose," the committee asserted: "Term limitations could . . . cost you your job, raise your electric rates, threaten our environment, take away your right to elect your own leaders."[81]

One issue on which voters were especially sensitive was the threat that California might use its growing numbers in Congress—one-eighth of the House of Representatives—to secure diversion of water from the Columbia River, something the state's congressional delegation always had opposed. Washington governor Booth Gardner summed up this argument: "When people realize that California is going to take our water if this thing passes . . . the day the vote comes, people will vote against term limits." Initiative backers called Gardner's remarks an exaggeration. "These guys are running scared," said John Burick, a spokesman for LIMIT. "The incumbents are grasping at straws."[82]

Yet initiative proponents unwittingly gave credence to the anti-California argument when they invited former California governor Jerry Brown, who planned to run for president in 1992, to speak in favor of the initiative. Bockwinkel said a friend of Brown's had suggested the visit. "I didn't have a problem with bringing him in, but his visit did get a lot of play in the papers," she said.[83] Brown's visit gave Foley an opportunity to counterattack. "It's wonderfully ironic that a former governor of California would favor term limits for Washington's members of Congress," Foley said. "Jerry Brown has supported diversions of water from the Northwest to California," a threat to the region that Foley had used to his benefit in the past. "It's not surprising he favors tilting the balance [in Congress]."[84]

The weekend before the 1991 election, Foley flew home to Spokane. In a series of speeches, he denounced the initiative, describing to voters the consequences of losing seniority in Congress. Other members of the delegation echoed his position. In Seattle, Representative Norm Dicks warned that losing Foley would hurt the Northwest on such issues as defense spending, electrical rates, and cleanup of the Hanford nuclear reservation in central Washington.[85] On Election Day, 54 percent of Washington voters cast ballots against the initiative. In Foley's home district, 62 percent of voters opposed it. "The role of Tom Foley in opposing term limits proved crucial to its defeat," University of Washington political scientist David Olson wrote. Olson also praised Foley's colleague Representative Al Swift, who said he would leave Congress after one more term rather than be forced out by term limits.[86]

Returning to Washington, DC, after the election, Foley praised the judgment of his home state's voters in rejecting the initiative. "I think one of the characteristics of the Washington State electorate is that they are not swept one way or the other by these proposals but consider them very, very carefully," he said at a press conference. Assessing the term-limits movement nationally, he said that, despite their popularity, such measures "are not a commanding, sweeping, irresistible force." When voters are exposed to "an aggressive presentation of both sides of the argument," he explained, "there is very often a rejection, as there was dramatically in Washington yesterday." And, he argued, the public appeared satisfied with steps he had taken to resolve problems with the House bank and restaurants that had been reported before the election. He then delivered a spirited defense of Congress and its members: "They certainly should not be typified or described as living in some kind of a lap of luxury. That [description] is totally false, misleading and erroneous, and people obviously have tried to spread it for political and other purposes."[87]

After the defeat of the 1991 initiative, Foley believed that Washington voters had dealt a fatal blow to the term-limits movement. "I don't believe that even in 2020 there will be term limitations on Congress," he told *Washington Post* columnist David Broder. Foley's remark prompted Broder, who respected Foley, to describe his attitude as "all too characteristic of incumbents in Congress, who have come to believe that nothing can disturb their comfortable occupancy of their jobs."[88] As the House bank scandal dragged into the spring of 1992, Foley discovered that image of Congress, however inaccurate, to be increasingly pervasive.

Within days of the 1991 election, I-553 backers began work on a second initiative. "The *Seattle Times* did our work for us," Sherry Bockwinkel said, by conducting an exit poll to determine why the initiative lost. The paper's polling discovered that voters did not want term limits applied retroactively. "We took that as gospel and rewrote the initiative" to reflect that sentiment, she explained. In January 1992, LIMIT filed the second initiative and revived its campaign to collect signatures. Given the number I-573, that measure took a slightly different form than the previous initiative. Instead of imposing a legal limit on time in office, the initiative prevented congressional incumbents from being listed on the ballot after serving six years for US representative or twelve years as a US senator. Sitting members of Congress who wanted to run after those periods expired would have to do so as write-in candidates. Opponents of the initiative said the effect would be the same as limiting terms because write-in candidates rarely win elections. Bockwinkel said her group decided against seeking funding from the Koch brothers' group, Citizens for Congressional Reform, and another national organization, U.S. Term Limits. "We had a lot of volunteers," she explained. "I collected seven thousand signatures personally—it was easy."[89]

Although the wording was different, the debate over the 1992 initiative echoed that of the previous year, with two main differences: both sides were better organized and financed, and Foley was up for reelection in November. Washington State's political climate was unsettled in other ways as well. For reasons unrelated to the term-limits issue, Governor Booth Gardner decided against running for a third term.[90] Senator Brock Adams, facing allegations of sexually harassing female staff members and campaign workers, also chose not to run for reelection.[91]

The leaders of LIMIT were confident that Foley's clout could not stop a second initiative. "Everyone likes Tom Foley, but it's the system he is a part of and is trying to protect. . . . If Foley were a newcomer he'd be appalled at the abuses of power," Bockwinkel asserted, referring to the Speaker's efforts to reform the House seniority system during his first decade in Congress. Arguments against term limits that worked in 1991 had lost their effectiveness, she said. "Last fall, people were talking about the loss of clout and experience of our senior members" if the initiative passed. Referring to the still-simmering House bank scandal, Bockwinkel scoffed, "Now we see they use their experience for cover-up, not for visionary problem solving and leadership."[92]

Heather Foley, the Speaker's wife and unpaid chief of staff, solicited contributions to the "No on 573" coalition, prompting a complaint to the House Ethics Committee by the U.S. Term Limits Council and the Term Limits Legal Institute. At issue was a $1,000 donation from the International Ladies' Garment Workers Union that had been sent to "Mrs. Tom Foley, c/o Speaker's Office, U.S. Capitol" and a list of potential contributors assembled by the Washington Federation of State Employees with the notation "per Heather Foley." Those documents led term-limits supporters to complain that Heather Foley improperly used the Speaker's office to solicit donations for the anti-term-limits group. Not so, the Speaker replied. All of Heather Foley's efforts "have been done without remuneration, after business hours and at home," he said in a press release.[93]

In Washington's September primary, John Sonneland defeated three other Republicans to earn the right to face Foley for a third time. Sonneland hoped the public outcry over the bad checks, the investigation of the House post office, and Foley's failure to act more decisively to curb abuses would work to the challenger's advantage. In Spokane, Sonneland's billboards asked: "Fed up with Congress? Fire the Speaker!" A Sonneland radio commercial suggested that Foley's constituents would not be invited to a fundraising party for him because "you live in the West. Tom and his friends live here with us, in the East, where Congress lives." Foley countered that sentiment with a brochure that showed him standing in a wheat field, wearing a plaid shirt and casual slacks instead of his characteristic dark suit. "One of Eastern Washington's Own," the caption read.[94] Sonneland, drawing on profitable investments in a cell phone company, said he was prepared to spend up to $500,000 of his own money on the campaign.[95]

Sonneland's tactics worried Ken Degerness, owner of a Spokane public relations agency that had worked for Foley's campaign in the past. "I don't want to sound paranoid, but I'm getting worried about the momentum of the campaign," he wrote in late October to Heather Foley and Janet Gilpatrick, manager of Foley's Spokane office. High-traffic intersections in Spokane lacked Foley yard signs, Degerness complained. His staff believed that many twenty-five- to thirty-five-year-old voters were supporting Sonneland out of a desire for change. He suggested that Foley do a live call-in TV program the weekend before the election as a way to demonstrate that he was in touch with issues.[96]

The 1992 election results validated Degerness's fears. Sonneland held Foley to only 55 percent of the vote, down from 69 percent two years earlier. Fifth District voters did give a plurality of votes to Bill Clinton, the Democratic presidential candidate, but third-party candidate Ross Perot drew 23 percent. In another indication of anti-incumbent sentiment, Washington voters narrowly approved I-573, the term-limits initiative. Statewide, the margin was 52 percent in favor and 48 percent opposed, almost reversing the previous year's split. In the Fifth Congressional District, opponents outnumbered supporters of the initiative by about ten thousand votes, a figure that Foley later cited as evidence that his constituents opposed term limits.[97] LIMIT's Bockwinkel said that radio advertising during the last week of the campaign calling attention to the House bank scandal made a difference in the outcome. Term-limits opponents could not raise enough money to counter those ads, she theorized. In addition, statewide campaigns for president, governor, and US senator preoccupied organized labor and other groups that had worked against the 1991 term-limits initiative.[98] Elsewhere, thirteen other states also imposed term limits by margins as high as 77 percent; in no state did voters defeat term limits.[99]

The Sunday after the election, Foley hinted at the next move for opponents of term limits. Appearing on ABC's *This Week with David Brinkley*, Foley said that the courts should decide whether states could legally impose term limits on members of Congress through initiatives. He also opposed bringing to the House floor a proposed constitutional amendment on term limits until after a court ruling on the various state initiatives.[100]

The court challenge began seven months later. In July 1993, Foley, two of his constituents, and the Washington League of Women Voters sued the state, claiming that the term-limits law violated the US Constitution. The Constitution says only that a member of the House must be a US citizen, at least twenty-five years old, and a resident of the state. Not only did the initiative impose an additional restriction by setting a limit on the number of terms a member could serve, Foley and the other plaintiffs argued, but it also infringed on a candidate's ability to express himself by running for office and on voters' rights to associate with candidates. "We believe voters should have an unrestricted choice of candidates," said Margaret Colony, president of the Washington State chapter of the League of Women Voters.[101]

Regardless of Foley's intentions, newspaper editorials and columns accused him of acting only in his self-interest. "Foley is obviously attempting to use the power and influence of his office to swing a court decision against term limits," the *Olympian*, the state capital's newspaper, scolded in an editorial. The paper said the issue should be decided on its legal merit without respect to "personalities and politics." Rather than interject himself into the lawsuit, Foley should have used his influence to resolve the impasse over logging in national forests, a major issue in the state that year, the editorial suggested.[102] In Spokane, the *Spokesman-Review* saw no harm in Foley's involvement, arguing that the courts properly should decide whether the state's term-limits law would go into effect.[103] Bockwinkel said she was thrilled when Foley joined the lawsuit. "I figured that would be his death knell," she explained. "As soon as that happened, it brought attention to him."[104]

Foley defended his decision to join the high-profile lawsuit. "I'm accused of going against the will of the people," he said. "But my interest is not to thwart anything. From my standpoint, I'm doing a service for everybody. This issue needs to be clarified."[105] Foley insisted that as Speaker of the House, he had an obligation to sue on behalf of the legislative branch. Representatives Al Swift and Jim McDermott (both Washington Democrats) later said they urged Foley not to put his name on the lawsuit, offering to be plaintiffs themselves. Swift already had declared his intent to leave Congress in 1994; McDermott, who represented a strong Democratic district in Seattle, could join the suit with little political risk. "I had a discussion with him [Foley] at one point," McDermott said, telling him, "'Tom, I should run that lawsuit . . . rather than you. I have a district where there's not going to be people who will think that's not right. Your district is going to be much harder.' And he said, 'I'm the Speaker and it's my responsibility to defend the House of Representatives.'" That distinction may have been lost on many of Foley's constituents, most of whom were not as well versed about the Constitution as their longtime representative.[106]

As McDermott had warned, Foley's position proved to be both unpopular and widely misunderstood. "This is absurd, a slap in the face of the voters," complained Rick Melanson, who had been involved in the pro-I-573 campaign in Spokane. "If Mr. Foley truly cared about the Constitution, he would honor the people's decision."[107] In October 1993, John Jacobs, the executive director of U.S. Term Limits, attacked Foley in a speech to the Spokane Rotary Club. "Is it right, does it make sense, that we're now in a society where our government officials are suing the voters?" Jacobs asked. "Isn't there something wrong with this picture?" But, until a reporter asked, Jacobs failed to mention that in both 1991 and 1992 a majority of Fifth District voters had opposed term limits. He then argued that, regardless of the district's preference, Foley "ought to do what's in the best interest of the country" and drop out of the lawsuit.[108] Nonetheless, Foley persisted, giving his next Republican opponent, George Nethercutt, a wedge issue. Nethercutt and his allies argued that Foley had been in office too long, and by 1994, many Fifth District voters were receptive to that argument.

The pro-term-limits forces hired Griffin Bell, a US attorney general under President Jimmy Carter, to represent them. Another Carter appointee, former White House counsel Lloyd Cutler, was the lead attorney opposed to term limits. In January 1994, US district judge William Dwyer of Seattle heard arguments. On February 10, 1994, he ruled that Initiative 573 was unconstitutional because it added a qualification for members of Congress beyond those specified in the Constitution. In a similar case, the Arkansas Supreme Court ruled in March against the term-limits measure that Arkansas voters had passed in 1992.[109] In November 1994, the US Supreme Court heard an appeal of the Arkansas case. In May 1995, the court ruled that only a constitutional amendment could limit terms of members of Congress—the argument that Foley and others had been making since 1991.[110] The ruling, which invalidated Washington's 1992 initiative, came too late to help Foley. Defeated for reelection in 1994 at least partially due to his opposition to term limits, he left Congress four months before the court's decision.

Tom Foley (*front row, right*) was a member of Gonzaga University's championship debate team in 1947–1948. Credit: Gonzaga University Library. Debating Society 1947–1948: champions, rg_1947_1948_37 (cn1402).

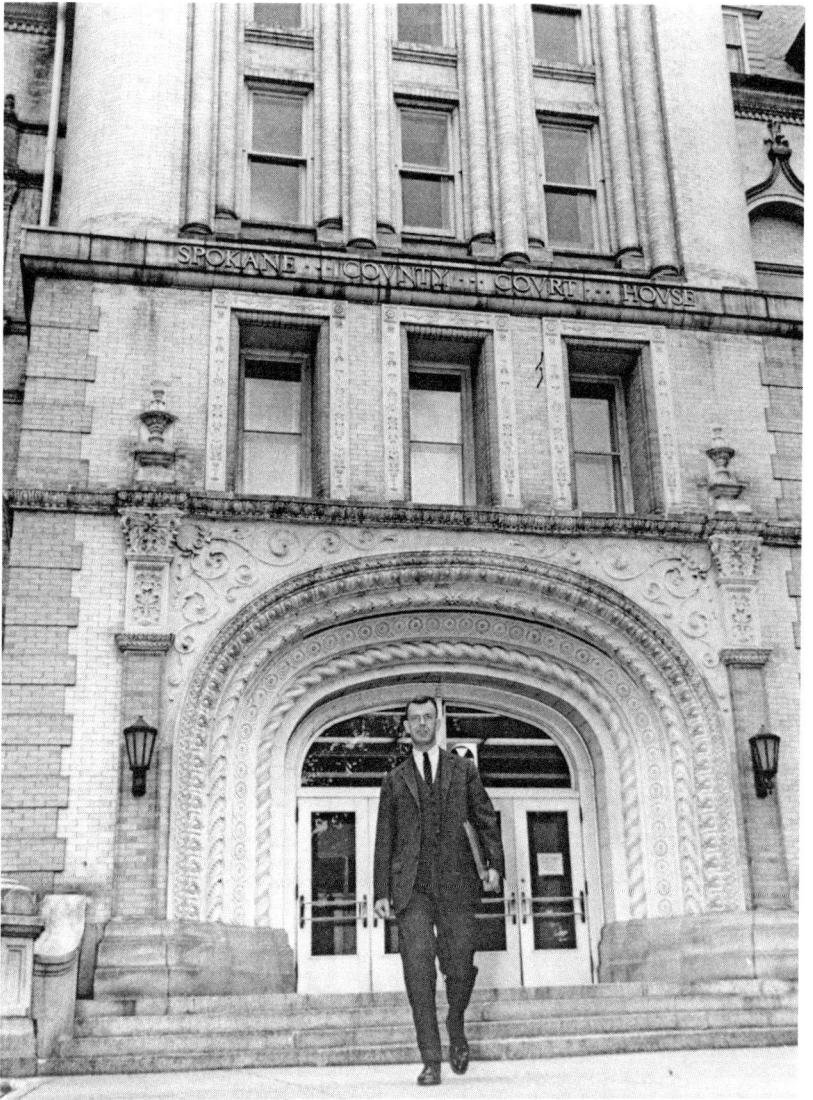

After graduating from the University of Washington law school, Foley returned to Spokane and became a deputy prosecutor for Spokane County in 1958. This photo was taken in front of the Spokane County Courthouse. Credit: Thomas S. Foley Photographs, Washington State University Libraries Special Collections.

Foley joined the staff of Senator Henry Jackson (D-WA) in 1961 as a special counsel to the Senate Committee on Interior and Insular Affairs. Jackson (*left*) encouraged Foley to run for the House of Representatives in 1964. Credit: Thomas S. Foley Photographs, Washington State University Libraries Special Collections.

Washington's powerful Democratic senators Henry Jackson (*front left*) and Warren Magnuson (*front right*) welcomed four newly elected members of the state's congressional delegation in 1964, posing with the latest edition of the Congressional Directory. The House members were (*from left*): Floyd Hicks, Lloyd Meeds, Tom Foley, and Brock Adams. Credit: University of Washington Libraries, Special Collections UW27204.

Arriving in Washington, DC, in 1964 after his election to the House, Foley posed for this photo on the steps of the US Capitol. Credit: Thomas S. Foley Photographs, Washington State University Libraries Special Collections.

In his second term in the House, Foley visited Omak in the northwest corner of the Fifth Congressional District to participate in the Omak Stampede rodeo. Mounted on this horse, Foley became the center of attention when the horse took off in the opposite direction of the other dignitaries. Foley was reunited with the horse several years later for this photo. Credit: Thomas S. Foley Photographs, Washington State University Libraries Special Collections.

Grand Coulee Dam, in the center of Foley's district, was the first major
hydroelectric dam on the Columbia River, constructed between 1933 and 1942.
The dam was originally built with only two powerhouses, and a third powerhouse
was proposed in the 1960s. Foley joined Senators Magnuson and Jackson (*left*)
and President Lyndon Johnson (*back to camera*) on a tour of the dam site in the
late 1960s to promote the third powerhouse, which was completed in 1974.
Credit: Thomas S. Foley Photographs, Washington State University Libraries
Special Collections.

Foley married Heather Strachan in 1968. They met on the staff of Senator Henry Jackson. After their marriage, Heather Foley became her husband's administrative assistant. This photo, taken in the early 1980s, shows her at work in the congressional office. Credit: Thomas S. Foley Photographs, Washington State University Libraries Special Collections.

Among the many constituents that Tom and Heather Foley met with in Washington, DC, was this delegation from W.I.F.E. (Women Involved in Farm Economics) in 1979, when Foley was chair of the House Committee on Agriculture. Credit: Thomas S. Foley Photographs, Washington State University Libraries Special Collections.

On election night in 1978, Foley spoke on the telephone while waiting for results in a Spokane hotel room. Foley won a three-way race for reelection, the only time he attracted less than 50 percent of the general election votes until his 1994 defeat. Credit: Barry Kough, *Lewiston Tribune*.

Tom and Heather Foley in a Spokane hotel elevator on Election Day 1978. Credit: Barry Kough, *Lewiston Tribune*.

House Speaker Tip O'Neill welcomes Helen and Ralph Foley (Tom's parents) to the US Capitol in 1986 when Tom Foley was the House Democratic whip, the last whip to be appointed by the Speaker rather than elected by the Democratic Caucus. Credit: Thomas S. Foley Photographs, Washington State University Libraries Special Collections.

Tom Foley appeared on the Sunday morning interview program *Meet the Press* in 1982. The program's moderator was Bill Monroe. Credit: Thomas S. Foley Photographs, Washington State University Libraries Special Collections.

At the 1992 Democratic National Convention in New York City, three former House speakers, (*from left*) Carl Albert, Tip O'Neill, and Jim Wright, posed for this photo with Foley, then in his third year as Speaker. Credit: Carl Albert Congressional Research and Studies Center Archives, University of Oklahoma.

As a member of the House who ran for reelection every two years, Foley often found himself visiting farms, ranches, and dairies, even taking a turn milking a cow. Credit: Thomas S. Foley Photographs, Washington State University Libraries Special Collections.

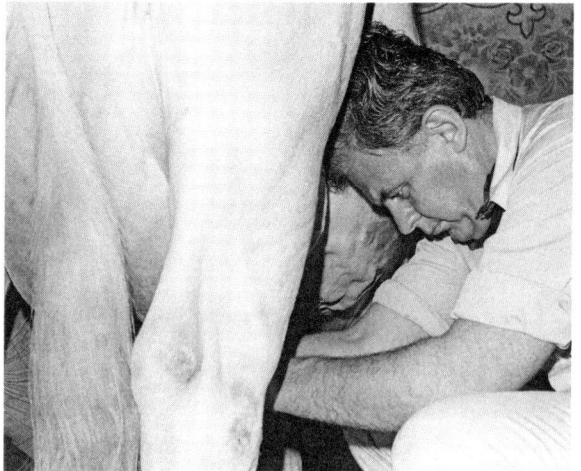

After Jim Wright became speaker in 1986, he assembled his leadership team. Foley (*to Wright's left*) was the majority leader, while Representative Tony Coelho of California (*holding the whip*) was the majority whip. Others in the photo (*from left*) are Representative David Bonior of Michigan, Representative Mary Rose Oakar of Ohio, an unidentified staff member, and Representative Richard Gephardt of Missouri. Credit: Thomas S. Foley Photographs, Washington State University Libraries Special Collections.

Foley enjoyed cordial relationships with Robert Michel, the House Republican leader when Foley was Speaker, and President George H. W. Bush. Credit: Thomas S. Foley Photographs, Washington State University Libraries Special Collections.

For Washington State's centennial in 1989, President George H. W. Bush visited Spokane and learned about the Centennial Trail through the city and Spokane Valley, a bicycle-pedestrian route for which Foley secured funding. Credit: Thomas S. Foley Photographs, Washington State University Libraries Special Collections.

The Foleys' beloved dog, Alice, was a Belgian Shepherd that Tom Foley rescued from John F. Kennedy Airport in New York, where she had been left unclaimed in an animal-holding area. She was at home in the Speaker's office and later appeared in a Foley campaign commercial. Credit: Thomas S. Foley Photographs, Washington State University Libraries Special Collections.

When actor Jimmy Stewart visited Speaker Foley at the Capitol, he was greeted by the Foleys' dog, Alice. Credit: Thomas S. Foley Photographs, Washington State University Libraries Special Collections.

Foley, a gun owner and occasional hunter, bagged a goose on a trip to eastern Washington. Credit: Thomas S. Foley Photographs, Washington State University Libraries Special Collections.

On a visit to Walla Walla County during wheat harvest in the late 1980s, Foley met with farmers and supporters Anne-Marie and Don Schwerin. Credit: Thomas S. Foley Photographs, Washington State University Libraries Special Collections.

Tom Foley was sworn in as Speaker of the House of Representatives on May 31, 1989, after the resignation of Speaker Jim Wright. Credit: Thomas S. Foley Photographs, Washington State University Libraries Special Collections.

When Soviet president Mikhail Gorbachev visited Washington, DC, his official appearances included an event at the US Capitol. Credit: Thomas S. Foley Photographs, Washington State University Libraries Special Collections.

After his election as Speaker in 1989, Foley greeted constituents in Clarkson, in the southeast corner of the Fifth Congressional District. Credit: Barry Kough, *Lewiston Tribune.*

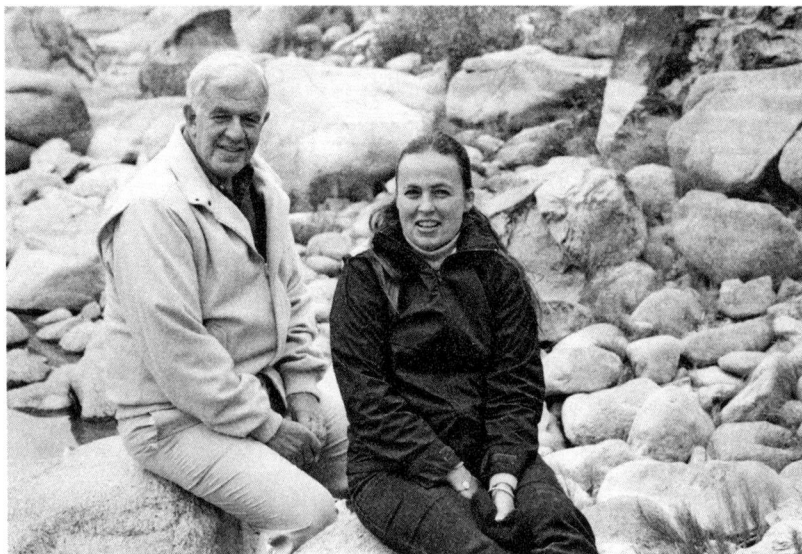

Tom and Heather Foley along the Centennial Trail in Spokane. Credit: Thomas S. Foley Photographs, Washington State University Libraries Special Collections.

Foley met with President Bill Clinton in the Oval Office after Clinton took office in January 1993. Credit: Thomas S. Foley Photographs, Washington State University Libraries Special Collections.

Foley with President Bill Clinton and First Lady Hillary Clinton at Statuary Hall in the US Capitol. Senate majority leader George Mitchell is at left. Credit: Thomas S. Foley Photographs, Washington State University Libraries Special Collections.

As Foley's 1994 race for reelection tightened, he met with supporters after a campaign debate in Spokane. Credit: Mary Ann McCurdy.

At an Oval Office meeting, Foley and Democratic leaders met with President Bill Clinton and Vice President Al Gore. Attending were (*from left*) Representative Leon Panetta (later Clinton's director of the Office of Management and Budget), Foley, Gore, Clinton, Senator George Mitchell, and Representative Richard Gephardt. Credit: Thomas S. Foley Photographs, Washington State University Libraries Special Collections.

After the passage of the Civil Rights and Women's Equity in Employment Act of 1991, a triumphant Foley met with reporters. Credit: Thomas S. Foley Photographs, Washington State University Libraries Special Collections.

Foley and his 1994 Republican opponent, George Nethercutt, debated eight times in the three weeks before the election. They posed for this photo before the final debate in October 1994. In 2022, Nethercutt, who served ten years in the House, joined the advisory board for the Foley Institute at Washington State University. Credit: Sandra Bancroft Billings, *Spokesman-Review*.

CHAPTER 8

THE PERFECT STORM

om Foley had never given a concession speech. The forty-ninth Speaker of the House of Representatives had never before needed one. In fifteen previous elections in his eastern Washington district, Foley always had been the victor, often by comfortable margins. But as the evening of November 8, 1994, wore on, his winning streak appeared to be over. As Spokane's daily newspaper, the *Spokesman-Review*, went to press at midnight, Foley was almost four thousand votes behind his Republican challenger, George Nethercutt, with 73 percent of the ballots counted.[1] Throughout election night, returns from across the country showed Republicans winning control of the House of Representatives for the first time since 1954. Even if Foley had managed to cling to his seat, his tenure as Speaker was over.

By noon the next day, the gap narrowed to twenty-two hundred votes, with nineteen thousand absentee votes still uncounted. Calculating that he would need nearly two-thirds of the remaining votes to win, Foley recognized the inevitable outcome.[2] He telephoned Nethercutt to offer his congratulations. Then, the highest-ranking Democrat in Congress stepped into the lobby of his district office in downtown Spokane to face the waiting TV cameras and microphones. Surrounded by aides and campaign workers, Foley began in characteristic fashion by thanking his constituents, who had just thrown him out of office. "I want to express my deepest appreciation to the people of the Fifth Congressional District who have given me the honor of representing them for 30 years," he said.[3] The most prominent Democrat to fall to a Republican challenger in 1994, Foley was the first Speaker of the House to lose in his home district since Abraham Lincoln was president.[4]

The election results reverberated across the American political landscape. The Republicans, led by Speaker-to-be Newt Gingrich of Georgia, gained fifty-two seats in the House of Representatives, the largest shift between parties since 1948.[5] Republicans also took control of the Senate. Along with Foley, dozens of longtime Democratic incumbents, including chairs of several powerful committees, lost their seats. They were targets of the voters' anger at Congress and President Bill Clinton over taxes, health care, and government in general. Amazingly, not a single Republican congressional incumbent on the 1994 general election ballot lost his or her seat. Gingrich and his allies had managed to persuade many voters that the Democrats were solely to blame for the nation's problems. As the most visible Democrat in Congress, Foley surely was among the most vulnerable.[6]

A set of complex and multipronged dynamics surrounded the 1994 midterm election. While those dynamics created significant nationwide effects, this storm of forces also led to Foley's defeat. This chapter focuses on the events that led to that outcome. Other chapters have examined the electoral history of the district (including the effects of redistricting), widely varying margins in support for Foley and his opponents across time, national political trends, the role of the district's political culture, and the public policy positions taken by Foley. In 1994, these forces coalesced into a perfect storm. Even though Foley had been reelected for three decades in a district whose voters were significantly more conservative than he, the storm of 1994 unseated him from the speakership and ended his congressional tenure.

Beyond the national shift to Republican candidates, Foley's defeat stemmed from a complicated mix of personality and policy. His positions on gun control and congressional term limits backfired, enabling his political opponents to use those issues against him. Foley also had difficulty convincing some of his constituents that he effectively represented them when, as Speaker, he did not cast a recorded vote. Finally, a late start to his campaign and Foley's old-school reluctance to immediately and forcefully respond to attacks on his integrity also cost him votes. While no single miscalculation on Foley's part caused his defeat, the cumulative effect of a half dozen issues—a perfect storm—toppled the Speaker.

Over the previous three decades, Foley had built a remarkable career in Congress. His conciliatory style was ideally suited for a House divided by bitter partisan warfare in the final months of Jim Wright's tenure. During nearly six years as Speaker, Foley assumed the role of consensus builder rather than an advocate for his party's positions, albeit that was a role some Democratic liberals saw as a liability. Throughout his career, Foley often defended his preference for compromise rather than confrontation. "I think I am a little cursed with seeing the other point of view and trying to understand it," he once explained.[7]

For his last two decades in Congress, Foley tried to hold the center. But as his district's demographics and economy changed in the 1980s, discerning the middle ground became more difficult. Often, his positions frustrated both sides. Yet his desire for compromise was consistent with his moderate ideology and his aversion to conflict. After Foley became part of the House leadership, he had a new constituency to please: the House Democratic Caucus with its diversity of positions. As Speaker, Foley walked a tightrope between the rural, conservative values of his district and the more liberal positions of the caucus. "It was extremely complicated for Foley, not only trying to get reelected, but also trying to be the leader of the Democratic Party," said Tom Nides, a key Foley aide. "In a lot of cases, they [the two positions] were diametrical opposites, and it was not always possible to reconcile them."[8] Bruce Reed, a domestic policy adviser to President Bill Clinton and later chief of staff to Vice President Joe Biden, agreed. "It was a long way from the center of the House Democratic Caucus to the center of the country," Reed said. "Speaker Foley, who was from a potentially heartland district—not that far from the coast, basically a rural district—just had to straddle two horses."[9]

One example was gun control. For most of his time in the House, Foley had resisted government attempts to restrict the sale and possession of firearms, earning awards and endorsements from the National Rifle Association (NRA).[10] As the NRA became more militant in the 1990s, Foley grew increasingly uncomfortable with the group's positions. Many House Democrats called for stricter gun laws, catching Foley in a tug-of-war between his two constituencies: the Washington State voters who elected him their representative and the caucus that elected him Speaker. His support for a ban on assault weapons drew the wrath of the NRA, which mobilized its members against Foley. His defense of Congress after the House bank and post office scandals in the early 1990s played into the hands of Newt Gingrich, whose strategy to take over Congress relied on convincing the public that the entire legislative branch was corrupt.

Foley and other Washington state Democrats enjoyed a banner year in 1992. Bill Clinton won the state's eleven electoral votes on his way to the White House. Voters also elected former representative Mike Lowry as governor and chose Patty Murray to become the state's first woman US senator, replacing Brock Adams, who did not seek reelection. Democrats carried all but one of the state's nine congressional districts.[11] Nonetheless, three outcomes of the 1992 election hinted at trouble ahead for Foley. First, his Republican challenger John Sonneland held Foley to only 55 percent of the vote, down from 69 percent two years earlier. Second, independent presidential candidate Ross Perot attracted 24 percent of the vote statewide, providing a potential reservoir of support for future Republican congressional candidates in Foley's district. Third, a Washington State initiative to limit the number of terms of legislators and the state's representatives in Congress narrowly passed. The measure would have prevented congressional incumbents from being listed on the ballot after serving six years as a representative or twelve years as a senator—essentially forcing longtime incumbents such as Foley to run as write-in candidates.[12] In retrospect, the statewide support for term limits and enthusiasm for Perot's candidacy were clear signs of voter disenchantment and frustration with the status quo.

After twelve years with Republicans in the White House, Foley relished the prospect of working with Democratic president Bill Clinton. He believed his knowledge of the legislative process and his ability to work out compromises would be assets to Clinton. "It's our role to react, not to initiate, to modify rather than create," he told an interviewer in 1993.[13] Foley wanted to demonstrate that Democrats could use their majorities in Congress to further the agenda of a Democratic president, unlike the experience of 1977–1980, when President Jimmy Carter and congressional leaders often were at odds. Foley did not always agree with Clinton's priorities or strategies. Yet, as the leader of the House Democrats, he needed to fully support the president's agenda, even as he looked forward to sharing some of the spotlight with Clinton. As congressional correspondent Ronald Elving wrote: "Freed from serving as the party's human symbol and media spokesman, the Speaker can concentrate on running the House and pressing a program with which he is in sympathy. Foley is far more likely to exert his powers in full to these ends than he was for the purposes of obstruction and delay. He says he expects to be 'more decisive' if 'not necessarily more controlling.'"[14]

Meanwhile, Foley took no chances in raising money for his 1994 reelection campaign. In 1993, he collected nearly $600,000 in contributions, exceeding the total of the previous years.[15] But issues about Foley's management of the House of Representatives continued to haunt him. That summer, *Mother Jones* magazine ran a cover story depicting Foley as a gladiator ready to swing a battle-ax. The headline read: "Killing Reform: The Inside Story on How House Speaker Foley Kept His Job." The article focused on his behind-the-scenes strategy to retain the speakership by undercutting potential challengers. But without major reforms in House procedures, the negative media coverage continued, and Foley did not mount an effective rebuttal. "In general, Foley's troubles stem from that inability to see Congress as outsiders do, the knee-jerk instinct to cover for the institution built up over twenty-eight years of working there," the magazine's Richard Blow concluded.[16]

A survey of district voters commissioned by Foley's campaign that October warned that the Democrat would have difficulty holding on to his seat the following year. "Speaker Tom Foley is in a precarious political position in Washington's 5th Congressional District," Mellman-Lazarus-Lake, a Washington, DC, consulting firm cautioned. Based on a survey of four hundred voters, the consultants found three main reasons for Foley's vulnerable position: strong Republican leanings among voters, growing antipolitics sentiment in the district, and the belief that Foley represented the worst attributes of incumbent politicians. "Voters are nearly unanimous in disliking the job that Congress is doing and in holding Foley responsible to some degree," the report said. The pollsters noted an alarming shift in voters' opinion of Foley since a survey taken a year earlier. "What has changed even more than the mood of the District is the closer alignment in voters' minds between Tom Foley the individual and the D.C. politics voters despise," the consultants warned. "It is as if last year (1992) voters could separate between Foley the person and Congress the institution. But this year voters see more and more overlap between the two."[17]

To overcome that sentiment, Mellman-Lazarus-Lake recommended that Foley frame his public statements and actions in terms demonstrating how he was working in the district's interest, "not on behalf of his party, his President, or his institution." In particular, the consultants suggested Foley should show the benefits of his clout, such as protecting Fairchild Air Force Base, the largest military installation in eastern Washington, against possible closure. Finally, the pollsters said Foley needed to rebuild his relationship with his constituents.[18] Foley heeded the consultants' advice, to a degree. In the next six months, his office issued press releases illustrating his protection of federal projects and jobs in the district. In February 1994, the Pentagon announced that Fairchild would become the nation's largest air-refueling base, with a fleet of KC-135 tankers to replace the aging B-52 bombers that were being removed from active duty. "The entire Spokane community and the civilian and military personnel at Fairchild should view this announcement as a big vote of confidence," Foley said in a prepared statement.[19] A month later, he announced that the Department of the Interior planned to merge two units of the US Bureau of Mines in Spokane but would keep both offices open. The offices provided valuable support to the Northwest mining industry, Foley said.[20] Neither press release, however, mentioned the number of jobs at stake at Fairchild and the Bureau of Mines office or attempted to document the economic benefits of the federal agencies to Spokane.

In March 1994, political observers predicted that based on the size of his campaign treasury and the lack of an announced Republican candidate, Foley would coast to another term. "I think he is safe. So far there is no indication of anyone emerging to seriously challenge him," said Blaine Garvin, a Gonzaga University political science professor.[21] Three months later, however, the *Seattle Times* reported that "the speaker of the House appears headed for his stiffest election challenge in more than a decade." A private poll indicated that nearly half of district voters wanted a new representative in Congress.[22]

By midsummer, three Republicans had lined up to challenge Foley: John Sonneland and Duane Alton, who had both previously run for the seat, and George Nethercutt, the Spokane County Republican chairman, who had never sought elected office. Sonneland, a physician, first ran in 1978 but lost to Alton in the primary. Sonneland was the Republican nominee in 1980, 1982, and 1992. Each challenger had once come within nine thousand votes of Foley; both hoped that 1994 would be the end of Foley's congressional career. Alton had high name recognition in the district as a result of television commercials for his chain of tire stores.[23] Moreover, during the sixteen years between his candidacies, he had rounded the sharp edges of his rhetoric. And Sonneland was encouraged by his showing in 1992, in which he held Foley to 55 percent of the vote; the Republican believed that his momentum would carry over to 1994.

Born in Spokane in 1944, Nethercutt was fifteen years younger than Foley. Like Foley, he was a lawyer and a former congressional staff member. He graduated from Washington State University with an English degree and from Gonzaga University's law school. After finishing law school, he worked as a clerk for a federal judge in Alaska. That job led him to

Washington, DC, where he worked on the staff of Alaska senator Ted Stevens for four and a half years. Nethercutt moved to Seattle in 1977 to open a branch of his family's law practice and to Spokane in 1979 after his father died. He became involved in Republican politics in Spokane County in 1980, the year Ronald Reagan defeated Jimmy Carter for president and Slade Gorton ousted longtime Washington senator Warren Magnuson. Over the next decade, Nethercutt worked for Republican candidates at the precinct and legislative district levels, eventually becoming Spokane County party chair in 1990.[24]

Reporters frequently asked Nethercutt about potential Republican candidates for Congress. "As 1994 came along, I got the question, 'Well, are you Republicans going to run anyone of any substance against Tom Foley?'" Nethercutt recalled, acknowledging that the party had not been competitive in previous elections. In late 1993, Randy Shaw, a news anchor for KHQ-TV in Spokane, expressed interest in running against Foley. Nethercutt remembered receiving a telephone call from Shaw that December asking to meet at a restaurant on Spokane's South Hill. "I went in there thinking he was going to tell me, 'I'm ready to run. Will you help me?'" Instead, Shaw said he would not run because his brother was ill. Nethercutt said, "I remember driving home, thinking, 'What are we going to do for a candidate?'"[25]

That week the *Spokesman-Review* reported on Shaw's decision not to challenge Foley and named Nethercutt as a possible contender. "The day it showed up in the paper I got something like eighty-three phone calls from friends of mine, who said, 'If you run, I'll help you.' I responded, 'I'm thinking about it, that's all.'" After discussing the idea with his wife, Mary Beth, he decided to fly to Washington, DC, to meet with political consultant Ed Rollins, who had managed Ross Perot's 1992 presidential campaign. As Nethercutt recalled the conversation, Rollins said, "If it was Tip O'Neill or Jim Wright or Sam Rayburn, I'd say, 'You're my good friend, stay home, practice law, enjoy your life.' But given the atmosphere of 1993–1994, Mr. Foley can be beaten."[26]

Rollins told Nethercutt he was reluctant to get involved in any 1994 campaign because of the controversy surrounding the New Jersey governor's race in November 1993 in which Rollins claimed to have paid Black ministers to encourage Democratic voters to stay at home on Election Day. (He later recanted that statement.) "George, I'm the last guy in the world you want involved. Foley would surely make me a campaign issue," Rollins said. Even so, the prospect of helping his friend, while taking on the

Speaker of the House, appealed to his competitive instincts. "I walked out onto Nineteenth Street [in Washington, DC] into the cold December wind thinking to myself, I'd love to do this fucking race," Rollins later wrote. "George would make a great candidate and congressman, and beating the speaker would be a nice way for me to finish my career."[27]

At Rollins's suggestion, Nethercutt commissioned a poll in February 1994 showing a high disapproval rating for Foley. In Rollins's analysis:

> The poll results had come back surprisingly positive [for Nethercutt]. Tom Foley *had* apparently lost touch with his district. The data suggested Foley was vulnerable to a conservative challenge if his opponent wasn't a right-wing extremist, as Foley's last two challengers had been. . . . Although he [Nethercutt] wasn't well known in the district, he fit perfectly the profile of the kind of candidate who could give Foley trouble."[28]

A month later, Nethercutt decided to run. "There was no crystallizing moment—it was a combination of a lot of things," he later explained. In mid-April, Nethercutt and his supporters organized a breakfast to launch his campaign. "I expected maybe 350 people; 1,000 people showed up," he said.[29]

By 1994, Foley had come to personify voters' complaints about the federal government: It was too big, too intrusive, and too slow to respond to the nation's problems. The irony was that those same voters took for granted the federal projects that long had flowed into eastern Washington as a direct result of Foley's seniority and leadership positions. Sid Morrison, a former Republican congressman from the neighboring Fourth District, said Foley often failed to seek credit for his work on behalf of the state's interests. "He did a lot behind the scenes—it was not his style to blow his own horn," Morrison said.[30]

Foley's opposition to term limits for members of Congress also hurt him. His involvement in a 1993 lawsuit challenging the 1992 Washington initiative prompted his critics to claim, "He sued his constituents!" and led national term-limits groups to pour thousands of dollars into ads attacking him. Foley insisted that as Speaker, he had an obligation to sue to clarify the constitutionality of congressional term limits, a distinction that may have been lost on many Fifth District voters during the 1994 campaign.[31]

When it came to gun control, Foley had long taken a position at odds with a majority of Democrats in Congress. The NRA had presented Foley with a "Defender of Individual Rights" award in 1978 and endorsed him for the first time in 1982.[32] Foley's longtime opposition to restrictions on individual gun ownership weakened after a fatal shooting in his home district. On June 20, 1994, a recently discharged airman went on a rampage at the hospital of Fairchild Air Force Base, eight miles west of Spokane. The man killed four people and wounded twenty-three others before military police killed him. The gunman used a MAK-90 semiautomatic rifle, a version of the Soviet-designed AK-47. Touring the base four days after the shooting with secretary of the air force Sheila Widnall, Foley said he supported a ban on such rifles as the one used in the shooting, commonly referred to as assault weapons.[33]

Although the Speaker rarely votes, Foley told reporters: "I would have broken [a tie] in support of legislation."[34] Banning the importation, manufacture, and most sales of semiautomatic weapons posed no threat to the rights of hunters or target shooters, Foley argued. "I think that these weapons are not essentially related to . . . sporting and other recreational uses, and they have found themselves increasingly into use by criminal elements in this country," he said.[35] Foley also said that he would have supported the Brady Bill the previous year, though he opposed high taxes on ammunition or other "elaborate restrictions on firearms."[36] Within weeks, the NRA added Foley to the list of Democrats it wanted to defeat.

That summer, Mellman-Lazarus-Lake, the consulting firm that conducted the 1993 voter survey, convened a series of focus group meetings at the request of the Foley campaign organization. Participants in Spokane and Walla Walla were asked to write down positive and negative comments about the congressman. One Walla Walla voter criticized Foley for sponsoring "pork-barrel projects" including the US Army Corps of Engineers headquarters and Veterans Administration hospital in Walla Walla. Projects once welcomed as beneficial to the district were now derided as pork, reflecting the change in public attitudes toward federal spending and its value to the district.[37]

About the same time the focus group was assessing his strengths and weaknesses, Foley was reflecting on public attitudes toward Congress. "All the polls indicate that people have a respect and regard for their own individual . . . House or Senate member, but the institution of Congress has come under a lot of complaint and criticism," he told National Public Radio's Elizabeth Arnold in an interview in July. "There's no question that there is some public cynicism—hostility wouldn't be too strong of a word—to the institution." Foley was genuinely puzzled about the source of this attitude. Pointing to restrictions on outside income passed in 1991, he said Congress had "the tightest ethical rules of any parliament in the world." Frustrated at the inability to communicate that theme to the public, Foley lamented: "This institution has undergone a lot of reform and improvement, and somehow . . . in a world of enormous media and communications, it's escaped notice. It's almost as if it didn't happen."[38]

One of the most frustrating issues to confront Speaker Foley in 1993 and 1994 was President Bill Clinton's ambitious goal to expand access and cut costs of health care for all Americans. The inability of Congress to pass any legislation after twenty-one months of debate ranks as the greatest setback of Clinton's first term—and cast the die for the defeat of Foley and dozens of congressional Democrats in the 1994 election. As Foley himself put it in his 1999 memoir: "The size, the complexity, and ambition of the health care program was simply indigestible and, as it turned out, unpassable."[39] One of Foley's closest allies in the House leadership, Representative David Bonior (D-MI), was more blunt: "The failed drive to provide health care to all Americans represented a spectacular failure for all Democrats: for the president, for the first lady and for every Democrat in Congress."[40] In many ways, the stalemate over health care foreshadowed the ways in which Republicans, when they were a minority in Congress, were able to capitalize on internal divisions within the Democratic Caucus to stymie legislation that had widespread public support.

In proposing comprehensive legislation to make health care more available to Americans without insurance, Clinton was building on a Democratic agenda that spanned most of the twentieth century and culminated in the passage of Medicare as part of President Lyndon B. Johnson's Great Society in 1965, during Foley's first term in the House.[41] In his acceptance speech at the 1992 Democratic national convention, Clinton criticized incumbent president George H. W. Bush for failing to fix weaknesses in the health care system. "He won't take on the big insurance companies and the bureaucracies to control health costs and give us affordable health care for all Americans, but I will," Clinton declared. In calling for a "new covenant" with the American people, he described his vision of a partnership between government and its citizens. He envisioned a nation "in which health care is a right, not a privilege, in which we say to all of our people: Your government has the courage finally to take on the health care profiteers and make health care affordable for every family." He advocated "saving lives, saving money, saving families from heartbreak."[42]

Clinton did not mention health care in his first inaugural address on January 20, 1993, but five days later he appointed First Lady Hillary Rodham Clinton to lead a task force devoted to health care reform. Its charge was to write legislation to be submitted to Congress by April 30—one hundred days after the president took office. The timetable proved overly ambitious, given the complexity of the proposals, the opposition that emerged to them, and the press of other business in Congress. The president appointed Ira Magaziner, a policy expert, fellow Rhodes scholar, and friend, to manage the task force's day-to-day operations. In an interview a year after leaving office, Foley recalled his first encounter with the presidential adviser: "When Mr. Magaziner came up [to Capitol Hill] and made some mention about the hundreds of decisions that had to be made before the bill could be written, I remember thinking to myself, 'This is not going to work,' to do this in a fundamental, ground-up, cover-every-problem way. And they wanted to do it that first year!"[43]

The president also underestimated the difficulty of bypassing the congressional committees that had jurisdiction over health care. In the spring and summer of 1993, the First Lady's task force and its advisers failed to engage key players on Capitol Hill. "They came over and saw us all the time, but ignored what we said," complained Representative Pete Stark (D-CA) chair of a House Ways and Means Committee Subcommittee on Health.[44] Heavy hitters such as Dan Rostenkowski (D-IL), chair of Ways and Means, and John Dingell (D-MI), chair of the Energy and Commerce Committee, were not consulted early in the process. Representative James McDermott (D-WA) recalled that Dingell's father, a member of the House before him, proposed a single-payer bill in 1945. "These were guys who had long histories of working an issue," and they could have been instrumental in bringing it to the floor.[45]

Meanwhile, by the fall of 1993, powerful business interests came out against Clinton's proposals. The Health Insurance Association of America commissioned a series of television commercials featuring a middle-aged white couple lamenting the loss of choice for patients provided under some future government plan. Known as the "Harry and Louise" ads for the first names of the actors who portrayed the couple, the commercials were broadcast intermittently from September 1993 until September 1994. Journalist Jonathan Cohn described them as "the lasting image of the Clinton health care fight for many of the people who lived through it."[46]

Nonetheless, Foley, as the leader of the president's party in the House, felt obliged to push forward with the legislation, regardless of the administration's clumsy approach to dealing with Congress. In March 1994, he introduced Hillary Clinton at a conference of senior citizens, in Washington, DC, intended to jump-start the stalled legislation. After warning of the consequences of failing to act, Foley declared: "There will continue to be debate, but from it will emerge a final Health Care Reform package that will be in the best interest of the American people." He praised the First Lady's leadership, calling her "the most convincing and compelling voice on health care reform in America."[47] That week, in what may have been the high-water mark for possible legislation, the House Ways and Means Committee Subcommittee on Health recommended passage of some elements of the Clinton health care plan.[48] But a little more than two months later, the White House lost a key ally on health care when Representative Dan Rostenkowski was indicted on seventeen criminal charges, accusing him of defrauding Congress of more than $500,000. He subsequently gave up the chairmanship of Ways and Means.[49]

Foley struggled to balance competing interests within his own caucus. McDermott was among a core of House liberals who wanted a government-sponsored single-payer system, similar to Canada's. Representative Jim Cooper (D-TN), a conservative Democrat, led a faction that argued in favor of a larger role for private insurers than the Clinton plan provided. "In between these extremes were Democrats holding a variety of positions consistent with their ideologically and parochial preferences," Jonathan Cohn wrote in a history of US health care legislation from 1991 to 2018 that "every position involved trade-offs that made agreement elusive." Cohn argued that had the Democrats been united, it would have been possible to pass some form of health care reform.[50]

By summer 1994, congressional Republicans closed ranks against any Democratic proposal. Republican strategist William Kristol wrote a memo (subtitled "opposition without apology") declaring that "the appropriate Republican response is to take the noble road of opposing any alternative the Democrats offer and insist on starting over in '95."[51] A frustrated Foley told reporters: "That they would be so obvious about their obstruction and about their desire to see any bill . . . defeated is a remarkable kind of confession of their putting politics above the interests of the people."[52] The final blow came in September after Foley made a last-ditch appeal to the Republican leadership to meet with Democrats. In characteristic fashion, he asked about any incremental legislation that both parties could agree on. House Republican leader Robert Michel (R-Il), who had long worked with Foley on bipartisan ventures, said through a spokesman he was "receptive to the idea" and would be "meeting with the speaker to discuss it." More tellingly, though, Representative Newt Gingrich (R-GA), building support for his candidacy to succeed Michel as the Republican leader, rebuffed Foley's offer. "I don't want to be suckered. I don't trust them," Gingrich said.[53] A month later, Senate Democratic leader George Mitchell of Maine told his Republican colleague, John Chafee of Rhode Island, that an attempt by the two to patch together a health care bill didn't have enough votes in the Senate to pass.[54] In their 1996 book analyzing the fate of health care legislation, *Washington Post* reporters Haynes Johnson and David Broder said Gingrich had been preparing for a battle over health care changes since 1991, even before Clinton declared his candidacy for president. Gingrich "realized health care would be the next great battleground in the political struggle and anticipated that denying Democrats victory on health reform would pave the way for Republicans to win back control of Congress," Johnson and Broder wrote.[55] Political scientist Theda Skocpol documented how the Clinton health plan intensified attacks on the president and "brought together more and more and more allies and channeled resources and support towards antigovernment conservatives within the Republican Party."[56] She drew a parallel to attacks by business groups in 1934 and 1935 on President Franklin Roosevelt's proposal for a Social Security system of insurance for older Americans. The hardening of the Republican position made it difficult for moderates such as Michel and Chafe to make compromises on legislation.

Reflecting later on the failure of the Clinton health plan, Foley acknowledged he didn't push the White House to scale back its approach. Foley believed that he and other congressional leaders should have been more assertive in telling the president that a less comprehensive package would fare better.[57] It was not the substance of the health care bill that hurt Democrats, Foley later said, but the perception that Congress could not come together to pass legislation that the country needed:

> The cacophony of voices, the vitriol with which the debate was carried on, the frustration with Congress's apparent inability to move forward and the symbolism that became attached to the bill due to the negative advertising surrounding it, all combined to turn what should have been a reasoned national debate into a muddle of confusion. . . . When, in the end, Democrats were unable to deliver on the promise of a health care reform bill, we paid the political price.[58]

The health care debate illustrated the challenges Foley faced at the center of his own party, as the leader of the House of Representatives in negotiations with the White House, and as a witness to the Republican leadership's refusal to work with Democrats on major legislation. Foley was caught between the diverse positions of his own caucus on health care. As Speaker, he couldn't push the president's plan too strongly without stepping on toes of powerful committee chairs (his longtime allies) who had their own visions of reform. Foley's cordial relationship with Michel faltered after Michel announced his retirement from Congress, allowing Gingrich and his insurgents to resist any Democratic proposal. They made a virtue of their obstructionism, turning the Democratic-controlled House's failure to pass a health reform bill into an argument for electing Republicans to Congress in 1992.

By September 1994, a fourth Republican candidate, Ed Larish of Walla Walla, had joined Nethercutt, Duane Alton, and John Sonneland on the primary ballot. They were helped by Representative Bill McCollum (R-FL), who spent $30,000 on Spokane television commercials attacking Foley. The ads criticized Foley's support of President Clinton's health care reform plan, urging voters to "send Bill Clinton a message by voting no on Tom Foley."[59] In the September 20 blanket primary, in which candidates of all parties competed against each other, Foley received only 35 percent of the total vote. Nethercutt, a fresh face with a moderate image, won the Republican nomination. He drew 29.5 percent, followed by Alton with 20 percent, Sonneland with 15 percent, and Larish with less than 1 percent.[60] That almost two-thirds of the total vote went to Republicans did not worry Foley—at least publicly. He theorized that the competitive race to unseat him inflated the turnout of Republican voters. "Every election I run," he stated, "predictions of my defeat have been made from the time of the primary onward, but I have won every election I have run."[61]

Clearly, though, in retrospect the fact that the Republicans outpolled Foley nearly two to one was an indication of voter dissatisfaction with the Speaker. A cartoon in the *Seattle Post-Intelligencer* showed a portrait of Foley defaced by spray-painted slogans that read: "Foley must go," "Term limits," and "Dump Incumbents." The perplexed Foley character says, "I had no idea we had such a graffiti problem in eastern Washington!"[62] A week later, a *Seattle Times* cartoonist took a similar jab, depicting Foley walking away from the Capitol, wondering, "Me? Out of touch with my district? It's not my fault some eastern Washington farmer doesn't carry a cellular phone or fax machine in the cab of [his] tractor."[63]

The day after the primary, the Reverend Frank Costello, a Gonzaga University professor and longtime Foley friend, called the Speaker's wife and trusted aide, Heather Foley, in Washington, DC. "What's going on?" Costello remembered asking. "We've got to get going," referring to the lack of campaign activity. Heather Foley's response to Costello was, "He has to stay back here and raise money for the campaign." Costello failed to persuade her that the congressman needed to be where the votes were—in the Fifth District.[64] In late September, Foley said congressional business would keep him in Washington, DC, for several weeks—a decision that proved to be a tactical error. Foley attempted to put a positive spin on the work of Congress, which he called "one of the most successful [sessions] of my career." In a press release, he listed his accomplishments as the following: deficit reduction, the North American Free Trade Agreement, income tax credits for the poor, and the crime-control bill, which included millions of dollars for hiring police officers, and the ban on assault weapons.[65] Not all of his constituents saw those pieces of legislation as accomplishments.

Foley's precarious position made the Fifth District contest a national story. In the next month, dozens of reporters from newspapers, magazines, and television networks visited Walla Walla, Spokane, and other towns in eastern Washington.[66] Joel Connelly of the *Seattle Post-Intelligencer*, who had covered Foley for nearly two decades, observed that his campaign organization did not run as smoothly in 1994 as it should have. Foley relied on a handful of trusted staff members to run his reelection campaigns, rather than building a strong district organization, he wrote. Carl Maxey, a prominent Spokane lawyer, offered a simple solution to Foley's problem: "He needs to get his butt out here [to the district] and campaign."[67] But the demands of being Speaker, or at least Foley's perception of those demands, kept him in Washington, DC, until mid-October. "Foley didn't particularly enjoy campaigning," said Tom Nides, who had become Foley's executive assistant in 1992. "It was always a struggle to get him to campaign."[68]

Foley's decision to remain in the nation's capital after Labor Day left his reelection campaign in the hands of outside consultants, paid campaign staff, and volunteers, some of them on leave from his congressional offices. Heather Foley was part of what some insiders called a "chaotic" campaign operation. Because she was not on the congressional payroll, she could roam back and forth between congressional and campaign offices without running afoul of federal laws.[69] Bill First, a former Foley staff member, and Ken Degerness, a Spokane media consultant, believed that the Foley campaign made a tactical blunder in early 1994 by failing to reserve billboards in advance. By fall, when Foley needed the exposure, Nethercutt or other advertisers had snapped up the best locations. Foley had only fourteen billboards in the entire district in 1994, down from almost fifty in Spokane alone during previous campaigns, Degerness said.[70]

For most of his career, Foley could count on winning the support of most farmers in the district. But by 1994, his agricultural base was in jeopardy. Judy Olson, a Garfield farmer and a former president of the National Association of Wheat Growers, traced the discontent to the 1990 farm bill, which specified requirements for crop rotations and types of tillage. Eventually, at Foley's urging, the US Department of Agriculture modified the rule.[71] Still, the episode contributed to the impression that Foley was not as valuable to farmers as he had been a decade and a half earlier when he chaired the Agriculture Committee. At a town meeting in Ritzville in Adams County two weeks before the election, Foley ran into disgruntled farmers who put sending a message to Congress ahead of their economic interests. Mike Largent, a farmer from Dusty and a member of the Washington Association of Wheat Growers, was described as "more concerned with the Clinton health plan and the cost of the crime bill than renewal of the Conservation Reserve Program," which paid farmers to leave land fallow. "A lot of us are not only wheat growers but American citizens," Largent said. A Reardan farmer, Fred Fleming, called Nethercutt "green as a gourd on agriculture," but said he would vote for him if it meant defeating Foley.[72]

Foley's seniority in Congress, long an advantage, worked against him in 1994. In contrast to the incumbent's opposition to term limits, Nethercutt pledged to leave the House after six years. "Three terms is long enough," Nethercutt wrote in a campaign brochure. "If you serve longer than that, you'll become part of the problem." Speaking in 1995 in favor of a national term-limits law, Nethercutt attributed his victory the previous year to "my recognizing the right of the people of the state of Washington to enact term limits."[73] (Nethercutt recanted his promise in 1999, announcing that he would seek a fourth term in the House. "I have changed my mind. The work I started will not be finished by the end of this term," Nethercutt said.)[74]

In late September, a poll for Seattle's KING-TV showed Nethercutt ahead of Foley by a 51–37 percent margin. A month later, a poll sponsored by the *Spokesman-Review* and KHQ-TV of Spokane showed Nethercutt with a lead of 46 percent to Foley's 44 percent, a virtual dead heat. With nine days remaining before the election, one voter in ten was undecided. Those voters held the outcome of the race in their hands. Pollster Del Ali said that undecided voters usually lean toward the challenger, which might give Nethercutt an edge. "The voters might be casting ballots not on who the candidates are, but who they're not. Nethercutt isn't Foley, and he isn't a whacko," Ali said.[75]

Nonetheless, Nethercutt was concerned that he was losing ground. Television commercials and direct-mail pieces sponsored by Foley's campaign were giving voters second thoughts about supporting the Republican. "I went from sixteen points ahead to two points, due to the tone of Mr. Foley's campaign," Nethercutt recalled. "As we got closer to election, all that mail, all that TV, all that radio—'He'll cut subsidies, he's going to hurt you'—that was the tone." Nethercutt believed his campaign had failed to respond effectively to the Foley strategy. "He's been hitting me hard on these issues for the last two weeks, and we haven't done a darn thing," Nethercutt complained to Ed Rollins and his key campaign advisers, "Doggone it, let's do something."[76]

The result was Nethercutt's most popular commercial, featuring his golden retriever, Chessie. Filmed in front of Nethercutt's Spokane home, it showed Nethercutt looking directly at the camera, denying that he planned to cut aid to education. "Tom Foley will say a lot of untruths about me. Next, Tom Foley's probably going to tell you I kick my dog. But, Chessie," he said, putting his arm around the dog as the camera drew back, "you know I'll never kick you."[77] Many viewers saw similarities to the successful Foley campaign commercials of 1988 that featured his Belgian shepherd, Alice. Nethercutt said the Chessie commercial showed "humor and humanity" and took the edge off a campaign that was escalating in harshness.[78] Foley supporters scoffed at the ad, calling the challenger "Golden Retriever George."

Nethercutt had the luxury of portraying himself as the victim of Foley's critical advertising because he took advantage of a relatively new trend in American campaigns, independent expenditures by interest groups. Several of these groups used harsher attacks on Foley than Nethercutt's own commercials did. An Indiana organization, Americans for Limited Terms, said in early November that it expected to spend $300,000 in Foley's district, attacking his stance against term limits. Although the group refused to disclose its donors, the *Wall Street Journal* reported that a major supporter of the group was California real estate developer Fred Sacher, a charter member of GOPAC, Newt Gingrich's personal political action committee.[79]

The NRA, which saw Foley's support for the 1994 assault weapons ban as a betrayal of his longtime opposition to gun control, poured thousands of dollars into the district and sent several staff members and board members to Spokane to campaign against Foley.[80] The most visible anti-Foley spokesman was actor Charlton Heston, who spoke at a Nethercutt fundraising dinner in Seattle and appeared in two anti-Foley commercials that were broadcast repeatedly during the last two weeks of the campaign.[81]

Two other independent groups joined the opposition camp. Even before Nethercutt won the Republican nomination, a political action committee opposed to statehood for the District of Columbia ran $25,000 worth of commercials critical of Foley. James Newberry, chairman of the Freedom Leadership PAC, said that Foley supported statehood for the nation's capital, a proposal opposed by many conservatives. In addition, Foley's opposition to term limits angered Newberry's group. Janet Gilpatrick, on leave from Foley's Spokane office to work on his campaign, did not dispute the group's characterization of Foley's position but was surprised to see the issue raised. "I've never heard it mentioned" in eastern Washington, she said.[82]

Meanwhile, the National Federation of Independent Business targeted Foley for defeat based on an analysis of selected roll call votes taken in 1991–1992 and 1993–1994. The votes included such bills as the Family and Medical Leave Act and a constitutional amendment to require a balanced federal budget. Even though, as Speaker, Foley cast recorded votes on only two of the eleven bills in 1991–1992 and three of ten in 1993–1994, the group considered his position on economic and workplace issues to be contrary to the interest of its members.[83]

Foley gave a spirited defense of his record—his most vigorous in years, friends said. But once again, he found himself balancing the national Democratic Party's position on some issues against the increasingly conservative sympathies of his district. Although Foley reluctantly agreed to run commercials criticizing Nethercutt and his positions, he insisted he could win on his own merits, not by denigrating his opponent. His gentlemanly approach was tested by a national political climate in which attacks on him were pointed, persistent, and personal. Nethercutt was reportedly uncomfortable with the commercials by the NRA and the other independent groups, but he insisted that he had no control over them.[84] By not formally disassociating himself from the NRA ads, however, he surely implicitly endorsed their message.

Television commercials were not the only source of anti-Foley sentiment. Throughout the fall, Spokane talk-radio announcers encouraged their listeners to vent their frustrations with Congress in general and Foley in particular. Talk show host Todd Herman of KSBN radio in Spokane once described Foley as "the odious eared one, the most corrupt man in the United States of America, Thomas S. Folly, the current sphincter [sic] of the House." Another announcer, KGA's Richard Clear, asked Foley on the air to address listener speculation that he was homosexual. "That's ridiculous," Foley responded. "I mean I think that's really bringing the campaign down to a pretty low level. . . . There is absolutely no truth to any of those terrible and slanderous suggestions." Later, Clear defended his decision to raise the topic, saying he simply asked Foley to respond to a question that others had raised.[85]

Following the model of Washington senators Warren Magnuson and Henry Jackson, Foley had assured a steady flow of federal dollars to his district.[86] But times had changed, and Foley could no longer successfully play the pork card. By 1994, voters no longer seemed to notice or care that Uncle Sam was providing jobs and new buildings. In Spokane, the money had gone to a research institute downtown and a new library at Gonzaga University, which the trustees gratefully named for Tom Foley's parents. Foley repeatedly blocked attempts to close Fairchild Air Force Base and to end the subsidized electrical rates that Spokane's Kaiser Aluminum enjoyed.[87] In Walla Walla, the US Army Corps of Engineers built a new district headquarters, and the Department of Veterans Affairs kept open a hospital that had been targeted for closure. At Washington State University in Pullman, federal money underwrote agricultural research laboratories that fueled the wheat-based agricultural economy of the district and an expansion of the veterinary hospital. Federal dollars helped widen US 395, the highway connecting the wheat-growing towns of Adams County to the Snake and Columbia River ports of the Tri-Cities, to four lanes.

When still-popular former independent presidential candidate Ross Perot stumped for Nethercutt the Friday before the 1994 general election, he told eastern Washington voters that they had paid for such pork with their taxes. In a brief Spokane visit, Perot equated Foley with Clinton's unpopular policies: "President Clinton says paint the Washington Monument pink, Speaker Foley salutes and it's painted." In contrast, Perot said, Nethercutt would "clean up the mess and balance the budget." Foley scoffed at

Perot's criticism, putting him in the category of Heston, former Republican congressman Jack Kemp, and other outsiders who were "coming into the district they know very little about, haven't been in very much and calmly attempting to tell the people of this district what their political interest is."[88]

The same day Perot visited Spokane, twenty corporate executives endorsed Foley, calling his clout essential to their efforts to sell products overseas. A who's who of Washington State's business establishment, the group included representatives from Boeing, Microsoft, Weyerhaeuser, Kaiser Aluminum, and Washington Water Power. "Having Speaker Foley in the other Washington only helps our ability to sell our products globally," Spokane businessman David Clack said. "No one but the voters of this district are best able to understand who should represent us," Paul Redmond, chair of the powerful Washington Water Power Company, added.[89]

Foley also won election-eve endorsements from several prominent environmental leaders, including John Osborn of the Inland Empire Public Lands Council, Jim Baker of the Sierra Club, and Tim Coleman of the Kettle Range Conservation Group. Speaking as individuals and not as representatives of their organizations, they said Foley was preferable to Nethercutt. "I said that Foley has made many great strides and that I was backing him," Coleman said. "My sense was that he wanted to go out [of office] doing good things for his district—fixing things that he had made mistakes on."[90] But the plea came too late for some activists, who had decided earlier not to support Foley in 1994 because of dissatisfaction with his positions on national forest management and wilderness designation. Many concluded that a novice Republican congressman would be better for the environment than a powerful fence-sitter.[91]

In the last three weeks before the election, Foley and Nethercutt debated eight times. The debates covered what by then had become familiar ground for candidates and the reporters covering them: health care, gun control, the federal deficit, health care reform, and term limits for members of Congress. Nethercutt repeatedly pledged that if elected, he would serve just three terms in the House of Representatives, the maximum allowed under the disputed Washington state term-limits initiative of 1992.[92] Nethercutt said the final debate, before the Spokane Rotary Club on November 3, was a turning point. For the first time, he had a sense that the momentum was on his side. "I remember people saying to me, 'That was the best you've done,'" Nethercutt recalled. "I showed myself equal to the task—not equal to Mr. Foley's experience—but a person they would not be afraid to vote for."[93]

Irrespective of his performance in the last debate, Foley won the editorial backing of the three largest daily newspapers in the district: the *Spokesman-Review*, the *Walla Walla Union Bulletin*, and the *Lewiston Morning Tribune*, an Idaho newspaper that circulated in the southeastern corner of the Fifth District. The *Spokesman-Review* called Nethercutt "a nice man. The sort of fellow you'd love to have for a neighbor." But Foley was "an underrated force behind the Fifth District's economic renaissance" and a force for bringing federal dollars to eastern Washington for needed projects. "There is no one—least of all an inexperienced, waffling freshman—who could represent this region's vital interests as effectively as the speaker of the House," the editorial concluded.[94]

In the end, Foley carried Spokane County, winning the city of Spokane but losing the suburban precincts of Spokane Valley. He also carried wheat-growing Whitman County, the home of Washington State University, by 115 votes. He lost the remaining counties, including Lincoln County west of Spokane, where his grandfather, Stephen Higgins, had settled nearly a hundred years earlier. Foley did not blame the voters for his defeat. "If I have any regret," he said, "I guess it is a regret that somehow I was not able to communicate the work that we [in Congress] do and some of the achievements that we have made."[95] After the 1994 election, one reporter observed: "Rather than pandering, as many other incumbents did, by claiming to run against Washington, he tried to convince Congress bashers that the institution was no den of corruption."[96] Pollster Mark Mellman, who advised Foley during the final campaign, agreed. "Tom Foley was a symbol in the mind of voters of the Democratic Congress that they did not like," Mellman said. "They felt he was out of touch with their needs and desires."[97] President Bill Clinton's approval ratings just before the 1994 election were in the mid-40 percent range, low but not unprecedented for a president in the middle of his term.[98] Yet Clinton's unpopularity alone did not explain Foley's defeat.[99]

A significant factor was Nethercutt's congenial personality. Unlike previous Republican candidates, many of whom took extreme positions, Nethercutt presented himself as a moderate and appealed to mainstream voters. Although Ross Perot, the NRA, and the term-limits groups showed no restraint in attacking Foley, Nethercutt himself was discreet, carefully tempering his criticism of Foley with respectful comments. Commentators drew parallels to Foley's first campaign in 1964, in which he unseated an eleven-term Republican incumbent. Echoing Foley's 1964 praise for Representative Walter Horan, Nethercutt was gracious in victory. "I'll be glad to turn to him for his wisdom and experience," the congressman-elect said of Foley. "He's made a wonderful contribution to this district. I wish there could be two winners."[100]

In many ways, Foley was the product of an earlier, less combative era of American politics. He seemed to neither comprehend the effects of nor adequately respond to the vicious, negative advertising aimed at him. Given the forces that were lined up against him, Foley probably could not have averted defeat. Under the circumstances, the closeness of his loss—fewer than four thousand votes out of more than two hundred thousand cast— was remarkable. Had it not been for the "perfect storm" that emerged in 1994, Foley might have held on to his seat. Reflecting later on the election results, he was philosophical about the voters' verdict. He took comfort in the fact that he carried Spokane County, where he had been born sixty-six years earlier. "I'm not ashamed to have lost an election. . . . It's not a disgrace to lose. It's part of the system. However, . . . in a way I wish, if I'd had a choice, I might have retired voluntarily than to have been caught up in the great earthquake of 1994."[101]

CHAPTER 9

HIS OWN STAMP?

What, then, can be said about Speaker Tom Foley as a "man in the middle"? This chapter offers several answers, identifying some of the characteristics that set him apart from the Speakers who preceded and followed him. Foley's career trajectory itself was distinctive. He was first elected to Congress from a conservative Republican district in eastern Washington, but unlike his immediate predecessor, he was a Democrat.

Second, Foley was the first Speaker from west of the Rocky Mountains, bringing a geographic perspective outside the "Boston-Austin axis."[1] To be sure, over the course of his thirty years in Congress, his electoral fortunes varied widely. But until his final race, Foley was never defeated, and then only by the barest of margins. Foley's 1994 defeat resulted from a conjunction of multiple forces he may not have foreseen, and even if he had, he may not have been able to deflect. These forces were primarily national in nature, led by the broad-based criticisms of Congress voiced by Representative Newt Gingrich (R-GA), independent presidential candidate Ross Perot, and others. But the political winds unleashed against Foley also reflected his willingness to take principled stands on policy at odds with portions of his electorate.

It is tempting to interpret much in Foley's career as striving to avoid the conflict and turmoil that comes from taking extreme positions. One of the few criticisms of his man-in-the-middle leadership style (as opposed to particular policy positions) was that he sometimes appeared hesitant to make decisions and was too conciliatory in his relationships with Republicans.

Indeed, Foley often defended his preference for compromise rather than confrontation. "I think I am a little cursed with seeing the other point of view and trying to understand it," he once explained.[2] Political columnist Joel Connelly, who covered Foley for most of his time in Congress, wrote: "Foley has brought a judicial temperament to the legislative process. He is cautious to a fault on major decisions, insisting that all arguments be heard and every party be allowed to speak."[3] At the same time, though, political scientist Roger Davidson suggested that "although his low-key style brought Republicans some relief from [Jim] Wright's tense partisanship, Foley faced criticism within his own party. Some Democrats faulted his tepid partisanship, his cautious approach, and during the Bush years, his reluctance to define and promote a clear partisan agenda."[4] Yet we believe that Foley's leadership posture arose not out of weakness but from adherence to a different role orientation and a different personality than that preferred by his critics. That role orientation made him more than just a partisan leader; he was the leader of Congress, "the people's institution."[5]

Colleagues described Foley as "seeing three sides of every issue," and that particular kaleidoscopic approach often brought him to two significant places. One was a position where it was necessary to serve the multiple interests of a diverse political party and a fairly heterogeneous electoral constituency. The other was a position of principle sometimes counter to the majority of the party that he led. Being "the man in the middle" meant that he would step outside the countervailing positions of the two parties and place himself independent of both. That dimension was a road map that led him to a distinctive style of leadership in the context of other speakers before and after him. Foley's leadership mode was both personal and political. Colleagues and observers agreed he was distinctive in his combination of deep intelligence, ethical foundations, and bipartisan reach on policy processes. His longtime House colleague Leon Panetta (D-CA), later President Bill Clinton's chief of staff, said Foley possessed "one of those remarkable combinations you rarely find in a legislator: a combination of brains, a likable personality and stature that kind of all comes together."[6] He also was a master tactician of the legislative process, which he demonstrated as whip and majority leader in the 1980s.

After becoming Speaker in 1989, "Tom Foley had the ability to extend the reach of the democratic speakership; it remained to be seen if the House of Representatives would give him the opportunity," wrote Ronald M. Peters Jr., a leading scholar on the speakership.[7] Looking forward, Peters predicted: "In confronting the conditions of the democratic speakership,

Foley will undoubtedly place his own stamp upon it as the office continues its evolution."[8] Was Peters correct in his judgment of Foley? If so, how did Foley accrue and exercise the power and influence throughout his career that enabled him to have the potential to extend the speakership? What kind of imprint did Foley have both on the speakership and on his role? What impact could Foley have had if the political environment had adapted fully to his values?

Including his nearly six-year speakership, Foley's thirty-year congressional career demonstrated both the benefits and the costs of following his own values. Foley generally stayed within the boundaries of conventional normative political practice, but he imprinted his stamp on those boundaries, mixing his personal values with the sometimes dissonant expectations of the context in which he operated. Where did this dissonance emerge? Several examples illustrate this pattern and how it was sustained throughout his career. Early in his career, Foley joined the Democratic Study Group (DSG), a reform-oriented organization of progressive Democrats, many of whom were elected along with Foley in Lyndon B. Johnson's presidential landslide of 1964. But because of the conservative nature of his home district, Foley asked that his membership not be publicized, although he later changed that posture.[9]

As DSG chair in 1974, Foley pushed to open House committee proceedings and change the way committee chairs were selected. In particular, committee assignments would be made by the Steering and Policy Committee instead of the Ways and the Means Committee. When it came time to choose a chair for the House Agriculture Committee in 1975, Foley nominated the incumbent, Representative William R. "Bob" Poage (D-TX). A conservative, Poage "had voted against the majority of House Democrats 63 percent of the time in the prior Congress."[10] Chair since 1967, Poage had been put in place by a system that excluded participation by the Democratic Caucus as a whole. Buoyed by the 1974 election results, which brought seventy-five new Democrats to the House, the caucus voted "narrowly to reject his [Poage's] reappointment as chairman by a 141–144 vote, undoubtedly influenced by the fact that the next in line was Washington State's popular Tom Foley, a former DSG chairman thirty years Poage's junior."[11]

Becoming chair of the Agriculture Committee elevated Foley to a position of influence and visibility in the Democratic leadership, cementing his capacity to provide transactional benefits to a significant portion of his diverse constituency, namely, the agricultural community. Moreover, the position enabled him to develop and support food and nutrition programs in ways that were responsive to progressive interests. But as a testament to the way others perceived Foley, no one publicly accused him of advocating reform of the committee process out of a self-serving desire to acquire more power in the committee system or in the House itself.

As Speaker, Foley could maneuver deftly through the potentially disruptive politics of his support role in regard to the policy initiatives of the president, especially when the president, Bill Clinton, came from his own party. Others in the party, including some of Foley's leadership team, were not always on the same side. A prime example of how Foley sorted through contending claims on his support was the North American Free Trade Agreement (NAFTA) of 1993, which created a free trade zone among Canada, Mexico, and the United States. Like most of his predecessors, President Clinton was a supporter of NAFTA, believing it "essential to our national interest." He said removing export barriers to Mexico represented "an enormous opportunity for businesses, our workers, and our farmers."[12]

As discussed in chapter 5, many factions of the Democratic Party, including organized labor, saw NAFTA as having significant negative consequences for Americans. While NAFTA would help some US agricultural interests (depending on existing tariffs for crops and livestock), many labor unions (including those in Foley's district) opposed the agreement, arguing it would move production to Mexico or Canada and create pressure to lower US wages in order to compete.[13]

Ross Perot's presidential candidacy in 1992 revealed the cross-pressures in the US political and economic environment, which were mirrored in the House of Representatives of which Foley was leader. Perot received nearly 24 percent of votes in Washington State and 21 percent in Foley's district.[14] A highly visible opponent of NAFTA, Perot campaigned against Foley in Spokane a few days before the 1994 election.

The deep policy division over NAFTA also tested the House leadership. While Foley supported the agreement (and President Clinton), majority leader Richard Gephardt and whip David Bonior opposed it. "Foley's support was consistent with his own long-held views on free trade," observed congressional scholar Barbara Sinclair. "To contain the long-run damage the split might do to the leadership team, the participants followed certain tacit ground rules."[15] Foley was challenged to balance the interests of his district's farmers, many of whom stood to benefit from increased exports, with that of blue-collar union members in Spokane and elsewhere, who believed NAFTA would cost them jobs. On the final House roll call, a majority of Democrats voted against NAFTA, reflecting the manufacturing base of many urban districts.

The NAFTA legislation illustrated three attributes of Foley's leadership style and actions. First, it demonstrated his commitment to his institutional position as leader of the House of Representatives by supporting a president of the same political party; second, it showed his courage in risking his leadership role by taking a position contrary to that of the majority of his party, including others on his leadership team; and third, it underscored his ability to avoid alienating those with whom he disagreed. Whip David Bonior was among the NAFTA opponents who maintained strong personal loyalty to Foley, writing:

> Fairness infused his style of debating. Tom was as judicial in discussion as he was in demeanor. . . . I was more partisan than most of my colleagues and I knew it. I also knew that I needed to work on seeing my colleagues' point of view. Foley helped me grow in this essential aspect of my institutional life. The entire Democratic Caucus experienced Speaker Foley's sense of fairness and loyalty.[16]

Taking pains not to impugn the motives of those who opposed him on NAFTA, Foley trusted the wisdom of his colleagues from both parties. In closing the House floor debate, he declared: "Let not this debate, or our decision, ruin the fabric of our democracy. Let it be something to strengthen us, as we face the challenges of the future. I go now to the chair to put this question to the House. And I do so with the prayer that it will be the right decision for our people and the right decision for this great institution."[17]

Foley remained committed to fundamental political principles, even when they conflicted with the opinions of many of his constituents. This commitment was expressed in his positions on highly visible, volatile, and unpopular issues. "When Foley does take a bold stand, it reflects devotion to the law," political columnist Joel Connelly wrote during Foley's next-to-last term in Congress. "He was out front in opposing President Bush's efforts to put an anti-flag-burning amendment in the U.S. Constitution."[18] On that flag-burning issue, Foley declared: "I do not favor an amendment to the First Amendment of the Constitution of the United States which provides the basis of the elemental freedoms of the country in terms of speech and press and religion. . . . If it is not conservative to protect the Bill of Rights, then I don't know what conservatism is today."[19]

As noted in several earlier chapters, unusual among twentieth-century Democratic Speakers, Foley balanced bipartisanship with his own party's position in a House that was often divided along party lines. Before becoming speaker, Foley's average party support scores on House votes were higher than the Democratic average, substantially so in the period right before he became Speaker. He operated with a high level of civility, even when he disagreed with the Republicans on fundamental issues. His bipartisanship usually surfaced in the context of process rather than in policy, although there also were times when he took a position at odds with the majority of his fellow Democrats. One example, described earlier, came in 1989, when Republicans won a voice vote based on Foley's ruling from the chair. As noted in chapter 6, Representative Mickey Edwards (R-OK) recalled that after Foley ruled the negative votes had prevailed, "every Republican on the floor rose spontaneously and gave Tom Foley a standing ovation."[20]

Foley and Robert Michel, the House minority leader from 1981 to 1995, worked together on many occasions, despite their significant differences on policy. According to Douglas B. Harris, "Michel had very strong personal relationships with both Tip O'Neill and Tom Foley."[21] More than ten years after Michel's retirement and Foley's defeat, the two longtime leaders were jointly interviewed by Ron Sarasin, a former Republican House member from Connecticut. The following is an excerpt from Michel's comments:

> Mr. Speaker, . . . things have changed considerably from the time you and I were leaders of our respective parties and even though we'd get involved in very vigorous debates on key issues, we never let it degenerate to a fight between personalities. Usually the Speaker gets the last call and as the Minority Leader, I would get the last call on my side. I'd make the windup argument as best I could, knowing full well my friend Tom Foley is going to take the other side and will listen very attentively and respectfully and vote [his] conscience, obviously. But the thing that I enjoyed so much during my tenure as Minority Leader, . . . even with Speaker Tip O'Neill, we had a great respect for one another personally. We could go at it hammer and tongs verbally during the course of the day and after it was all over go back to the office and play a little gin rummy and have a brew or something. Or even play golf on weekends.[22]

According to Michel, Foley suggested they take turns hosting House leadership meetings. "We'll have one in my office and the next week, we'll have one in your office," Michel recalled Foley suggesting. Michel said that cordial relationship filtered down to members: "Well, if they [the party leaders] are getting together and talking socially and being civil to one another, maybe we ought to."[23]

Describing Foley's ability to work across the aisle, congressional scholar Ronald Peters wrote: "While his voting record had shifted to the left during his years in the Democratic leadership, he remained moderate in disposition and had established excellent relations on the Republican side of the aisle."[24] Unfortunately, with few exceptions, the opportunities for harmony among House members diminished in 1995 after Michel retired from the House and Foley was defeated for reelection. Since then, the near parity of the two parties in Congress has worked against cooperation and compromise on legislation. Following the Republican takeover of the House in 1995, the majority has flipped between parties four times, most recently when Republicans regained control after the 2022 election. Explaining the consequences of frequent turnover, political scientist Frances Lee noted: "Competition fuels party conflict by raising the political stakes of every policy dispute." The minority party has no incentive to cooperate on legislation in the national interest because it might result in a policy victory for the majority, Lee observed. "How can a party wage an effective campaign after . . . collaborating with its opposition?"[25]

Given this hyperpartisan stalemate and the inability of either party to hold a decisive majority, are there lessons from Foley's leadership style for Congress in the twenty-first century? For one viewpoint, we return to President Barack Obama's remarks at Foley's memorial service in 2013:

At a time when our political system can seem more polarized and more divided than ever before, it can be tempting to see the possibility of bipartisan progress as a thing of the past—old school as Bob [Michel] said. It can be tempting to wonder if we still have room for leaders like Tom; whether the environment, the media, the way the districts are drawn, and the pressures that those of us in elected office are under somehow preclude the possibility of that brand of leadership. Well, I believe we have to find our way back there. Now, more than ever, America needs public servants who are willing to place problem solving ahead of politics. . . . We are sent here to do what's right, and sometimes doing what's right is hard . . . and yet that's the measure of leadership.[26]

Finally, can we describe Tom Foley as a truly transformational leader throughout his congressional career? Or was he simply a "man in the middle," trading off pressures from multiple sides? As is the case with most people in public life, the answers are complicated. It seems clear that Tom Foley entered Congress with a portfolio of transformational values, perhaps at least in part a result of his Jesuit education and his family background. Those values were especially visible with regard to civility and inclusion, but they also appeared in some of the most visible and conflict-producing issues he faced.

One example is his early involvement in the progressive DSG. Foley chaired the group in the pivotal year of 1974, and several of its reforms later worked to his benefit in moving up the leadership ladder. Yet there is no record of other legislators suggesting that his early support for the reforms was designed to advance Foley's own ambitions. Foley was in his early forties when he became a subcommittee chair; when he became chair of the House Agriculture Committee in 1975 at age forty-five, he became the youngest chair of a major congressional committee. Even so, upon assuming that chair position, he appointed as vice chair the longtime previous incumbent southern member who had been ousted under a significantly altered selection process for committee chairs that resulted from the DSG reforms.

It also was the case that Foley largely was a transactional leader in his relationship with his district. Foley delivered economic and infrastructure benefits to his constituents—to the farmers, to the energy interests, to the forest products industry, and to labor unions. Those benefits provided the foundation for his thirty-year congressional career. The Fifth District (and Washington State as a whole) no doubt appreciated his upward march on the leadership path, as long as those benefits continued, even if many of his constituents either did not know or did not care about his progressive, transformational values. However, in his last election, Foley was criticized by detractors for directing tax dollars into his own district as a sign of "pork-barrel" politics.

Foley may have discovered that it is more challenging to be transformational from the middle than from policy or organizational extremes—and not just in the middle between contending interests but also in the middle between elements of his own party. But Foley's transformational tilt was perhaps most challenging for him when his values led him to policy positions contrary to his district. Thus, his positions against term limits, in favor of banning assault weapons, in support of NAFTA, and in opposition to a constitutional amendment to prohibit flag burning all were in opposition to substantial portions of his constituency. That Tom Foley could survive in office at the highest political levels for thirty years was a testament to his capacity to meld his transformational values and positions with transactional district-oriented policy actions and a political acumen that served him well.

EPILOGUE

In a cynical age, I still believe that we must summon people to a vision of public service. For, in the end, this ethic determines more than anything else whether we will have citizens and leaders of honor, judgment, wisdom, and heart. These are the qualities this institute will nurture and advance, helping this nation become what it has always been destined to be, the best hope of a free people to live in an open and just society.

—Tom Foley, 1996, at the dedication of the Foley Institute at Washington State University

A fter thirty years in Congress—the last fifteen in the national spotlight—Tom Foley did not retreat into private life. He chaired the President's Foreign Intelligence Advisory Board for two years before being appointed US ambassador to Japan by President Bill Clinton in 1997. He also supported a public policy institute at Washington State University that bears his name. Consistent with his gracious acceptance of the voters' decision in 1994, Foley rarely spoke publicly about his successors as House Speaker or the increased polarization and rancor that became the norm in Congress starting in the late 1990s.

Before leaving the Speaker's office, Foley arranged to transfer his congressional papers to Washington State University (WSU) in Pullman, seventy-five miles south of Spokane, the largest public institution of higher education in his district. In January 1995, three long-haul trucks arrived at the loading dock of WSU's Holland-Terrell Library. They carried 604 boxes of documents, with an estimated 2,000 sheets of paper per box, and 174 cartons of books from Foley's personal library.[1] The documents, photographs, videos, and books eventually filled 480 boxes, occupying 550 linear feet of shelf space.[2]

In April of the following year, WSU dedicated the Thomas S. Foley Institute for Public Policy and Public Service, committed to fostering civic education and public policy research. At the dedication, Foley was joined by three other former members of the House from Washington State, Mike Kreidler, Sid Morrison, and Al Swift, in a panel discussion about politics in America. Looking back at his time in Congress, Foley said, "If I regret anything, it's that there wasn't a greater opportunity to give a greater sense of this political institution that we were all part of—the Congress. I think that's partly our fault." He and the other panelists lamented the lack of public understanding of and appreciation for Congress.[3] To address that deficiency, the Foley Institute sponsors speakers, panels, and symposia on the role of Congress, media and politics, foreign policy, and other topics that attract audiences of up to four thousand people annually. It offers internships and graduate fellowships to WSU students and supports research on democratic institutions and public policy.[4]

Former vice president Walter Mondale stepped down as US ambassador to Japan in December 1996, shortly after President Clinton won reelection. After months of speculation, Clinton first publicly mentioned Foley's name as Mondale's successor. "Speaker Foley is one of the most distinguished men in America," Clinton told a Japanese reporter in June 1997, "and I think he will be unanimously and quickly confirmed as we push this process forward."[5] It was another two months, however, before the nomination was sent to the Senate. At the time, DC insiders said the Clinton administration wanted to be sure the Senate Foreign Relations Committee, then chaired by Senator Jesse Helms (R-NC), would support Foley's nomination.[6]

In an interview before his confirmation, Foley indicated he would follow the same deliberate path as he had taken as Speaker of the House. To those pushing him to open Japan to US exports, Foley cautioned against impatience. "An American business representative comes in, lays the cards on the table and makes the case for the contract, then wants a quick decision," Foley said. "The Japanese, on the other hand, don't favor the quick. You can easily be considered too abrupt, too quick, to want results too fast."[7]

Japanese officials were delighted to learn of Foley's appointment after the long delay. "We welcome the nomination of an influential ambassador, which shows that the Clinton administration continues to emphasize relations with Japan," Foreign Ministry spokesman Hiroshi Hashimoto said. Prime Minister Ryutaro Hashimoto also praised the selection.[8]

The caution in submitting Foley's nomination proved unnecessary. When the appointment went to a Foreign Relations subcommittee, Washington's two senators, Democrat Patty Murray and Republican Slade Gorton, spoke on his behalf. Gorton called him "not simply a good nominee for the post, but the best nominee for the post that the president could possibly have picked."[9] The Senate voted on October 27, 1997, to confirm his appointment, with ninety-one votes in favor and none opposed. "The futures of our two countries [Japan and the United States] are tied together," he said after he was confirmed. "To be the U.S. ambassador at this time is a great honor and a great challenge."[10]

Less than three weeks later, Foley arrived in Tokyo and quickly settled into his new position. A *New York Times* reporter described him as taking a softer line on US-Japanese trade than officials in Washington, including the secretaries of Treasury and Commerce, the US trade representative, and the chair of the Federal Reserve Board. "For some critics, Mr. Foley and his bosses in Washington appear to be performing a good cop, bad cop routine, but for others, results are what count, and the jury is still out," the *Times* reporter wrote.[11] Otherwise, Foley's time as ambassador was marked by cutting ribbons at trade shows and welcoming US business delegations. An exception came in 2001, when the new president, George W. Bush, asked him to remain in Japan to calm tensions after a US submarine accidentally sank a Japanese fishery training ship in the Pacific Ocean about ten miles south of Honolulu, killing nine aboard the Japanese ship, including four high school students.[12]

George Nethercutt, the Republican who ousted Foley from Congress in 1994, introduced legislation in 1999 to name the US Courthouse in Spokane in Foley's honor and the plaza on its south side for Walt Horan, the Republican who previously held the seat for twenty-two years. "The long and distinguished careers of both Ambassador Foley and Rep. Horan merit this important recognition," Nethercutt said before the House voted unanimously to support the proposal.[13] Foley traveled to Spokane after his return to the United States for a dedication of the federal building and plaza in April 2001. Seeing the new sign on the building, Foley quipped with characteristic modesty, "I expected a small but impressive plaque near the front. The letters are way too big. My father would have said the same thing. Although my mother would have said they're just about right."[14]

After Foley stepped down as ambassador in 2001, he returned to Washington, DC. He rejoined the law firm of Akin Gump Strauss Hauer & Feld, with which he had been associated from 1995 to 1997. He retired in 2008. Tom and Heather Foley lived on Capitol Hill, a short walk from the building where he spent most of his legislative career. After a stroke in December 2012 and months of declining health, Foley died at his home on October 18, 2013. He was eighty-four.[15]

At a memorial service at Statuary Hall in the Capitol, Foley was praised as a model of leadership by President Barack Obama, former president Bill Clinton, Vice President Joe Biden, House Speaker John Boehner, former and future Speaker Nancy Pelosi, and other congressional leaders. "Now, more than ever, America needs public servants who are willing to place problem-solving ahead of politics," Obama said. "We are sent here to do what's right, and sometimes doing what's right is hard. . . . But it is the measure of leadership."[16] Former representative Robert Michel, minority leader when Foley was Speaker, recalled a visit to Foley's home a few days before he died. "We thought it was going to be just a visit of a couple of minutes, and it ended up we were speaking for an hour about the days gone by. . . . We were both able to say our piece in an atmosphere of mutual respect, open-mindedness, and most of all, trust."[17] Pelosi, during her first term as House Speaker from 2007 to 2011, called him "the quintessential champion of the common good." She quoted from Foley's first floor speech in the House in 1965, in which he declared: "Public service is a free gift of a free people and a challenge for all of us in public life to do what we can to make our service useful for those who have sent us here." Pelosi added, "Few fulfilled that charge with more courage, more conviction, more civility than he."[18]

Three days later, hundreds of mourners filled St. Aloysius Church on the campus of Gonzaga University in Spokane, Foley's hometown. Speakers included Washington governor Jay Inslee (who earlier served in the House of Representatives); the state's two US senators, Patty Murray and Maria Cantwell, both Democrats; and the current Fifth District representative, Cathy McMorris Rodgers. Inslee praised Foley's civility and compassion, saying, "I don't think you can point to another leader that we have been blessed with in our nation's history that combines such a strong heart for his people with such a strong backbone for constitutional democracy."[19] Murray told of a telephone call from Foley when she was first elected to the Senate in 1992. "The powerful speaker of the House . . . immediately called me, the brand-new back-bench senator who'd just been elected. Not because he had to, but just because I was from Washington State, and so was he."[20]

Foley's ashes were placed in the historical Congressional Cemetery on the west bank of the Anacostia River, less than two miles from the Capitol, the final resting place of dozens of members of the House of Representatives and the Senate. A dramatic ten-foot stainless steel sculpture by Wenquin Chen, *The Endless Curve*, was placed at Foley's grave site in the fall of 2020.[21] Heather Foley recalled that after returning to Washington from Japan, her husband often took their dog walking through the cemetery grounds. The marker is near the entrance of the cemetery "among other former members of Congress, as I thought he would want to be found among his peers," she said.[22]

BIOGRAPHICAL HIGHLIGHTS: THOMAS STEPHEN FOLEY

1929 (March 6): Born in Spokane, Washington. Parents: Helen Foley, a teacher, and Ralph Foley, then Spokane County prosecutor and later a superior court judge.

1946: Graduates from Gonzaga Preparatory School, Spokane.

1946–1949: Attends Gonzaga University, Spokane, where he is a member of the debate team, which wins the national championship in 1948.

1947: Enlists in US Naval Reserve, Spokane. Serves three years; receives honorable discharge, 1950.

1950: Transfers to the University of Washington, Seattle; earns bachelor's degree in history in 1951.

1957: Earns law degree from the University of Washington, returns to Spokane.

1958: Deputy prosecutor, Spokane County; instructor, Gonzaga School of Law.

1960: Moves to Olympia, works as assistant state attorney general.

1961: Moves to Washington, DC, joins staff of Senator Henry Jackson (D-WA) as special counsel to the Senate Committee on Interior and Insular Affairs.

1964: Files for Democratic nomination for US House of Representatives, Fifth Congressional District. Unopposed in Democratic primary. Defeats incumbent Republican representative Walt Horan by more than ten thousand votes. He is reelected fourteen times.

1965: Appointed to the House Agriculture Committee and the House Committee on Interior and Insular Affairs.

1968 (December 19): Marries Heather Strachan, a former staff member in Senator Jackson's office, in Colombo, Ceylon (now Sri Lanka).

1973–1976: Member of the House Committee on Standards of Official Conduct (now the House Ethics Committee).

1973: Awarded honorary degree, Gonzaga University, Spokane.

1974: Elected chair of the Agriculture Committee, a position he holds until 1980.

1974: Awarded honorary degree, Whitman College, Walla Walla.

1975: Elected chair of the House Democratic Study Group.

1981: Appointed House majority whip by Speaker Tip O'Neill. (Foley was the Democrats' last appointed whip.)

1987: Elected House majority leader.

1989: Elected Speaker of the House after the resignation of Speaker Jim Wright. Legislative accomplishments as speaker: Americans with Disabilities Act (1990), Omnibus Budget Reconciliation Act (1990), Family Medical Leave Act (1993), Assault Weapons Ban (1993), and North American Free Trade Agreement (1993).

1994: Defeated by Republican challenger George Nethercutt by fewer than 4,000 votes (of more than 216,000 votes cast). Foley became the first Speaker of the House to be defeated in his home district since 1862.

1995: Joins the Washington, DC, law firm of Akin Gump Strauss Hauer & Feld. (He rejoined the law firm in 2001 and was of counsel until 2008.) Appointed by President Bill Clinton to chair the President's Foreign Intelligence Advisory Board.

1996: Speaks at the dedication of the Thomas S. Foley Institute for Public Policy and Public Service at Washington State University, Pullman, Washington.

1997: Nominated by President Clinton to be the twenty-fifth US ambassador to Japan in 1997, a position he holds until March 2001.

2001: US courthouse in Spokane, also known as the Federal Building, is named in Foley's honor; the adjoining plaza is named for Walt Horan, the House member Foley defeated in 1964.

2013 (October 18): Dies at his home in Washington, DC, after a series of strokes.

2013 (October 29): Memorial service in Statuary Hall, Washington, DC, attended by President Barack Obama, former president Bill Clinton, House Speaker John Boehner, and current and former members of Congress.

2013 (November 1): Memorial service at St. Aloysius Church, Spokane, adjoining Gonzaga University, attended by Governor Jay Inslee, Senators Patty Murray and Maria Cantwell, Representative Cathy McMorris Rodgers, and other current and former members of Congress.

Sources: Charles Apple, "Man of the House," *Spokesman-Review*, June 20, 2019; *Thomas S. Foley, Late a Speaker of the House and a Representative from Washington, Memorial Addresses and Other Tributes* (Washington, DC: US Government Printing Office, 2014), v–x.

NOTES

Prologue and Acknowledgments

1. Tom Kenworthy, "Wright Timetable Not Settled; Criminal Inquiry Begun," *Washington Post*, May 31, 1989, A4.

2. Tom Kenworthy, "Wright to Resign Speaker's Post, House Seat; Texan Again Rebuts Charges, Decries Conflict over Ethics," *Washington Post*, June 1, 1989, A1.

3. See Stephen Gettinger, "The Defeated Speakers," *CQ Weekly Report* 52, no. 44 (November 12, 1994): 3291.

4. See the discussion in Kenton Bird, "Tom Foley's Last Campaign: Why Eastern Washington Voters Ousted the Speaker of the House," *Pacific Northwest Quarterly* 95, no. 1 (Winter 2003–2004): 3–15.

5. Philip D. Duncan and Christine C. Lawrence, *Politics in America 1996: The 104th Congress* (Washington, DC: Congressional Quarterly Press, 1994), quoted in Kenneth R. Mayer and David T. Canon, *The Dysfunctional Congress? The Individual Roots of an Institutional Dilemma* (Boulder, CO: Westview Press, 1999), 33.

1. The Man in the Middle

Epigraph: Barack H. Obama, *Thomas S. Foley: Late a Speaker of the House and a Representative from Washington, Memorial Addresses and Other Tributes* (Washington, DC: Government Printing Office, 2014), 30–31.

1. Sean M. Theriault, *Party Polarization in Congress* (New York: Cambridge University Press, 2008), 5. See also James E. Campbell, *Polarized: Making Sense of a Divided America* (Princeton, NJ: Princeton University Press, 2016), 29–35.

2. Jeffrey R. Biggs and Thomas S. Foley, *Honor in the House: Speaker Tom Foley* (Pullman: Washington State University Press, 1999), 51.

3. Michael Oreskes, "Foley's Law," *New York Times Magazine*, November 11, 1990, sec. 6, 64.

4. David W. Rohde, *Parties and Leaders in the Postreform House* (Chicago: University of Chicago Press, 1991), 184.

5. Sarah A. Binder and Thomas E. Mann, "Constraints on Leadership in Washington," *Issues in Governance Studies* 41 (July 2011): 3–4. See also James MacGregor Burns, *Leadership* (New York: Harper & Row, 1978).

6. Ronald M. Peters and Craig A. Williams, "The Demise of Newt Gingrich as a Transformational Leader: Does Organizational Leadership Theory Apply to Legislative Leaders?," *Organizational Dynamics* 30, no. 3 (March 2002): 257–268.

7. James MacGregor Burns, *Transforming Leadership* (New York: Grove Press, 2003), 211.

8. Burns, 213.

9. Theresa Bullard, "Six Core Values of a Transformational Leader," November 25, 2014, https://www.slideshare.net/quantumleapalchemy/6-core-values-of-a-transformational-leader.

10. See Sean M. Theriault, *The Gingrich Senators: The Roots of Partisan Warfare in Congress* (New York: Oxford University Press, 2013). See also Peters and Williams, "The Demise of Newt Gingrich," 257.

11. Barbara Sinclair, *Legislators, Leaders, and Lawmaking: The U.S. House of Representatives in the Postreform Era* (Baltimore: Johns Hopkins University Press, 1995), 280, citing Alan Ehrenhalt, "Media, Power Shifts Dominate O'Neill's House," *CQ Weekly Report*, September 13, 1986, 2134.

12. Biggs and Foley, *Honor in the House*, 137.

13. Roger H. Davidson, "The Emergence of the Postreform Congress," in *The Postreform Congress*, ed. Roger H. Davidson (College Park, MD: St. Martin's Press, 1992), 22.

14. Biggs and Foley, *Honor in the House*, 137.

15. Biggs and Foley, 137.

2. You Can Get There from Here!

1. Frank M. Dallam, founding editor of *Spokane Falls Review*, used the term "Inland Empire" in his first issue, of May 19, 1883, calling it "an immense region of unlimited resources and possibilities"; quoted in Ralph E. Dyar, *News for an Empire: The Story of the* Spokesman Review *of Spokane, Washington, and of the Field It Serves* (Caldwell, ID: Caxton Printers, 1952), 5. For a full discussion of the emergence of this regional identity, see Katherine G. Morrissey, *Mental Territories: Mapping the Inland Empire* (Ithaca, NY: Cornell University Press, 1997).

2. Tom Foley, interview by Kenton Bird, June 20, 1995.

3. Ralph Foley, interview, 1980 (n.d.), Audio Collection, Foley Papers, Washington State University Library.

4. Maureen Latimer, interview by Kenton Bird, June 22, 1998.

5. Ralph Foley, interview.

6. After Foley's defeat in 1994, John Pierce, coauthor of this book, asked Foley's

staff for copies of speeches Foley had given as Speaker. He was told, "Oh, there aren't any; Tom almost never wrote down anything."

7. House Speaker Tip O'Neill once complained Foley could "argue three sides of every issue." David E. Rosenbaum, "Man in the News: Thomas Stephen Foley; A Politician Outside the Mold," *New York Times*, June 2, 1989, A1.

8. Robinson and Lyons quotations are from O. Casey Corr, "Little Boy with Lisp Will Lead the House, Young Foley Is Recalled in His Native Spokane," *Seattle Post-Intelligencer*, June 1, 1989, A6.

9. Latimer, interview.

10. Latimer, interview.

11. One account says Foley was disciplined for tardiness at Gonzaga. See Louise Sweeney, "King of the Hill," *Christian Science Monitor*, February 22, 1990, 15. Another indicates that Foley was told to improve his grades. See *Current Biography*, September 1989, 7.

12. John Newhouse, "Profiles: The Navigator," *New Yorker*, April 10, 1989, 62.

13. Jacqueline Trescott, "The Gentleman from Washington, True to Form," *Washington Post*, June 1, 1989, C13.

14. Latimer, interview. See also Corr, "Little Boy with Lisp," A6.

15. Joel Connelly, "Foley's Dawg Years," *Columns: The University of Washington Alumni Magazine*, June 1, 1992, 15.

16. Scott Lukins, interview by Kenton Bird, May 23, 1996.

17. Lukins, interview.

18. Carlton Smith, "Foley Proceeding with Caution," *Seattle Times*, June 1, 1989, A6.

19. Ralph Foley, interview.

20. Foley's job history comes from various sources, including a biographical questionnaire he filled out for *Congressional Quarterly* when he was running for re-election in 1966. See 1966 campaign file, Foley Papers.

21. Herb Legg, interview by Kenton Bird, August 13, 1995.

22. Foley, biographical questionnaire.

23. Tom Foley, interview, June 20, 1995.

24. "Foley Talking Congress Bid," *Spokane Daily Chronicle*, March 31, 1964, 5.

25. Tom Foley, interview, June 20, 1995. Additional details are contained in several newspaper and magazine accounts, including Robert L. Rose, "Foley Labels First Race a Mad Scheme," *Spokesman-Review*, December 8, 1986, A1; Newhouse, "Profiles: The Navigator," 48.

26. Tom Foley, interview, June 20, 1995.

27. Tom Foley, interview, June 20, 1995.

28. William Prochnau and Richard W. Larsen, *A Certain Democrat: Senator Henry M. Jackson* (Englewood Cliffs, NJ: Prentice-Hall, 1972), 314.

29. Roberta Ulrich, "Horan, Foley Are Staging Gentlemanly Political Campaign

East of Cascades," United Press International dispatch, *Bellingham Herald*, October 27, 1964. The same story appeared in the *Bremerton Sun*, October 27, 1964, under the headline "Refreshing Campaign—Horan vs. Foley." Both clippings in the Foley Papers.

30. Tom Foley, interview, June 20, 1995.

31. "Democrats Gain Four Congressional Seats," *Wenatchee Daily World*, November 4, 1964, 17.

32. Richard Larsen, "Heather Foley Keeps Tom's Office Running," *Walla Walla Union Bulletin*, July 2, 1989, 30.

33. "Foley to Wed Law Student in November," *Spokesman-Review*, August 24, 1968, 6; Lois Romano, "Tom Foley's Right Hand," *Washington Post*, February 9, 1990; Martin Tolchin, "Foley's Spouse No Stranger to Power," *New York Times*, March 27, 1992, A12.

34. Betsy Trainor, "Congressman's Wife: I'm Forced to Be Aggressive," *Walla Walla Union Bulletin*, March 28, 1974, 15.

35. Romano, "Tom Foley's Right Hand."

36. John Jacobs, *A Rage for Justice: The Passion and Politics of Phillip Burton* (Berkeley: University of California Press, 1995), 230.

37. Emily C. Baer-Bositis, "Organizing for Reform: The Democratic Study Group and the Role of Party Factions in Driving Institutional Change in the House of Representatives" (PhD diss., University of Minnesota, 2017), 73.

38. Legg, interview.

39. Tom Foley, interview by Kenton Bird, March 20, 1996.

40. Tim Wirth, interview by Kenton Bird, February 23, 1998.

41. John Lawrence, interview by Kenton Bird, March 4, 2018.

42. Tom Foley, interview, March 20, 1996.

43. Hebert angered the freshman members with a condescending comment: "Okay, boys and girls. Let me tell you what it's like around here"; quoted in Jacobs, *Rage for Justice*, 268.

44. Common Cause, "Report on House Committee Chairmen," January 13, 1975, quoted in Jacobs, 268.

45. *CQ Weekly Report*, January 18, 1975, 166.

46. Mike McCormack, interview by Kenton Bird, July 25, 1997.

47. Tom Foley, interview, March 20, 1996.

48. "Foley's Rise Rapid to Power Position," *Spokesman-Review*, January 18, 1975, 16.

49. Jacobs, *Rage for Justice*, 268.

50. Two other committee chairs, Edward Hebert and Wright Patman of the Banking Committee, were ousted. Wayne Hays and George Mahon narrowly kept their chair positions.

51. William R. Poage, letter to Foley, November 8, 1978, Foley Papers.

52. Tom Foley, interview, March 20, 1996.

53. William Schneider, "JFK's Children: The Class of 1974," *Atlantic Monthly*, March 1989, 42.

3. A Bipartisan Speaker

1. Pat Williams, interview by Kenton Bird, June 26, 1997, Foley Papers, Washington State University Library.

2. Gloria Borger, "The Rise of the Accidental Speaker," *US News & World Report*, June 5, 1989, 38.

3. Hays Gorey, "Waiting for Opportunity to Knock: Tom Foley Is the Accidental Tourist of American Politics," *Time*, June 5, 1989, 36.

4. Werner Brandt, interview by Kenton Bird, March 23, 1996. Foley appointed Brandt sergeant at arms of the House in 1992.

5. John J. Barry, *The Ambition and the Power* (New York: Viking Penguin, 1989), 132.

6. Among the casualties in the Senate was Foley's friend and longtime Washington senator, Warren Magnuson.

7. For a thorough analysis of the Democrats' difficulties in the early Reagan years, see Barbara Sinclair, "Tip O'Neill and Contemporary House Leadership," in *Masters of the House: Congressional Leadership over Two Centuries*, ed. Roger H. Davidson, Susan Webb Hammond, and Raymond W. Smock (Boulder, CO: Westview Press, 1998), 302–305.

8. For a concise overview of the founding of NCPAC, see Marc C. Johnson, *Tuesday Night Massacre: Four Senate Elections and the Radicalization of the Republican Party* (Norman: University of Oklahoma Press, 2021), esp. chap. 1, "A Group Like Ours Could Lie through Its Teeth," 8–26.

9. Jim Wright, interview by Kenton Bird, May 8, 1997.

10. Richard E. Cohen, *Rostenkowski: The Pursuit of Power and the End of the Old Politics* (Chicago: Ivan R. Dee, 1999), 117–118.

11. Cohen, 119. See also Christopher Madison, "The Heir Presumptive," *National Journal*, April 29, 1989, 1034–1038.

12. Wright, interview.

13. Brandt, interview.

14. Wright, interview.

15. Robert L. Rose, "Foley Gets Majority Whip Job," *Spokesman-Review*, December 9, 1980.

16. At Reagan's request, Congress approved a huge tax cut in 1981, but the large tax reductions drained the federal Treasury. As the federal deficit worsened, Reagan proposed tax increases in his State of the Union address on January 26, 1982. See *CQ Almanac* (Washington, DC: Congressional Quarterly Publishing, 1982), 32.

17. David S. Broder, "Democrats Voice Mixed Reaction to Reagan's Tax Boost Appeal," *Washington Post*, August 17, 1982, A7.

18. Dale Tate, "Congress Clears $98.3 Billion Tax Increase," *CQ Weekly Report,* August 21, 1982, 2035.

19. Judith Miller, "Respected by the House," *New York Times,* August 18, 1982.

20. Ari Posner, "Friendly Foley," *New Republic,* August 8 and 15, 1988, 12.

21. Laura Parker, "A Powerful Leader in a Shaky District," *Seattle Post-Intelligencer,* October 17, 1982.

22. Tom Foley, interview by Kenton Bird, June 30, 1995. For a discussion of some of the tensions that Foley faced between leadership responsibilities and local expectations, see Baodi Zhou, "Thomas S. Foley and the Politics of Wheat: U.S. Wheat Trade with Japan, China and the Soviet Union, 1965–1986" (PhD diss., Washington State University, 1999).

23. Tip O'Neill with William Novak, *Man of the House: The Life and Political Memoirs of Speaker Tip O'Neill* (New York: Random House, 1987), 355.

24. Democrat Walter Mondale's loss to Ronald Reagan in the 1984 presidential election kept O'Neill in the House for two more years.

25. O'Neill with Novak, *Man of the House,* 373.

26. John Jacobs, *A Rage for Justice: The Passion and Politics of Phillip Burton* (Berkeley: University of California Press, 1995), 296–297. Former Washington State Democratic chair Herb Legg explained to Kenton Bird that Burton told him that six members originally pledged to him instead voted for Wright. See also J. Brooks Flippen, *Speaker Jim Wright: Power, Scandal, and the Birth of Modern Politics* (Austin: University of Texas Press, 2018), esp. 242–280.

27. Barry, *The Ambition and the Power,* 137.

28. Richard E. Cohen, email to Kenton Bird, July 15, 1998.

29. Posner, "Friendly Foley," 13.

30. Barry, *The Ambition and the Power,* 137.

31. Cohen, email to Kenton Bird.

32. Richard E. Cohen, "Democratic Whip Foley May Become a Party Leader Who Shuns Partisanship," *National Journal,* September 28, 1985.

33. Eric Pryne, "The House Is His castle: Deft Maneuvering, Quiet Style Pay Off for Tom Foley and State," *Seattle Times,* December 7, 1986, A1.

34. Joel Connelly, "Tom Foley: The Student and Storyteller," *Seattle Post-Intelligencer,* September 25, 1986.

35. "Foley Elected Majority Leader," press release, 1986, Foley Papers.

36. Wright, interview.

37. Tom Kenworthy, "Braking Partisanship: Majority Leader's Pragmatism Finds Respect," *Washington Post,* March 30, 1987, A1.

38. Fred Barnes, "The Wright Stuff," *New Republic,* May 15, 1989, 13–16.

39. Foley press release, December 5, 1988, Foley Papers.

40. John Newhouse, "The Navigator," *New Yorker,* April 10, 1989, 48.

41. A description of the procedure is found in John J. Pitney Jr. and William F. Connelly Jr., "The Speaker: A Republican Perspective," in *The Speaker: Leadership in*

the U.S. House of Representatives, ed. Ronald M. Peters Jr. (Washington, DC: CQ Press, 1995), 73. Wright gives his own version of what happened and expresses some regret in an essay in the same book, "Challenges That Speakers Face," 341.

42. The Republican Conference is the equivalent of the House Democratic Caucus.

43. Dick Cheney, interview by Kenton Bird, December 12, 1996. Cheney elaborated on his grievances with Wright in "What's Wrong about Wright: When the House Speaker Manipulates the Rules, Democracy Suffers," *Washington Post*, April 9, 1989, B2.

44. O'Neill with Novak, *Man of the House*, 353–354.

45. O'Neill with Novak, 94.

46. Julian E. Zelizer, *Burning Down the House: Newt Gingrich, the Fall of a Speaker, and the Rise of the New Republican Party* (New York: Penguin Press, 2020), 162.

47. A concise summary of the Ethics Committee's investigation of Wright is contained in *Congressional Quarterly's Guide to Congress* (Washington, DC: Congressional Quarterly Books, 1991), 769–771.

48. Norman J. Ornstein, "Can Congress Be Led?," in *Leading Congress: New Styles, New Strategies*, ed. John J. Kornacki (Washington, DC: CQ Press, 1990), 24.

49. According to Wright, a House Republican said the failure of Tower's nomination had alienated many Republicans. "We're under heavy pressure to make an example of you," the representative told Wright. See Jim Wright, *Worth It All: My War for Peace* (Washington, DC: Brassey's, 1993), 231.

50. Gingrich defeated Madigan, the favorite of minority leader Robert Michel, by a vote of 87 to 85 in the Republican Conference. For an account of Gingrich's maneuvering for the whip job, see Dan Balz and Ronald Brownstein, *Storming the Gates: Protest Politics and the Republican Revival* (Boston: Little, Brown, 1996), 131–133; Zelizer, *Burning Down the House*, 180–193.

51. *Boston Globe* dispatch, "New Republican Whip Has a New Target: Tom Foley," *Spokesman-Review*, March 28, 1989.

52. Robin Toner, "Around Wright, a Loyalty Dance," *New York Times*, April 7, 1989, A14.

53. Karen Dorn Steele, "Majority Leader Commands Respect," *Spokesman-Review*, April 2, 1989, A1.

54. Madison, "The Heir Presumptive," 1034–1038. Frank's praise would take on additional significance two months later when a Republican National Committee press release linked the two men's positions in a clumsy attempt to imply that Foley was gay, a charge for which the RNC never offered evidence and later retracted.

55. A California savings and loan official bought and held the bonds while Coelho arranged financing. During that period, the price of the bonds increased, but Coelho paid the original price. When he sold them, he made a profit of $6,882. He also misstated the dates that he bought and sold the bonds on his congressional financial statement. See *CQ Almanac* (Washington, DC: CQ Press, 1989), 41–42.

56. Don Phillips, "Foley: The Speaker Is Still the Speaker," *Washington Post*, May 28, 1989, A24.

57. Wright, interview.

58. Tom Kenworthy, "Wright to Resign Speaker's Post, House Seat," *Washington Post*, June 1, 1989, A1.

59. Tom Kenworthy and Charles R. Babcock, "Wright Acknowledges 'Mistakes' of Judgment," *Washington Post*, June 1, 1989, A18.

60. Jacqueline Trescott, "Tom Foley and the Changing of the Guard," *Washington Post*, June 1, 1989, C1.

61. David E. Rosenbaum, "A Politician Outside the Mold: Thomas Stephen Foley," *New York Times*, June 2, 1989, A1.

62. Barry, *The Ambition and the Power*, 757.

63. Jim Camden, "Foley New House Speaker," *Spokane Daily Chronicle*, June 6, 1989, A1.

64. Draft of speech, Acceptance of Speakership, June 6, 1989, Foley Papers.

65. Douglas B. Harris and Matthew N. Green, "Michel as Minority Leader: Minority Party Strategies and Tactics in the Post-reform House," in *Robert H. Michel: Leading the Republican House Minority*, ed. Frank H. Mackaman and Sean Q Kelly (Lawrence: University Press of Kansas, 2019), 107.

66. "Demos Too Pushy in the House? Foley Says GOP Has a Point," Associated Press dispatch, *Spokesman-Review*, June 8, 1989.

67. Matthew N. Green, *The Speaker of the House: A Study of Leadership* (New Haven, CT: Yale University Press, 2010), 28, 31.

68. Thomas S. Foley, "Speaking for the House," in *The Speaker: Leadership in the U.S. House of Representatives*, ed. Ronald M. Peters Jr. (Washington, D.C.: CQ Press, 1996), 249.

69. David Schaefer, "Tom Foley as 'Healer of the House,' Two Months in New Job Have Bought Peace," *Seattle Times*, August 17, 1989, B4.

70. Jim Wright, *Balance of Power: Presidents and Congress from the Era of McCarthy to the Age of Gingrich* (Atlanta: Turner Publishing, 1996), 490. See also Flippen, *Speaker Jim Wright*.

71. William Poage, letter to Tom Foley, November 8, 1978, Foley Papers.

72. Les Blumenthal, "Foley Puts Northwest in Spotlight," *Walla Walla Union Bulletin*, November 24, 1989.

73. Ornstein, "Can Congress Be Led?," 24.

74. Adam Clymer, "Thomas Foley, House Speaker, Dies at 84; Democrat Urged Parties to Collaborate," *New York Times*, October 18, 2013, B9.

75. Green, *Speaker of the House*, 103.

76. Jeffrey R. Biggs and Thomas S. Foley, *Honor in the House: Speaker Tom Foley* (Pullman: Washington State University Press, 1999), 272.

77. Emily Langer, "Thomas S. Foley, Former House Speaker, Dies at 84," *Wash-*

ington Post, October 18, 2013. See also Burdett A. Loomis and Wendy J. Schiller, *The Contemporary Congress*, 7th ed. (Boulder, CO: Rowman and Littlefield, 2018), 108.

78. Sean M. Theriault, *The Gingrich Senators: The Roots of Partisan Warfare in Congress* (New York: Oxford University Press, 2013), 17.

79. Chris Buskirk, "The Russian Fun-House Mirror," *New York Times*, August 20, 2018, https://www.nytimes.com/2018/08/20/opinion/john-brennan-clearance -trump-russia.html. Buskirk, a contributing opinion writer for the *Times*, was described as editor and publisher of the journal *American Greatness*, a conservative publication.

4. Mapping the Fifth District Landscape

1. Martin Wattenberg, email to John Pierce, June 16, 2020.

2. Walter Nugent, *Color Coded: Party Politics in the American West, 1950–2016* (Norman: University of Oklahoma Press, 2018), 241–250.

3. Justin C. Williams Jr., "Political Redistricting: A Review," *Papers in Regional Science* 74, no. 1 (January 1995): 13.

4. Michael P. McDonald, "A Comparative Analysis of Redistricting Institutions in the United States," *State Politics and Policy* 4, no. 4 (Winter 2004): 371. See also Bruce E. Cain, "Assessing the Partisan Effects of Redistricting," *American Political Science Review* 79, no. 2 (June 1985): 320–333; Alan I. Abramowitz, Brad Alexander, and Matthew Gunning, "Incumbency, Redistricting, and the Decline of Competition in U.S. House Elections," *Journal of Politics* 68, no. 1 (February 2006): 75–88.

5. *Reynolds v. Sims*, 377 U.S. 533 (1964).

6. Nugent, *Color Coded*, 248–249. Cathy McMorris Rodgers served three terms as chair of the House Republican Conference, 2013–2019.

7. For a historical dive into Washington State's redistricting past, see Howard Mc-Curdy, "Redistricting Wars," in *Turning Points in Washington's Public Life*, ed. George Scott (Folsom, CA: Civitas Press, 2011), 219–246.

8. Jim Camden, interview by Kenton Bird, July 30, 2020.

9. Camden, interview.

10. Richard Larsen, "The Sparring Starts over Redistricting," *Seattle Times*, March 1, 1971, A4.

11. Editorial, "People Just Pawns When Politicians Redistrict," *Wenatchee Daily World*, March 3, 1971, 4.

12. Editorial, "People Just Pawns," 4.

13. Tom Foley, letter to James Davenport, March 14, 1972, Foley Papers, Washington State University Library.

14. Washington Secretary of State's Office, "Redistricting & Census Information," accessed November 1, 2022, https://www.sos.wa.gov/elections/redistricting/redistricting-information.aspx.

15. Marjie High, "History of Redistricting in Washington State," *Washington State Wire*, February 4, 2019, 1.

16. McGovern carried only Massachusetts and the District of Columbia. Republican incumbent Richard Nixon won every other state on his way to an Electoral College landslide, capturing 520 electoral votes to McGovern's 17.

17. Associated Press, "UW Geography Professor to Plan State Redistricting; Told to Shun Politicians," *Wenatchee Daily World*, February 28, 1972.

18. "Foley Won't Seek Appeal: Eastern Part of State Two Districts," *Spokane Daily Chronicle*, March 28, 1972.

19. Daniel J. Elazar, *American Federalism: A View from the States* (New York: Thomas Y. Crowell, 1966); Daniel J. Elazar, *The American Mosaic: The Impact of Space, Time, and Culture on American Politics* (Boulder, CO: Westview Press, 1994).

20. See the discussion in Robert D. Putnam, *Making Democracy Work: Civic Traditions in Modern Italy* (Princeton, NJ: Princeton University Press, 1993).

21. Elazar, *American Mosaic*, 237.

22. Elazar, 237.

23. Jim Camden, "Foley's Rise: A Look Back; Thirty Years Ago Spokane's Congressman Became the 57th Speaker of the House," *Spokesman Review*, June 2, 2019, 9.

24. Lee Drutman, "How Hatred Came to Dominate American Politics," *Five Thirty-Eight*, October 5, 2020, https://fivethirtyeight.com/features/how-hatred-negative-partisanship-came-to-dominate-american-politics/.

25. Mike Prager, "NRA Commits $50,000 for Ads against Foley," *Spokesman-Review*, October 13, 1994; Jim Camden, "National Groups Attack Foley in Localized Ads," *Spokesman-Review*, September 16, 1994, B2.

26. Nicholas P. Lovrich, John C. Pierce, and Stuart Elway, "Two Washingtons? Political Culture in the Evergreen State," in *Governing the Evergreen State: Political Life in Washington*, ed. Cornell W. Clayton, Todd Donovan, and Nicholas P. Lovrich (Pullman: Washington State University Press, 2018), 1–21.

27. The size of the sample was too small to segregate Fifth District respondents from others in the "Other Washington" cluster and by counties in the Fifth District, so these differences are by implication. See Lovrich, Pierce, and Elway, "Two Washingtons?"

28. Judy Olson, interview by Kenton Bird, July 30, 2019. Olson, president of the National Association of Wheat Growers in 1994–1995, ran for Foley's seat in 1996, earning nearly as many votes as Foley did in 1994 but capturing only 44 percent of the district's vote in the higher-turnout presidential election year.

29. One of McGovern's rivals for the Democratic nomination in 1972 was Foley's mentor and friend Washington senator Henry Jackson. A conservative Democrat considered a hawk on foreign policy issues, Jackson dropped out of the race in May 1972 after a poor finish in the Ohio primary.

30. The Republican candidate in 1972 was Clarice Privette, an eccentric Spokane businesswoman who had challenged Senator Henry Jackson in the Democratic

primary two years earlier. Privette's picture and biography did not appear in Washington's official state voter pamphlet because she refused to pay the $200 fee to the Secretary of State's Office. "Foley Faces Spokane Woman for Congress Seat," *Pullman Herald*, November 2, 1972.

31. Julian E. Zelizer, *Burning Down the House: Newt Gingrich, the Fall of a Speaker, and the Rise of the New Republican Party* (New York: Penguin Press, 2020), 288.

32. Thomas E. Mann and Norman J. Ornstein, *The Broken Branch: How Congress Is Failing America and How to Get It Back on Track* (New York: Oxford University Press, 2006), 91.

33. Martin P. Wattenberg, *The Decline of American Political Parties, 1952–1996* (Cambridge, MA: Harvard University Press, 1998), 201, 216.

34. Jim Camden and Jess Walter, "Perot Stumps for Nethercutt in Spokane," *Spokesman-Review*, November 5, 1994, A1.

35. Shawn Vestal, "Nethercutt Looks Back on His Time as a 'Giant Killer,'" *Spokesman-Review*, April 20, 2018.

36. "Foley Leaves County Legacy," *Newport Miner*, October 23, 2013, 1A.

37. "Foley Leaves County Legacy."

38. Thomas E. Mann and Norm Ornstein, "Supply-Side Congressional Reform," Brookings Institution, *Fixgov* (blog), July 25, 2018, https://www.brookings.edu/blog/fixgov/2018/07/25/supply-side-congressional-reform/.

39. Sean M. Theriault, *Party Polarization in Congress* (New York: Cambridge University Press, 2008), 7.

40. Theriault, 3.

41. Theriault, 138.

42. James E. Campbell, *Polarized: Making Sense of a Divided America* (Princeton, NJ: Princeton University Press, 2016), 191.

43. Campbell, 191–192.

44. Theriault, *Party Polarization in Congress*, 108.

45. Dan Balz and Ronald Brownstein, *Storming the Gates: Protest Politics and the Republican Revival* (Boston: Little, Brown, 1996), 365.

46. Emily Langer, "Thomas S. Foley, Former House Speaker, Dies at 84," *Washington Post*, October 18, 2013, A1. See also Burdett A. Loomis and Wendy J. Schiller, *The Contemporary Congress*, 7th ed. (Boulder, CO: Rowman & Littlefield, 2018), 108.

47. Theriault, *Party Polarization in Congress*, 3.

48. Theriault, 3.

5. Holding the Center

1. Richard F. Fenno Jr., *Home Style: Members in Their Districts* (Boston: Little, Brown, 1978), 7.

2. Keith C. Petersen, *River of Life, Channel of Death: Fish and Dams on the Lower Snake* (Lewiston, ID: Confluence Press, 1995).

3. Tim Coleman, interview by Kenton Bird, February 1, 1999; Jim Baker, interview by Kenton Bird, July 25, 1997; John Osborn, interview by Kenton Bird, August 3, 1996.

4. Richard E. Cohen, "From Foley, a Rare Show of Raw Power," *National Journal*, May 22, 1993, 1247.

5. Kenton Bird, "Tom Foley's Last Campaign: Why Eastern Washington Voters Ousted the Speaker of the House," *Pacific Northwest Quarterly* 95, no. 1 (Winter 2003/2004): 3–15.

6. See Nicholas P. Lovrich, John C. Pierce, and Stuart Elway, "Two Washingtons? Political Culture in the Evergreen State," in *Governing the Evergreen State: Political Life in Washington,* ed. Cornell W. Clayton, Todd Donovan, and Nicholas P. Lovrich (Pullman: Washington State University Press, 2018), 1–22. See also George Scott, ed., *Turning Points in Washington's Public Life* (Folsom, CA: Civitas Press, 2011).

7. Ronald M. Peters Jr., *The American Speakership: The Office in Historical Perspective* (Baltimore: Johns Hopkins University Press, 1990), 281.

8. Burdett A. Loomis and Wendy J. Schiller, *The Contemporary Congress,* 7th ed. (Boulder, CO: Rowman & Littlefield, 2018), 51.

9. Fenno, *Home Style,* 56.

10. Jeffrey R. Biggs and Thomas S. Foley, *Honor in the House: Speaker Tom Foley* (Pullman: Washington State University Press, 1999), 48–49.

11. Richard Larsen, interview by Kenton Bird, May 29, 1996; Jim Camden, "The Tale of the Runaway Wrangler and Other Enlightening Anecdotes," *Spokesman-Review,* June 7, 1989, 2.

12. Jim Lynch and Jess Walter, "Why Wasn't Berserk Airman Ousted? Secretary of Air Force Will Order Investigation Today," *Spokesman-Review,* June 23, 1994, A1.

13. *Congress Daily,* June 27, 1994, 4.

14. Mike Prager, "NRA Commits $50,000 for Ads against Foley," *Spokesman-Review,* October 13, 1994, B1.

15. Stuart Elway, "Speaker Foley Faces Uphill Battle, Nethercutt Holds Lead," Elway Poll, October 1994, 3. See also Timothy Egan, "Foley, Behind in Polls, Plays Gingrich Card," *New York Times,* October 27, 1994, A26.

16. Elway, "Speaker Foley Faces Uphill Battle," 3.

17. Shelby Scates, "Should Man Offer (Congress) Seat to Lady?," *Seattle Post-Intelligencer,* October 12, 1966, 22. The headline is a reference to Foley's 1966 opponent, Republican Dorothy Powers.

18. Scates, 22. Foley later hired Gene Moos as a staff member at the House Agriculture Committee.

19. Tom Foley, interview by Kenton Bird, March 20, 1996.

20. Nick Kotz, "Meat Industry Stand on Inspection Bill Assailed," *Minneapolis Tribune,* July 18, 1967, 16; Nick Kotz, "Meat Inspection: The New Jungle," *The Nation,* September 18, 1967, 230–231. See also "Wholesome Meat Act Reported to House," *CQ Weekly Report,* November 3, 1967, 2207.

21. United States Department of Agriculture, Census of Agriculture Historical Archive, "1964 Washington," accessed November 1, 2022, https://agcensus.library.co rnell.edu/census_parts/1964-washington; United States Department of Agriculture, Census of Agriculture Historical Archive, "1992 Washington," accessed November 2, 2022, https://agcensus.library.cornell.edu/census_parts/1992-washington/.

22. Art Hanson, Trip Log, January 12–18, 1970, District Files, Foley Papers, Washington State University Library.

23. Jack Fischer, "Foley, Gamble Square Off," *Spokesman-Review*, October 25, 1970, 6.

24. Paul E. Pitzer, *Grand Coulee: Harnessing a Dream* (Pullman: Washington State University Press, 1994), 347.

25. National Park Service, "Washington: Grand Coulee Dam," accessed November 1, 2022, https://www.nps.gov/articles/washington-grand-coulee-dam.htm.

26. Tom Foley, interview by Kenton Bird, June 20, 1995.

27. News report, KEPR-TV, Pasco, WA, September 27, 1974, interview transcript in Foley Papers.

28. John Jacobs, *A Rage for Justice: The Passion and Politics of Phillip Burton* (Berkeley: University of California Press, 1995), 230.

29. Leon Panetta, interview by Kenton Bird, June 25, 2020.

30. Dan Glickman, interview by John Pierce and Kenton Bird, December 21, 2020.

31. Karen Elliot House, "How Rep. Foley Played a Key Role in Shaping Disputed Farm Bill," *Wall Street Journal*, September 14, 1977, 1.

32. Mary Link, "Wheat Bloc Wins Victory on Price Supports," *CQ Weekly Report*, July 23, 1977, 1566–1557; Mary Link, "Conferees, Carter Compromise on Farm Bill," *CQ Weekly Report*, August 6, 1977, 1651.

33. House, "How Rep. Foley Played a Key Role," 1.

34. Kevin Roche, "Crowd Cheers on Roy Cochran in Attack on Rep. Tom Foley," *Lewiston Morning Tribune*, December 11, 1977, 1A.

35. Jim McDermott, interview by Kenton Bird and John Pierce, August 19, 2020.

36. McDermott, interview. In fact, Foley's maternal grandfather owned farmland and a stake in a grain elevator in the Big Bend region of central Washington, about ninety miles west of Spokane.

37. Frederick W. Mayer, *Interpreting NAFTA: The Science and Art of Political Analysis* (New York: Columbia University Press, 1998), 3.

38. Maxwell A. Cameron and Brian W. Tomlin, *The Making of NAFTA: How the Deal Was Done* (Ithaca, NY: Cornell University Press, 2000), 125.

39. For a detailed chronology, see Cameron and Tomlin, xi–xiv.

40. Cameron and Tomlin, 110.

41. "H.R. 3450 (103rd): North American Free Trade Agreement Implementation Act," November 17, 1993, 10:36 p.m. ET, https://www.govtrack.us/congress/votes/103 -1993/h575.

42. Kenneth J. Cooper, "House Approves U.S.-Canada-Mexico Trade Pact on 234 to 230 Vote, Giving Clinton Big Victory," *Washington Post*, November 18, 1993, A1.

43. "H.R. 3450 (103rd): North American Free Trade Agreement Implementation Act," November 20, 1993, 7:28 p.m. ET, https://www.govtrack.us/congress/votes/103 -1993/s395.

44. Leo H. Kahane, "Congressional Voting Patterns on NAFTA: An Empirical Analysis," *American Journal of Economics and Sociology* 55, no. 4 (October 1996): 395.

45. Cameron and Tomlin, *Making of NAFTA*, 110.

46. Ken Casavant, interview by Kenton Bird, January 18, 2021.

47. William P. Avery, "Domestic Interests in NAFTA Bargaining," *Political Science Quarterly* 113, no. 2 (Summer 1998): 285–286.

48. Gwen Ifill, "Clinton Defends Trade Pact to Skeptical AFL-CIO," *New York Times*, October 5, 1993, B10.

49. David E. Bonior, *Whip: Leading the Progressive Battle during the Rise of the Right* (Westport, CT: City Point Press, 2018), 257.

50. "After NAFTA: What's Next for Us?," *AFL-CIO Reports*, Washington State Labor Council, November 22, 1993, 1, 6.

51. Jolene Unsoeld, "Floor Speech in Opposition to NAFTA Passage," November 17, 1993, Unsoeld Congressional Papers, Evergreen College, Olympia, WA.

52. Mary Ann Grimes, "NAFTA: Jobs Lost or Gained? Free-Trade Agreement Gets Mixed Reviews on Benefits to U.S., Canada and Mexico," *Seattle Times*, January 29, 1995.

53. Mayer, *Interpreting NAFTA*, 299.

54. Norm Dicks, interview by Kenton Bird, May 11, 2021.

55. Barbara Sinclair, *Legislators, Leaders, and Lawmaking: The U.S. House of Representatives in the Postreform Era* (Baltimore: Johns Hopkins University Press, 1995), 88.

56. Andrew Taylor, "Leading the Minority: Guiding Policy Change through Legislative Waters," in *Robert H. Michel: Leading the Republican House Minority*, ed. Frank H. Mackaman and Sean Q Kelly (Lawrence: University Press of Kansas, 2019), 125.

57. Douglas B. Harris, "Anticipating the Revolution: Michel and Republican Congressional Reform," in *Robert H. Michel: Leading the Republican House Minority*, ed. Frank H. Mackaman and Sean Q Kelly (Lawrence: University Press of Kansas, 2019), 193.

58. Taylor, "Leading the Minority," 125.

59. Panetta, interview.

60. Karen Hosler, "Gephardt Opposition Could Doom NAFTA: Many Democrats Would Follow His Lead," *Baltimore Sun*, September 11, 1993.

61. Cooper, "House Approves U.S.-Canada-Mexico Trade Pact," A1.

62. Remarks by Speaker Foley, transcript of US House of Representatives, floor debate, November 17, 1993, Foley Papers.

63. Taylor, "Leading the Minority," 124.

64. Taylor, 124.

65. Matthew N. Green, *The Speaker of the House: A Study of Leadership* (New Haven, CT: Yale University Press, 2010), 128–129.

66. Biggs and Foley, *Honor in the House*, 278.

67. David Groves, email to Kenton Bird, January 19, 2021. In addition to Foley, four Democrats (Maria Cantwell, Jolene Unsoeld, Jay Inslee, and Mike Kreidler) lost their House seats in 1994, and Republicans captured an open seat formerly held by Democrat Al Swift, who did not seek reelection. As a result, the state's delegation went from eight Democrats and one Republican in 1994 to seven Republicans and two Democrats in 1995.

68. Stuart Elway, *Elway Report*, November 1992, 4.

69. Eric M. Uslaner, "Let the Chits Fall Where They May? Executive and Constituency Influences on Congressional Voting on NAFTA," *Legislative Studies Quarterly* 27, no. 3 (1998): 347–371.

70. Casavant, interview by Kenton Bird.

71. Sinclair, *Legislators, Leaders, and Lawmaking*, 88.

72. President Bill Clinton, letter to Speaker Tom Foley, November 15, 1993, Foley Papers.

73. Sinclair, *Legislators, Leaders, and Lawmaking*, 88.

74. Bonior, *Whip*, 308–309.

75. George Kundanis, email to Kenton Bird, May 11, 2021.

76. Cooper, "House Approves U.S.-Canada-Mexico Trade Pact," A1.

77. Martin P. Wattenberg, *The Decline of American Political Parties, 1952–1996* (Cambridge, MA: Harvard University Press, 1998), 204–205.

78. Elway, "Speaker Foley Faces Uphill Battle," 4.

79. Biggs and Foley, *Honor in the House*, 220.

80. Richard Gephardt, interview by John Pierce and Kenton Bird, June 5, 2020.

81. Robert Crow, interview by Kenton Bird, July 18, 1997.

6. The Pinnacle of Power

1. Susan Page, *Madam Speaker: Nancy Pelosi and the Lessons of Power* (New York: Twelve, 2021), 168.

2. Sarah A. Binder and Thomas E. Mann, "Constraints on Leadership in Washington," *Issues in Governance Studies* 41 (July 2011): 3–4. See also James MacGregor Burns, *Leadership* (New York: Harper & Row, 1978).

3. Thomas S. Foley, "Speaking for the House," in *The Speaker: Leadership in the U.S. House of Representatives*, ed. Ronald M. Peters Jr. (Washington, DC: CQ Press, 1995), 249.

4. David Schaefer, "Tom Foley as 'Healer of the House,' Two Months in New Job Have Bought Peace," *Seattle Times*, August 17, 1989, B4.

5. Jim Wright, *Balance of Power: Presidents and Congress from the Era of McCarthy to the Age of Gingrich* (Atlanta: Turner Publishing, 1996), 490.

6. William Poage, letter to Foley, November 8, 1978, Foley Papers, Washington State University Library.

7. Edwards recounted the episode in a speech to the American Enterprise Institute, December 6, 1989, quoted in John J. Pitney Jr. and William Connelly Jr., "The Speaker: A Republican Perspective," in *The Speaker: Leadership in the U.S. House of Representatives*, ed. Ronald M. Peters Jr. (Washington, DC: CQ Press), 75. Foley said the Democrats on the floor were "confused and murmuring among themselves" because they never before had lost a voice vote. See Michael Orestes, "Speaker Tom Foley, Leading the House without Partisanship, Has Passion for the Process," *Eugene Register-Guard*, November 11, 1989, 1C.

8. Schaefer, "Tom Foley as 'Healer of the House,'" B4.

9. Peter Osterlund, "House Ways Friendlier with Foley as Speaker," *Baltimore Sun*, August 7, 1989.

10. Don Phillips, "House Passes Pay-Ethics Bill, 252–174; Plan Bars Keeping Speech Honoraria," *Washington Post*, November 17, 1989, A1.

11. Phillips, A1.

12. *Congressional Quarterly Almanac* (Washington, DC: CQ Press, 1989), 51.

13. Jim Camden, "Foley Steers House through Turbulence; Restoring Civility a Top Achievement," *Spokesman-Review*, November 26, 1989, C1–C2.

14. Phillips, "House Passes Pay-Ethics Bill," A1.

15. David Worley, interview by Kenton Bird, April 8, 1999. Democrats kept their promise not to help candidates such as Worley who criticized the raise. He received a $5,000 contribution from the Democratic National Campaign Committee in the last week of the 1990 campaign after another Georgia Democrat declined the money. Worley lost to Gingrich by only 974 votes that year.

16. Osterlund, "House Ways Friendlier."

17. Foley press conference transcript, June 13, 1989, 1, Foley Papers.

18. Roberta Ulrich, "Foley the Peacemaker Takes on a Fractious House," *Oregonian*, May 5, 1991.

19. Kyung M. Song and Jim Brunner, "Ex-House Speaker Tom Foley Reigned in Friendlier Political Era," *Seattle Times*, October 19, 2013.

20. Barry Surman, "New Leaders Pick Veterans for Key Roles on Staffs," *CQ Weekly Report*, August 19, 1989, 2164–2165.

21. Christopher Hanson and Joel Connelly, "Foley Still Must Answer to District," *Seattle Post-Intelligencer*, August 18, 1989, B1.

22. Jacqueline McRae, "The Speaker Comes Home; Tom Foley Vows Continued Visits," *Walla Walla Union Bulletin*, August 18, 1989, 1.

23. For a description of how Foley blocked closure of the VA Medical Center in 1987, see Bill McAllister, "Congress Wields Heavy Hand in Reversing Agency Decisions; Legislation Prevented Conversion of Hospital to Clinic," *Washington Post*, March 15, 1989, A16.

24. "Foley Wants Corps' Headquarters Downtown," *Walla Walla Union Bulletin*, August 18, 1989, 1.

25. Robin Toner, "Foley Shows He Is Speaker for Both Washingtons," *New York Times*, August 21, 1989. See also John E. Yang, "House Speaker Foley, Very Much the Product of His State, Hasn't Fallen Far from the Tree," *Wall Street Journal*, August 23, 1989, A12.

26. Les Blumenthal, "Foley Puts Northwest in Spotlight," *Walla Walla Union Bulletin*, November 24, 1989.

27. Blumenthal.

28. Tom Kenworthy, "Democratic Critics Wait for Foley to Push Back: Speaker Given Credit for House in Order," *Washington Post*, June 7, 1990, A1. See also David Schaefer, "Foley Downplays 1st-Year Success; House Speaker Sees Trouble Ahead," *Seattle Times*, June 7, 1990, B1.

29. Foley, "Speaking for the House," 250–251.

30. George H. W. Bush, letter to Kenton Bird, February 16, 1999.

31. Associated Press, "A Tree with Roots in Early Democracy," *Seattle Times*, September 19, 1989, A1.

32. Jim Camden, "Bush Settles Up by Paying Cash for Dinner Tab," *Spokesman-Review*, September 20, 1989, B1.

33. The assassinations came at the height of an urban offensive launched by the Farabundo Martí National Liberation Front guerrillas, abbreviated in Spanish as FMLN. Documents released later showed that senior officers in the Salvadoran military decided to settle scores with people they suspected of collaborating with the guerrillas. See William M. LeoGrande, *Our Own Backyard: The United States in Central America, 1977–1992* (Chapel Hill: University of North Carolina Press, 1998), 569.

34. LeoGrande, 570.

35. Foley press conference transcript, November 22, 1989, 19, Foley Papers.

36. The ad ran on April 16, 1990, in the limited-circulation national edition of the *Times*, costing sponsors $2,142. Had it run in the New York edition of the paper, the cost would have been between $39,000 and $44,453.

37. Laurel Darrow, "Foley Gets a Page of Advice on El Salvador: Stop the Aid," *Lewiston Morning Tribune*, April 17, 1990, 5A.

38. Jim Camden, "Northwest Group Targets Foley on Salvador Aid," *Spokesman-Review*, April 16, 1990, A6.

39. Editorial, "Foley Hears from Home," *Seattle Post-Intelligencer*, April 17, 1990, A10.

40. Camden, "Northwest Group Targets Foley," A6.

41. Human Rights Watch, "El Salvador: Human Rights Developments," 1990, accessed October 24, 2022, https://www.hrw.org/reports/1990/WR90/AMER.BOU-07.htm#P415_104868. See also Angela Sanbrano, unpublished op-ed essay, issued April 30, 1990, by the Committee in Solidarity with the People of El Salvador, archived at https://cispes.org/article/statement-30th-anniversary-killing-jesuits.

42. Editorial, "Pressure to End El Salvador War," *Idahonian/Daily News*, May 24, 1990. See also LeoGrande, *Our Own Backyard*, 573–575.

43. Foley press conference transcript, May 23, 1990, 3, Foley Papers.

44. Dan Balz and Tom Kenworthy, "Bush Again Calls for Flag Amendment," *Washington Post*, June 13, 1990, A9.

45. Foley press conference transcript, June 12, 1990, 2, Foley Papers.

46. Tom Foley, interview by Kenton Bird, May 20, 1997.

47. Susan Rasky, "Foley Vindicated by Vote on Flag," *New York Times*, June 22, 1990, A14.

48. The June 26 vote in the Senate was 58–42 in favor, 9 votes short of two-thirds.

49. In 1995 and 1997, the Republican-controlled House gave a two-thirds majority to the amendment, only to see it die in the Senate. In June 1999, the House endorsed a similar amendment by a 305–124 vote, 19 votes more than two-thirds (*CQ Weekly Report*, June 26, 1999, 1532).

50. Foley press conference transcript, June 12, 1990, 4.

51. Richard E. Cohen, "Flag Debate Enhances Foley's Stature," *National Journal*, June 30, 1990, 1618.

52. Foley press conference transcript, October 27, 1990, 3, Foley Papers.

53. For background on US relations with Iraq before the invasion, see Bruce W. Jentleson, *With Friends Like These: Reagan, Bush, and Saddam, 1982–1990* (New York: W. W. Norton, 1994). See also *Triumph without Victory: The Unreported History of the Persian Gulf War*, edited by the staff of *U.S. News & World Report* (New York: Times Books, 1992), 13–20; Jean Edward Smith, *George Bush's War* (New York: Henry Holt, 1992), 41–49.

54. The transcript of Glaspie's meeting with Saddam Hussein was published in the *New York Times*, September 23, 1990; it is quoted in Smith, *George Bush's War*, 56. See also *Triumph without Victory*, 25.

55. *Wall Street Journal*, September 6, 1990, quoted in Smith, *George Bush's War*, 60.

56. Smith, *George Bush's War*, 7.

57. Dan Goodgame, "What If We Do Nothing?," *Time*, January 7, 1991, 20.

58. Judith Miller and Laurie Mylorie, *Saddam Hussein and the Crisis in the Gulf* (New York: Times Books, 1990), 144.

59. Foley press conference transcript, August 2, 1990, 1–2, Foley Papers. Five months later, though, Foley argued that UN economic sanctions, if given time, could pressure Iraq to withdraw from Kuwait.

60. Foley press conference transcript, August 3, 1990, 2, 4, Foley Papers.

61. Smith, *George Bush's War*, 92.

62. Smith, 96–97.

63. Associated Press, "Foley Supports Decision to Send in Troops," *Spokesman-Review*, August 9, 1990.

64. Smith, *George Bush's War*, 99.

65. *Washington Post*, August 9, 1990, quoted in Smith, 103.

66. Smith, 106.

67. Ramsey Clark, *The Fire This Time: U.S. War Crimes in the Gulf* (New York: Thunder's Mouth Press, 1992), 204.

68. Foley press conference transcript, October 27, 1990, 1–2.

69. See table 4.1 for votes cast for Foley and his opponents from 1964 to 1994.

70. Eric Sorensen, "Farmers Are Hot in Dusty, Where Foley Vote Dried Up," *Spokesman-Review*, November 8, 1990, A1.

71. Smith, *George Bush's War*, 201.

72. Smith, 202.

73. Foley made this remark in an interview for a 1991 television documentary on the Gulf crisis, produced by the American Enterprise Institute and the BBC. Quoted in David Mervin, *George Bush and the Guardianship Presidency* (New York: St. Martin's Press, 1996), 189.

74. *CQ Weekly Report*, November 17, 1990, 3881.

75. "Foley Says Congress Supportive of Buildup," *Walla Walla Union Bulletin*, November 18, 1990.

76. Associated Press, "Foley to Join Middle East Tour," *Yakima Herald Republic*, November 21, 1990.

77. William Safire, "The Hitler Analogy," *New York Times*, August 24, 1990, A29.

78. Clark, *The Fire This Time*, 30.

79. "Foley Has Doubts about Iraq; Speaker Skeptical of Nuke Threat," *Idahonian/ Daily News*, November 28, 1990, 1A. Foley's information was accurate. In May 1992, a year after the war's end, a UN investigation determined that Iraq was two to three years away from building a usable bomb because its design was "fundamentally flawed." See Eric Alterman, *Sound and Fury: The Washington Punditocracy and the Collapse of American Politics* (New York: HarperCollins, 1992), 261n.

80. Alterman, *Sound and Fury*, 216. See also *Triumph without Victory*, 181.

81. Alterman, *Sound and Fury*, 220.

82. *Triumph without Victory*, 188.

83. Letter to Foley, signed by Bob Wayne, Walt Miller, and twenty-two others, December 1990, copy in Kenton Bird Papers, Washington State University Library.

84. Foley press conference transcript, January 3, 1991, 12, Foley Papers.

85. Foley press conference transcript, January 7, 1991, 6, Foley Papers.

86. Smith, *George Bush's War*, 243.

87. Prepared text of Foley's remarks, January 12, 1991, Foley Papers. See also *Congressional Record*, January 12, 1991, H441.

88. Foley press conference transcript, January 16, 1991, 5, Foley Papers. (The file copy of the transcript is misdated January 10; however, it is clear from press reports that Yeutter's remarks were made after the January 12 vote in the House.)

89. Foley press conference transcript, January 14, 1991, 6, Foley Papers.

90. Alterman, *Sound and Fury*, 262.

91. The Polling Game," *Extra!*, May 1991, 11.

92. Tom Foley, letter to Kenton Bird, February 22, 1991.

93. Ken Olsen, "Foley: Extend War Unity to Peace," *Idahonian/Daily News*, January 30, 1991, 1A.

94. The chronology of the fighting and cease-fire comes from *Triumph without Victory*, esp. 399–415.

95. *Triumph without Victory*, 373.

96. *Triumph Without Victory*, 406–408.

97. Foley press conference transcript, February 28, 1991, 1, Foley Papers.

98. Joel Connelly, "The U.S. Needs a 'Domestic Desert Storm,' Foley says," *Seattle Post-Intelligencer*, March 27, 1991, A1, A6.

99. "Gulf Session May Delay Foley's Town Meetings," *Idahonian/Daily News*, January 2, 1991.

100. Ken Olsen, "Grilling the Speaker; Foley Hears Critics on War, Trip to Barbados," *Idahonian/Daily News*, March 27, 1991, 1A.

101. Roberta Ulrich, "Foley the Peacemaker Takes on a Fractious House," *Oregonian*, May 5, 1991.

102. David Lambro, "Foley Calls GOP Divisive in Use of Gulf War Issue," *Washington Times*, April 22, 1991, A3.

103. Richard Marin, "George Bush Could Set a Record," *Washington Post*, National Weekly Edition, March 16–22, 1990, 37.

104. The Democrats lost ten seats in the House, however, which diminished their majority to 258–176. One House member, Bernie Sanders of Vermont, an independent, usually voted with the Democrats.

105. Bush also pardoned Elliot Abrams, Alan Fiers, Clair George, and Robert McFarlane, all of whom had been convicted of withholding information from Congress, and Duane Clarridge, who, like Weinberger, had not yet gone on trial.

106. David Johnston, "Bush Pardons 6 in Iran Affair, Averting a Weinberger Trial; Prosecutor Assails 'Cover-Up,'" *New York Times*, December 25, 1992, A1.

107. Robert L. Jackson and Ronald J. Ostrow, "Key Democrats Backed Pardon of Weinberger," *Los Angeles Times*, December 26, 1992, A1.

108. William J. Eaton, "Presidential Pardons Shake Up Political Establishment," *Los Angeles Times*, December 25, 1992, A19.

109. Editorial, "Congressional Complicity in the Pardons," *New York Times*, January 5, 1992, A14.

110. Walsh wrote that Weinberger's supporters "had managed to silence Colin Powell [chairman of the Joint Chiefs of Staff], House Speaker Tom Foley, and Congressman [Les] Aspin, who chaired the House Armed Services Committee. Lawrence Walsh, *Firewall: The Iran-Contra Conspiracy and Cover-Up* (New York: W. W. Norton, 1997), 506.

111. Jim Camden, "Foley's Aide Says Pardon Not Supported," *Spokesman-Review*, December 29, 1992, A4.

7. Defending the Reputation of the House

1. Dan Balz and Ronald Brownstein, *Storming the Gates: Protest Politics and the Republican Revival* (Boston: Little, Brown, 1996), 27.

2. The first allegations that House members had overdrawn their accounts came in 1832. See "History of the House Bank," *CQ Almanac* (Washington, DC: Congressional Quarterly Press, 1992), 43. Additional background on the bank comes from Foley press conference transcript, March 19, 1992, 7–9, Foley Papers, Washington State University Library. The US Senate had no similar office.

3. Guy Gugliotta, "Foley Saw House Bank Problems as Correctable," *Washington Post*, April 2, 1992. See also Guy Gugliotta, "Speaker Needed to Speak Up; Foley's Low-Key Approach Didn't Halt Bank Scandal," *Spokesman-Review*, April 5, 1992, A13.

4. Gugliotta, "Speaker Needed to Speak Up," A13.

5. Gugliotta.

6. Gugliotta.

7. Guy Gugliotta, "Foley Lowers Boom on Check-Bouncers," *Washington Post*, September 25, 1991. See also Gloria Borger and Stephen J. Hughes, "Day of the Living Deadbeats," *U.S. News & World Report*, October 14, 1991, 32.

8. Phil Kuntz, "Uproar over Bank Scandal Goads House to Cut Perks," *CQ Weekly Report*, October 5, 1991, 2844. Foley said at his October 3 press conference that the check to a Spokane stereo equipment store was held for twenty-four hours by the bank and paid when a deposit was received. "They probably didn't miss it," he said.

9. Foley press conference transcript, October 3, 1991, Foley Papers.

10. Foley press conference transcript, October 3, 1991.

11. Foley press conference transcript, October 3, 1991.

12. Kuntz, "Uproar over Bank Scandal," 2844.

13. Associated Press dispatch, "Idahoans Say They Didn't Have House Bank Overdrafts," September 26, 1991, Foley Papers. LaRocco was defeated for reelection in 1994, the same year Foley lost his seat.

14. Associated Press dispatch, "Idahoans Say They Didn't Have House Bank Overdrafts,"

15. Foley press conference, October 3, 1991.

16. Nancy Gibbs, "Perk City," *Time*, October 14, 1991, 18, quoted in Mark J. Rozell, *In Contempt of Congress: Postwar Press Coverage on Capitol Hill* (Westport, CT: Praeger, 1996), 95.

17. Kuntz, "Uproar over Bank Scandal," 2844.

18. Kuntz.

19. Editorial, "The Speaker's Credibility Problem," *Washington Times*, October 7, 1991, D2.

20. Editorial, "Blame 'Bank,' Not All House Members," *Albany Democrat-Herald*, March 19, 1992, 10.

21. David Broder, "House-Keeping Habits Hurt Integrity," *Oregonian*, March 18, 1992, B7.

22. Broder, B7.

23. Steven Komarow, "Foley's Capitol Remodeling Wakes Up Fiscal Watchdogs," Associated Press dispatch, *Spokesman-Review*, February 10, 1992, A8–A9.

24. "Post Office Probe Hints at Larger Scandal," *CQ Almanac*, 1992, 47–51.

25. Mitchell Locin, "Speaker under Attack," *Chicago Tribune* dispatch in *Spokesman-Review*, March 27, 1992, A10.

26. Martin Tolchin, "Foley's Spouse No Stranger to Power," *New York Times*, March 27, 1992; William J. Eaton, "Scandals Shove Speaker's Wife into Spotlight," *Los Angeles Times*, April 19, 1992.

27. Foley press conference transcript, March 26, 1992, 6, Foley Papers.

28. "Voters Enraged over House Bank Abuses," *CQ Almanac*, 1992, 24. Russ later pleaded guilty to embezzlement, fraud, and filing a false report. Prosecutors alleged he embezzled $75,300 from the House bank by cashing seventeen checks for which he had insufficient funds on deposit to cover them. See William J. Eaton, "Ex-House Sergeant-at-Arms Sentenced to 2 Years," *Los Angeles Times*, December 18, 1993.

29. *Congressional Record*, March 12, 1992, H1255.

30. *Congressional Record*, H1256.

31. Julian E. Zelizer, *Burning Down the House: Newt Gingrich, the Fall of a Speaker, and the Rise of the New Republican Party* (New York: Penguin Press, 2020), 290.

32. Jack Anderson and Michael Einstein, "How Foley Should Have Handled Gingrich," *Washington Post*, April 9, 1992, B11.

33. Nancy Traver, "Why Foley Stood Idle," *Time*, April 13, 1992, 29. Traver's article also suggested, without evidence, that Foley was worried about calling attention to a 1989 FBI report of baseless allegations from a jail inmate about a relationship with Foley and a threat to kill the Speaker. Russ apparently circulated a copy of the report, even after the FBI determined that there was no truth to the inmate's claims.

34. Karen Dorn Steele and Jim Camden, "Heather Foley Rebuts Criticism," *Spokesman-Review*, April 8, 1992, A1, A8.

35. "House Names 303 More Who Wrote Bad Checks," Associated Press dispatch, *Seattle Post-Intelligencer*, April 17, 1992, A1.

36. Adam Clymer, "For Foley and the Democrats, Political Damage Is Overdrawn," *New York Times*, April 17, 1992, A11.

37. Steven Komarow, "Phew! Speaker Foley Tries to Perfume a Stench," Associated Press dispatch, *Tennessean*, April 1992.

38. "House Names 303 More Who Wrote Bad Checks," A1.

39. Al Swift, interview by Kenton Bird, March 20, 1996.

40. In Georgia, Gingrich himself came under attack for his own overdrafts from the House bank and fought off a stiff primary challenge from fellow Republican Herman Clark. Gingrich prevailed by 980 votes after a recount. "Gingrich Is Declared Winner after Recount in a Primary," *New York Times*, July 29, 1992.

41. "Foley Faces Heat in Both Washingtons," Associated Press dispatch, *Lewiston Morning Tribune*, March 30, 1992, 7A.

42. Locin, "Speaker under Attack," A10.

43. Roberta Ulrich, "Foley Tries to Deflect Attention from Uproar over House Bank," *Oregonian*, April 5, 1992.

44. Ulrich.

45. Kenneth J. Cooper, "Foley, Pummeled Last Spring, Again Paramount in the House," *Washington Post*, August 11, 1992, A8.

46. Kenneth J. Cooper, "Foley Scapegoat for Congress," *Washington Post* dispatch, *Spokesman-Review*, May 1, 1992, A4; Steven Komarow, "Tom Foley Quiets His Critics," Associated Press dispatch, *Lewiston Morning Tribune*, July 7, 1992, 5A.

47. David Ammons, "Foley's Woes, Voter Anger Boost New Term-Limits Drive," Associated Press dispatch, April 4, 1992, Foley Papers.

48. James H. Fund, "The Hill's Most Powerful Staffer," *Wall Street Journal*, March 27, 1992, editorial page.

49. Foley press conference transcript, March 26, 1992, 8.

50. Jeffrey R. Biggs and Thomas S. Foley, *Honor in the House: Speaker Tom Foley* (Pullman: Washington State University Press, 1999), 184.

51. Peter Callaghan, "Speaker Tom Foley Ponders the Weight of Defending the House," *Morning News Tribune* (Tacoma, WA), April 23, 1992, 1.

52. Becky Kramer, "Foley Faces Friendly Crowd in Walla Walla," *Walla Walla Union-Bulletin*, April 22, 1992.

53. Joel Connelly, "Foley Goes on Attack," *Seattle Post-Intelligencer*, April 21, 1992.

54. Jim Camden, "Poll: There's No Place Like Home for Foley," *Spokesman-Review*, April 19, 1992.

55. Bill Hall, interview by Kenton Bird, July 8, 1996.

56. Biggs and Foley, *Honor in the House*, 182.

57. Komarow, "Phew! Speaker Foley Tries to Perfume a Stench."

58. Komarow.

59. Rostenkowski's endorsement may have been of mixed value, especially given subsequent events. The representative from Illinois was indicted in June 1994 for alleged financial misconduct, some related to the operations of the House post office. He was narrowly defeated in November of that year, convicted in 1996, and served fifteen months in prison. President Bill Clinton pardoned Rostenkowski on December 23, 2000.

60. Cooper, "Foley, Pummeled Last Spring, Again Paramount in House."

61. Sherry Bockwinkel, interview by Kenton Bird, November 19, 1998.

62. Background on the 1991 initiative comes from David J. Olson, "Term Limits Fail in Washington: The 1991 Battleground," in *Limiting Legislative Terms*, ed. Gerald Benjamin and Michael Malbin (Washington, DC: CQ Press, 1992), 65–96.

63. *Seattle Post-Intelligencer*, July 18, 1992, A8.

64. Olson, "Term Limits Fail in Washington," 71.

65. Bockwinkel, interview.

66. Kenneth Jost, "Testing Term Limits," *CQ Researcher*, November 18, 1994, 1023.

67. Patti Epler and Les Blumenthal, "Push for Limits: Is It the People or the Powerful?," *Morning News Tribune* (Tacoma, WA), October 13, 1991, A8.

68. Olson, "Term Limits Fail in Washington," 69.

69. Olson, 73–74.

70. Epler and Blumenthal, "Push for Limits," A1, A8. See also "Well-Funded Group Backed by Libertarians Directed the Campaign to Pass Term Limits," *Congressional Quarterly Researcher*, November 18, 1994, 1020–1021.

71. Bockwinkel, interview.

72. The main contributor to "No on 553" was Philip Morris USA, followed closely by the Washington State Labor Council. Akin Gump Hauer & Feld, the Washington, DC, law firm Foley joined after leaving the House, gave $5,000. (Figures from the Washington Public Disclosure Commission, cited in Olson, "Term Limits Fail in Washington," 88–89.)

73. *Seattle Times*, July 20, 1991, A8.

74. "NRA Salutes Rep. Foley," press release, NRA Institute for Legislative Action, October 3, 1978, Foley Papers.

75. Neal Knox, interview by Kenton Bird, February 26, 1998.

76. Stanley Greenberg and Celinda Lake, "Washington Term Limits: Too Much to Lose," August–September 1991, the Analysis Group, Inc., 3, Foley Papers.

77. Greenberg and Lake, "Washington Term Limits," 30.

78. David Ammons, "Hard to Fathom, but Term-Limits Proposal Would Likely Be the End to Foley's Career," *Spokesman-Review*, August 4, 1991, 20.

79. Ammons, 20.

80. Dan Balz, "In Washington State, Politicians Face Showdown on Term Limits," *Washington Post*, September 3, 1991, A3.

81. "No on 553" campaign brochure, 1991, "Term Limits," Kenton Bird's research file, Washington State University Library.

82. Associated Press, "Gardner Blasts Term-Limit Initiative," *Idahonian/Daily News*, September 5, 1991, 3A.

83. Bockwinkel, interview.

84. *San Diego Union*, November 3, 1991, A1.

85. George Tibbits, "Foley Now Actively Fighting I-553," Associated Press dispatch, *Spokesman-Review*, November 3, 1991, B1.

86. Olson, "Term Limits Fail in Washington," 82 and notes 41, 96.

87. Foley press conference transcript, November 6, 1991, 3–4, Foley Papers.

88. David Broder, "Resistance to Campaign Reforms Makes Foley Part of the Problem," *Spokesman-Review*, December 9, 1991.

89. Both quotations come from Bockwinkel, interview.

90. Rebecca Boren and Scott Sude, "No Race for Gardner; Governor Stands

by Plan to Take Time Off, Won't Try for Senate," *Seattle Post-Intelligencer*, May 1, 1992, A1.

91. "Brock Adams Quits Senate Race Amid Sex Misconduct Allegations," *New York Times*, March 2, 1992, A1.

92. Ammons, "Foley's Woes," 20.

93. Editorial, "The Speaker Panics," *Wall Street Journal*, October 29, 1992; "Response to 'LIMIT' assertions," Foley press release, October 28, 1992, Foley Papers.

94. Jim Lynch, "Foley Counters Charges He's Out of Touch," *Spokesman-Review*, October 19, 1992, A1.

95. Timothy Egan, "House Speaker Facing a Well-Financed Rival," *New York Times*, October 31, 1992, sec. 1, 5.

96. Ken Degerness memorandum, October 27, 1992, Foley Papers.

97. Election results are based on county-by-county figures in the Official Abstract of the 1992 General Election, Washington Secretary of State's Office.

98. Bockwinkel, interview.

99. Jost, "Testing Term Limits," 1024.

100. "This Week with David Brinkley," transcript, November 8, 1992, 5, Foley Papers.

101. The other two plaintiffs were John Clute, dean of the Law School at Gonzaga University, and George Cheek, a Spokane community activist. Cynthia Flash, "Foley Takes Legal Aim at Term Limits," *News Tribune*, June 8, 1993, B1; Angela Bruscas, "A New Suit against Term Limits," *Seattle Post-Intelligencer*, June 8, 1993, B1.

102. Editorial, "Forget It, Tom Foley," *Olympian*, June 15, 1993.

103. Editorial, "Give Court the Chance to Toss Out Term Limits," *Spokesman-Review*, June 24, 1993.

104. Bockwinkel, interview.

105. Egan, "House Speaker Facing a Well-Financed Rival," 5.

106. Swift, interview; Jim McDermott, interview by Kenton Bird, May 26, 1996.

107. Timothy Egan, "House Speaker and Ex-Attorney General Dueling over Term Limits," *New York Times*, July 29, 1993, A16.

108. Jim Camden, "Term-Limits Backer Attacks Foley," *Spokesman-Review*, October 1, 1993, A1.

109. John Arthur Wilson, "The Outer Limits," *Seattle Weekly*, January 19, 1994; Jost, "Testing Term Limits," 1024.

110. Jim Camden and Lynda Mapes, "Tom Foley Says Ruling Vindicates His Position," *Spokesman-Review*, May 23, 1995, A1.

8. The Perfect Storm

Portions of this chapter appeared in *Pacific Northwest Quarterly* 95 (Winter 2003–2004): 3–15, and are reprinted with permission.

1. Jim Camden and Jess Walter, "Nethercutt Leads Foley; Speaker Clings to Hope

amid Rising GOP Tide," *Spokesman-Review*, November 9, 1994, A1. See also Christopher Hanson, "Foley Faltering against Newcomer," *Seattle Post-Intelligencer*, November 9, 1994, B12; Jim Simon, "Foley Loses Clout before Losing Seat," *Seattle Times*, November 9, 1994, B4.

2. Foley received 45 percent of the absentee votes. Nethercutt's final margin of victory was 3,983 votes out of 216,131 cast. Washington Secretary of State's Office, *Abstract of Votes, 1994 General Election*.

3. Jess Walter, "Foley Departs, as Ever a Voice of Conciliation," *Spokesman-Review*, November 10, 1994, A1, A7.

4. See Stephen Gettinger, "The Defeated Speakers," *CQ Weekly Report*, November 12, 1994, 3291.

5. Significantly, the total number of votes for Republican House candidates surpassed the number cast for Democrats for the first time since 1952. For a detailed numerical analysis of the Republican gains in 1994, see James E. Campbell, *Cheap Seats: The Democratic Party's Advantage in U.S. House Elections* (Columbus: Ohio State University Press, 1996), esp. chap. 8.

6. An excellent overview of the Republican strategy to take control of Congress is Dan Balz and Ronald Brownstein, *Storming the Gates: Protest Politics and the Republican Revival* (Boston: Little, Brown, 1996). See also Julian E. Zelizer, *Burning Down the House: Newt Gingrich, the Fall of a Speaker, and the Rise of the New Republican Party* (New York: Penguin Press, 2020), 294–298.

7. Ross Anderson, "Tom Foley: The Liberal Democrat from Conservative Spokane Caters to Hometown Issues While Climbing the Political Ladder," *Seattle Times*, April 22, 1984, magazine section, 12.

8. Tom Nides, interview by Kenton Bird, February 13, 1997.

9. Bruce Reed, interview by Kenton Bird, October 3, 2018.

10. In his third term, Foley voted against the House-Senate conference report that was the basis for the 1968 Gun Control Act. See "NRA Salutes Rep. Foley," news release, NRA Institute for Legislative Action, October 3, 1978, Foley Papers, Washington State University Library.

11. Richard E. Cohen, *Changing Course in Washington: Clinton and the New Congress* (New York: Macmillan, 1994), 58–59; Tom Foley, "Speaking for the House," in *The Speaker: Leadership in the U.S. House of Representatives*, ed. Ronald M. Peters Jr. (Washington, DC: CQ Press, 1995), 254.

12. Terry McDermott, "Six Years and Counting, *Seattle Times*, November 5, 1992.

13. Ronald D. Elving, "Era of a Firmer Hand: Foley at the Fore," *CQ Weekly Report*, January 23, 1993, 194.

14. Elving, 194.

15. "Foley Ready for '94 with Ample Funds, Little Competition," *CQ's Congressional Monitor*, March 1, 1994, 4.

16. Richard Blow, "Killing Reform: The Inside Story on How House Speaker Foley Kept His Job," *Mother Jones*, July–August 1993, 33.

17. Mellman-Lazarus-Lake, "Report and Analysis from a Survey of 400 Registered Voters in Washington's 5th CD," October 1993, 1–4, Washington State University Library.

18. Mellman-Lazarus-Lake, 4–5.

19. "Important Force Structure Changes Announced for Fairchild," press release, February 28, 1994, Press Files, Foley Papers.

20. "Foley Confirms Interior's Commitment to Bureau of Mines," press release, March 31, 1994, Foley Papers.

21. "Foley Ready for '94," 4.

22. David Schaefer, "Election May Be Toughest for Foley," *Seattle Times*, June 5, 1994, B1.

23. Jim Camden, "Foley Challengers Capitalize on Tide against Democrats," *Spokesman-Review*, September 11, 1994, C2.

24. George Nethercutt, interview by Kenton Bird, December 5, 1996.

25. Nethercutt, interview.

26. Nethercutt, interview.

27. Ed Rollins with Tom DeFrank, *Bare Knuckles and Back Rooms: My Life in American Politics* (New York: Broadway Books, 1996), 304, 305. Rollins previously had been the White House political director under President Ronald Reagan and executive director of the National Republican Campaign Committee in 1989–1990.

28. Rollins with DeFrank, 305.

29. Nethercutt, interview.

30. Sid Morrison, interview by Kenton Bird, May 29, 1996.

31. Timothy Egan, "House Speaker and Ex-Attorney General Dueling over Term Limits," *New York Times*, July 29, 1993, A16; Jim Camden, "Term-Limits Backer Attacks Foley," *Spokesman-Review*, October 1, 1993.

32. Jeffrey R. Biggs and Thomas S. Foley, *Honor in the House: Speaker Tom Foley* (Pullman: Washington State University Press, 1999), 77.

33. *Spokesman-Review*, June 23, 1994.

34. *CQ's Congress Daily*, June 27, 1994, 4. The House passed a bill to prohibit certain semiautomatic assault weapons in May 1994 by a vote of 216 to 214, so Foley's vote was not needed. The Senate incorporated the assault weapons ban into a wide-ranging anticrime bill; the two versions were reconciled by a conference committee, and a final version passed both houses of Congress in August 1994. President Clinton signed the bill into law on September 13, 1994.

35. Kenneth J. Cooper, "Spokane Shootings Persuaded Foley to Endorse Weapons Ban," *Washington Post*, July 3, 1994, A20.

36. "Foley Breaks Silence and Backs Assault Weapons Ban," *CQ's Congress Daily*, June 27, 1994, 5–6. The 1993 legislation was named for James Brady, a former presidential press secretary who was wounded in a 1981 assassination attempt on Reagan. It required states to conduct background checks of persons seeking to purchase firearms from federally licensed gun dealers and gave states the right to block convicted felons from purchasing guns.

37. Mellman-Lazarus-Lake, focus group transcripts, June 1994, Foley Papers.

38. Tom Foley, interview by Elizabeth Arnold, July 6, 1994, transcript, 1–2 (copy of transcript in author Kenton Bird's files). Arnold said she intended to use his comments in an election-year mood story, but in the press of covering the campaign, she never produced the story. For more about public discontent with Congress in the early 1990s, see Phil Kintz, "Uproar over Bank Scandal Goads House to Cut Perks," *CQ Weekly Report*, October 5, 1991, 2844; Nancy Gibbs, "Perk City," *Time*, October 14, 1991, 18; Kenneth Cooper, "Speaker Took Lead in Vote on Subpoena; But Not Enough Lawmakers Followed, and Foley Continues to Energize Critics," *Washington Post*, May 1, 1992, A4.

39. Biggs and Foley, *Honor in the House*, 230.

40. David E. Bonior, *Whip: Leading the Progressive Battle during the Rise of the Right* (Westport, CT: City Point Press, 2018), 383.

41. A health insurance program for senior citizens was proposed by President Harry S Truman in 1945. "Medicare signed into law, July 30, 1965," U.S. Senate, Historical Highlights, https://www.senate.gov/artandhistory/history/minute/Medicare_Signed_Into_Law.htm.

42. William J. Clinton, "Address Accepting the Presidential Nomination at the Democratic National Convention in New York, the American Presidency Project, University of California, Santa Barbara, https://www.presidency.ucsb.edu/documents/address-accepting-the-presidential-nomination-the-democratic-national-convention-new-york.

43. Tom Foley, interview with Kenton Bird, March 20, 1996.

44. Adam Clymer, Robert Pear, and Robin Toner, "The Health Care Debate: What Went Wrong," *New York Times*, August 29, 1994, A1.

45. James McDermott, interview with Kenton Bird and John Pierce, August 19, 2020.

46. Jonathan Cohn, *The Ten Year War: Obamacare and the Unfinished Crusade for Universal Coverage* (New York: St. Martin's Press, 2021), 38–39. See also Clymer, Pear, and Toner, "The Health Care Debate," A12.

47. "Health Right, Introduction of Hillary Rodham Clinton," March 23, 1994, Foley Papers.

48. "House Subcommittee Passes Clinton-Style Health Care Plan," *Washington Post*, March 24, 1994, A1. The photo accompanying the *Post*'s article showed Foley kissing Rodham Clinton on the cheek at the conference the previous day.

49. Pierre Thomas, "Rostenkowski Indicted on Charges He Defrauded the U.S. of $500,00," *Washington Post*, June 1, 1994. Rostenkowski pleaded guilty to two counts of mail fraud in 1996, served fifteen months in prison and performed two months of community service, and was pardoned by President Clinton on December 23, 2000. See Neil A. Lewis, "Clinton Issues a Pardon to Ex-Rep. Rostenkowski," *New York Times*, December 2, 2000, A12.

50. Cohn, *Ten Year War*, 42–43.

51. David Rogers, "Foley Says GOP Aims to Scuttle Any Health Bill," *Wall Street Journal*, July 27, 1994, A2.

52. Rogers.

53. Adam Clymer, "Foley Urges Republicans to Meet with Democrats on Health care," *New York Times*, September 4, 1994, A13.

54. Dana Priest and Michael Weisskopf, "Health Care Reform: The Collapse of a Quest," *Washington Post*, October 11, 1994.

55. Haynes Johnson and David Broder, *The System: The American Way of Politics at the Breaking Point* (Boston: Little, Brown, 1996), xi.

56. Theda Skocpol, "The Rise and Resounding Demise of the Clinton Plan," *Health Affairs*, Spring 1995, 76.

57. Tom Foley, interview by Kenton Bird, May 20, 1997.

58. Foley, "Speaking for the House," 257–258.

59. Craig Crawford, "Washington Letter," *Orlando Sentinel*, September 25, 1994, A12.

60. Foley received 44,829 votes; Nethercutt, 37,844; Alton, 25,177; Sonneland, 19,415; and Larish, 1,085. Washington Secretary of State's Office, *Abstract of Votes, 1994 Primary Election*. In 2003, a federal appeals court declared Washington's primary system unconstitutional, ending the "blanket primary." *Seattle Post-Intelligencer*, September 16, 2003.

61. John K. Wiley, Associated Press dispatch, "This Could Turn Out to Be Tom Foley's Toughest Campaign," *Lewiston Morning Tribune*, September 23, 1994, 1A.

62. *Seattle Post-Intelligencer*, September 25, 1994.

63. *Seattle Times*, October 2, 1994.

64. Frank Costello, interview by Kenton Bird, July 28, 1997.

65. "Results of the Primary Election," press release, September 21, 1994, Press Files, Foley Papers.

66. Rick Eskil, "Primary Shows Foley's Vulnerability," *Walla Walla Union Bulletin*, September 20, 1994, 4. See also Tom Kenworthy, "Rumbles of Discontent Shake Democrats Like a Quake," *Washington Post*, October 9, 1994, A23; Timothy Egan, "The No. 1 Congressman and His No. 1 Test," *New York Times*, October 29, 1994, A1.

67. Joel Connelly, "Eastern Washington Wonders If Foley Is Friend or Foe," *Seattle Post-Intelligencer*, October 5, 1994, A8.

68. Nides, interview.

69. Nides interview.

70. Bill First, interview by Kenton Bird, June 23, 1997; Ken Degerness, interview by Kenton Bird, August 1, 1996.

71. Judy Olson, interview by Kenton Bird, June 23, 1997.

72. Eric Sorensen, "Foley's Farm Vote Wilts," *Spokesman-Review*, October 26, 1994, A1. See also Eric Sorensen, "Farmers Are Hot in Dusty, Where Foley Vote Dried Up," *Spokesman-Review*, November 8, 1990.

73. Larry Swisher, "Term Limits Turncoat Takes to the Tube," *Lewiston Morning Tribune*, June 20, 1999, 3C.

74. Jim Camden, "Nethercutt Says He'll Run for Fourth Term; Lawmaker Says He Still Has Work to Do," *Spokesman-Review*, June 14, 1999, A1. He was elected to two more terms, a total of five, before running for the US Senate in 2004 against two-term Democrat Patty Murray. He lost the Senate bid, leaving Congress in 2005 after ten years.

75. Connelly, "Eastern Washington Wonders," A8; Jim Camden, "Nethercutt, Foley Campaign to Standstill," *Spokesman-Review*, October 30, 1994, B1.

76. Nethercutt, interview

77. Rollins with DeFrank, *Bare Knuckles and Back Rooms*, 329.

78. Nethercutt, interview.

79. David Rogers, "Conservatives Fund Campaign to Limit Terms," *Wall Street Journal*, November 4, 1994, A14.

80. In addition to donating $10,900 directly to Nethercutt's campaign, the NRA spent $70,000 in the Fifth District to oppose Foley. See Linda Killian, *The Freshmen: What Happened to the Republican Revolution?* (Boulder, CO: Westview Press, 1998), 284.

81. Mike Prager, "NRA Commits $50,000 for Ads against Foley," *Spokesman-Review*, October 13, 1994, B1.

82. Jim Camden, "National Groups Attack Foley in Localized Ads," *Spokesman-Review*, September 16, 1994, B2.

83. National Federation of Independent Business, "Small Business Report Card," 1991–1992 and 1993–1994 (copy in author Kenton Bird's files).

84. Camden, "National Groups Attack Foley," B2.

85. Herman and Clear quotations and Foley's response, Jim Kershner, "Network Piggybacks on Our Very Own Fox," *Spokesman-Review*, January 15, 1996, arts section, 3.

86. Magnuson served in the Senate from 1944 until his defeat in 1980; Jackson served from 1953 until his death in 1983.

87. For a behind-the-scenes look at how Foley worked to exempt the aluminum industry from Clinton's proposed energy tax in 1993, see Richard E. Cohen, "From Foley, a Rare Show of Raw Power," *National Journal*, May 22, 1993.

88. Jim Camden and Jess Walter, "Perot Stumps for Nethercutt in Spokane," *Spokesman-Review*, November 5, 1994, A1.

89. Tom Sowa, "Corporate Leaders Endorse Tom Foley," *Spokesman Review*, November 5, 1994, A1.

90. Tim Coleman, interview by Kenton Bird, February 1, 1999.

91. Jim Baker, interview by Kenton Bird, July 25, 1997; John Osborn, interview by Kenton Bird, August 3, 1996. Both relayed impressions of how some environmental activists viewed the congressional candidates in 1994.

92. "Foley and Challenger Both Score in Debate," *Seattle Post-Intelligencer*, October 18, 1994, B5.

93. Nethercutt, interview.

94. Editorial, *Spokesman-Review*, October 23, 1994. See also *Walla Walla Union-Bulletin*, October 23, 1994; *Lewiston Morning Tribune*, October 19, 1994, and November 1, 1994.

95. Christopher Hanson, "Foley Steps Down in Typical Style," *Seattle Post-Intelligencer*, November 30, 1994, A1.

96. Christopher Hanson, "A Good Man at a Bad Time," *Seattle Post-Intelligencer*, November 10, 1994, A1.

97. Mark Mellman, interview by Kenton Bird, April 16, 1999.

98. For example, a Gallup Poll taken on November 2–6, 1994, showed that 46 percent of respondents approved of the president's job performance, up from 39 percent in polls taken on August 15–16 and September 6–7. https://news.gallup.com/poll /116584/presidential-approval-ratings-bill-clinton.aspx.

99. Foley, "Speaking for the House," 258.

100. Jess Walter and Jim Camden, "Foley Concedes to Nethercutt," *Spokesman-Review*, November 10, 1994, A1. In 2022, Nethercutt joined the advisory board for the Thomas S. Foley Institute of Public Policy and Public Service at Washington State University. See Jim Camden, "Spin Control: Former Opponents Nethercutt and Foley Linked in Effort to Improve Civil Discourse," *Spokesman-Review*, April 10, 2022.

101. Biggs and Foley, *Honor in the House*, 289. See also Bruce Selcraig, "The New Politics Has No Room for a Giant Gentleman," *High Country News*, May 29, 1995, 12.

9. His Own Stamp?

1. Four of the five Speakers who preceded Foley came from Texas (Sam Rayburn and Jim Wright) or Massachusetts (John McCormack and Tip O'Neill). The exception was Carl Albert (Oklahoma).

2. Ross Anderson, "Tom Foley: The Liberal Democrat from Conservative Spokane Caters to Hometown Issues While Climbing the Political Ladder," *Seattle Times*, April 22, 1984, magazine section, 12.

3. Joel Connelly, "Tom Foley, '51, '57, Keeps the 'People's House' in Order," *Columns: The University of Washington Alumni Magazine*, June 1992, https://magazine.wa shington.edu/feature/tom-foley-51-57-keeps-the-peoples-house-in-order/.

4. Roger H. Davidson, "The Speaker and Institutional Change," in *The Speaker: Leadership in the U.S. House of Representatives*, ed. Ronald M. Peters Jr. (Washington, DC: CQ Press, 1995), 172.

5. Ronald M. Peters, *The American Speakership: The Office in Historical Perspective* (Baltimore: Johns Hopkins University Press, 1990), 5.

6. Quoted in Christopher Madison, "The Heir Presumptive," *National Journal*, April 23, 1989, 1036.

7. Peters, *American Speakership*, 5.

8. Peters, 286.

9. Emily C. Baer-Bositis, "Organizing for Reform: The Democratic Study Group and the Role of Party Factions in Driving Institutional Change in the House of Representatives (PhD diss., University of Minnesota, 2017), 73.

10. John A. Lawrence, *The Class of '74: Congress after Watergate and the Roots of Partisanship* (Baltimore: Johns Hopkins University Press, 2018), 111.

11. Lawrence, 111. See also Thomas E. Mann and Norman J. Ornstein, *The Broken Branch: How Congress Is Failing America and How to Get It Back on Track* (New York: Oxford University Press, 2006), 62.

12. Bill Clinton, letter to Tom Foley, November 15, 1993, Foley Papers, Washington State University Library. See also Frederick W. Mayer, *Interpreting NAFTA: The Science and Art of Political Analysis* (New York: Columbia University Press, 1998), 65.

13. David E. Bonior, *Whip: Leading the Progressive Battle during the Rise of the Right* (Westport, CT: City Point Press, 2018), 356–357.

14. Martin P. Wattenberg, *The Decline of American Political Parties, 1952–1996* (Cambridge, MA: Harvard University Press, 1998), 208.

15. Barbara Sinclair, *Legislators, Leaders, and Lawmaking* (Baltimore: Johns Hopkins University Press, 1995), 88.

16. Bonior, *Whip*, 310.

17. Tom Foley, remarks on the floor of the House of Representatives, November 17, 1993, audio recording in Foley Papers.

18. Connelly, "Tom Foley, '51, '57, Keeps the 'People's House' in Order."

19. Press conference with the Speaker of the House, April 3, 1990, quoted in Jeffrey R. Biggs and Thomas S. Foley, *Honor in the House: Speaker Tom Foley* (Pullman: Washington State University Press, 1999), 134.

20. Edwards spoke on December 6, 1989, to the American Enterprise Institute, quoted in John J. Pitney Jr., and William F. Connelly Jr., "The Speaker: A Republican Perspective," in *The Speaker: Leadership in the U.S. House of Representatives*, ed. Ronald M. Peters Jr. (Washington, DC: CQ Press, 1995), 75.

21. Douglas B. Harris, "Anticipating the Revolution: Michel and Republican Congressional Reform Efforts," in *Robert H. Michel: Leading the Republican House Minority*, ed. Frank H. Mackaman and Sean Q Kelly (Lawrence: University Press of Kansas, 2019), 193.

22. Ron Sarasin, oral history interview with Bob Michel and Tom Foley, June 14, 2006, United States Capitol Historical Society, 7, https://uschs.org/wp-content/uploads/2017/03/USCHS-Oral-History-Thomas-Foley-Robert-Michel.pdf.

23. Sarasin, 7.

24. Peters, *American Speakership*, 282.

25. Frances Lee, "American Politics Is More Competitive Than Ever. That's Making Partisanship Worse," *Washington Post*, January 9, 2014, https://www.washingtonpost.com/news/monkey-cage/wp/2014/01/09/american-politics-is-more-competitive-than-ever-thats-making-partisanship-worse/. See also Frances E. Lee, *Insecure Majorities: Congress and the Perpetual Campaign* (Chicago: University of Chicago Press, 2016), esp. 198–209.

26. Barack H. Obama, in *Thomas S. Foley: Late a Speaker of the House and a Representative from Washington, Memorial Addresses and Other Tributes* (Washington, DC: Government Printing Office, 2014), 31.

Epilogue

Epigraph: Thomas S. Foley Institute for Public Policy and Public Service, informational brochure, March 1998, https://foley.wsu.edu/.

1. Jim Jacobs, "Tom Foley's Papers Will Go to WSU," *Lewiston Morning Tribune*, December 9, 1994; Kenton Bird, "WSU to Be Site of Foley Institute for Public Policy," *Cornerstone*, College of Liberal Arts, Washington State University, Spring 1995.

2. Guide to the Thomas S. Foley Congressional Papers 1964–1997, Washington State University Libraries, Manuscripts, Archives and Special Collections, http://ntser ver1.wsulibs.wsu.edu/masc/finders/cg655.htm.

3. Eric Sorensen, "Foley, Three Comrades Launch WSU Institute," *Spokesman-Review*, April 4, 1996, B1.

4. "About the Institute," Foley Institute for Public Policy and Public Service, https://foley.wsu.edu/about/.

5. Al Kamen, "Virtually Blushing," *Washington Post*, June 23, 1997.

6. Jim Camden and Hannelore Sudermann, "It's Official, Foley Picked as Japan Envoy," *Spokesman-Review*, August 30, 1997.

7. Laurie Snyder, "Senate Sends Foley Back to Public Life," *Spokesman-Review*, October 28, 1997.

8. Braven Smillie, Associated Press, "Japanese Delighted with Foley Nomination; Officials Overlook Post's Long Vacancy in Praising Choice for Ambassador," *Spokesman-Review*, August 31, 1997.

9. Jeffrey R. Biggs and Thomas S. Foley, *Honor in the House: Speaker Tom Foley* (Pullman: Washington State University Press, 1999), 283.

10. Snyder, "Senate Sends Foley Back to Public Life."

11. Sheryl Wudunn, "New U.S. Diplomat Tries to Speak Japan's Language," *New York Times*, April 8, 1998, A10.

12. Thomas E. Ricks and Paul Arnett, "U.S. Sub and Japanese Boat Collide," *Washington Post*, February 10, 2001.

13. Jim Camden, "House OKs Naming Building for Foley," *Spokesman-Review*, August 3, 1999.

14. Jim Camden, "Courthouse Named for Foley," *Spokesman-Review*, April 7, 2021.

15. Adam Clymer, "Thomas Foley, House Speaker, Dies at 84; Democrat Urged Parties to Cooperate," *New York Times*, October 18, 2013.

16. Jim Camden, "Tom Foley Remembered at D.C. Memorial Service," *Spokesman-Review*, October 30, 2013, A1.

17. Robert Michel, in *Thomas S. Foley, Late a Speaker of the House and a Representative from Washington, Memorial Addresses and Other Tributes* (Washington, DC:

US Government Printing Office, 2014), 24. See also https://www.govinfo.gov/content /pkg/CHRG-113hhrg85201/html/CHRG-113hhrg85201.htm.

18. Thomas S. Foley, Late a Speaker of the House, 19, 21.

19. Thomas S. Foley, Late a Speaker of the House, 55.

20. Thomas S. Foley, Late a Speaker of the House, 57.

21. "A New Installation," Heritage Gazette, Association for the Preservation of Historical Congressional Cemetery, Fall 2020, 5, https://congressionalcemetery.org /wp-content/uploads/2021/01/CongCemeteryFall2020.FINAL_.pdf.

22. "Speaker Foley's Final Resting Place," Foley Institute Report, 2020, 3, https:// s3.wp.wsu.edu/uploads/sites/104/2021/07/Foley-Report-2020-Final.pdf.

BIBLIOGRAPHY

Alterman, Eric. *Sound and Fury: The Washington Punditocracy and the Collapse of American Politics*. New York: HarperCollins, 1992.

Baer-Bositis, Emily C. "Organizing for Reform: The Democratic Study Group and the Role of Party Factions in Driving Institutional Change in the House of Representatives." PhD diss., University of Minnesota, 2017.

Ball, Molly. *Pelosi*. New York: Henry Holt, 2020.

Balz, Dan, and Ronald Brownstein. *Storming the Gates: Protest Politics and the Republican Revival*. Boston: Little, Brown, 1996.

Barry, John M. *The Ambition and the Power*. New York: Viking Penguin, 1989.

Benjamin, Gerald, and Michael Malbin. *Limiting Legislative Terms*. Washington, DC: CQ Press, 1992.

Biggs, Jeffrey R., and Thomas S. Foley. *Honor in the House: Speaker Tom Foley*. Pullman: Washington State University Press, 1999.

Bird, R. Kenton. "The Speaker from Spokane: The Rise and Fall of Tom Foley as a Congressional Leader." PhD diss., Washington State University, 1999.

Bishop, Bill. *The Big Sort: Why the Clustering of Likeminded America Is Tearing Us Apart*. Boston: Houghton Mifflin Harcourt, 2009.

Bonior, David E. *Whip: Leading the Progressive Battle during the Rise of the Right*. Westport, CT: City Point Press, 2018.

Bonker, Don, with David Applefield. *A Higher Calling: Faith and Politics in the Public Square*. Nashville, TN: Elm Hill, 2019.

Burns, James MacGregor. *Leadership*. New York: Harper & Row, 1978.

Burns, James MacGregor. *Transforming Leadership*. New York: Grove Press, 2003.

Cameron, Maxwell A., and Brian W. Tomlin. *The Making of NAFTA: How the Deal Was Done*. Ithaca, NY: Cornell University Press, 2000.

Campbell, James E. *Cheap Seats: The Democratic Party's Advantage in U.S. House Elections*. Columbus: Ohio State University Press, 1996.

Campbell, James E. *Polarized: Making Sense of a Divided America*. Princeton, NJ: Princeton University Press, 2016.

Clark, Ramsey. *The Fire This Time: U.S. War Crimes in the Gulf.* New York: Thunder's Mouth Press, 1992.

Clayton, Cornell W., Todd Donovan, and Nicholas P. Lovrich, eds. *Governing the Evergreen State: Political Life in Washington.* Pullman: Washington State University Press, 2018.

Cohen, Richard E. *Changing Course in Washington: Clinton and the New Congress.* New York: Macmillan, 1994.

Cohen, Richard E. *Rostenkowski: The Pursuit of Power and the End of the Old Politics.* Chicago: Ivan R. Dee, 1999.

Cohn, Jonathan. *The Ten Year War: Obamacare and the Unfinished Crusade for Universal Coverage.* New York: St. Martin's Press, 2021.

Davidson, Roger H., ed. *The Postreform Congress.* College Park, MD: St. Martin's Press, 1992.

Davidson, Roger H., Susan Webb Hammond, and Raymond W. Smock, eds. *Masters of the House: Congressional Leadership over Two Centuries.* Boulder, CO: Westview Press, 1998.

Dyar, Ralph E. *News for an Empire: The Story of the* Spokesman Review *of Spokane, Washington, and of the Field It Serves.* Caldwell, ID: Caxton Printers, 1952.

Eilperin, Juliet. *Fight Club Politics: How Partisanship Is Poisoning the House of Representatives.* Lanham, MD: Rowman & Littlefield, 2006.

Elazar, Daniel J. *American Federalism: A View from the States.* New York: Thomas Y. Crowell, 1966.

Elazar, Daniel J. *The American Mosaic: The Impact of Space, Time, and Culture on American Politics.* Boulder, CO: Westview Press, 1994.

Farrell, John Aloysius. *Tip O'Neill and the Democratic Century.* Boston: Little, Brown, 2001.

Fenno, Richard F., Jr. *Home Style: House Members in Their Districts.* Boston: Little, Brown, 1978.

Fiorina, Morris P., and David W. Rohde, eds. *Home Style and Washington Work: Studies of Congressional Politics.* Ann Arbor: University of Michigan Press, 1989.

Flippen, J. Brooks. *Speaker Jim Wright: Power, Scandal, and the Birth of Modern Politics.* Austin: University of Texas Press, 2018.

Gephardt, Richard. *An Even Better Place: America in the 21st Century.* New York: Public Affairs, 1999.

Green, Matthew N. *The Speaker of the House: A Study of Leadership.* New Haven, CT: Yale University Press, 2010.

Hughes, John C. *Julia Butler Hansen: A Trailblazing Washington Politician.* Olympia, WA: Legacy Washington, 2020.

Jacobs, John. *A Rage for Justice: The Passion and Politics of Phillip Burton.* Berkeley: University of California Press, 1995.

Jenkins, Jeffery A., and Charles Stewart III. *Fighting for the Speakership: The House and the Rise of Party Government.* Princeton, NJ: Princeton University Press, 2013.

Jentleson, Bruce W. *With Friends Like These: Reagan, Bush, and Saddam, 1982–1990*. New York: W. W. Norton, 1994.

Johnson, Haynes, and David Broder. *The System: The American Way of Politics at the Breaking Point*. Boston: Little, Brown, 1996.

Johnson, Marc C. *Tuesday Night Massacre: Four Senate Elections and the Radicalization of the Republican Party*. Norman: University of Oklahoma Press, 2021.

Jones, Frank Leith. *Sam Nunn: Statesman of the Nuclear Age*. Lawrence: University Press of Kansas, 2020.

Killian, Linda. *The Freshmen: What Happened to the Republican Revolution?* Boulder, CO: Westview Press, 1998.

Kornacki, John J., ed. *Leading Congress: New Styles, New Strategies*. Washington, DC: CQ Press, 1990.

Lawrence, John A. *The Class of '74: Congress after Watergate and the Roots of Partisanship*. Baltimore: Johns Hopkins University Press, 2018.

Lee, Frances E. *Insecure Majorities: Congress and the Perpetual Campaign*. Chicago: University of Chicago Press, 2016.

LeoGrande, William M. *Our Own Backyard: The United States in Central America, 1977–1992*. Chapel Hill: University of North Carolina Press, 1998.

Loomis, Burdett A. *Time, Politics and Policies: A Legislative Year*. 2nd ed. Lawrence: University Press of Kansas, 2001.

Loomis, Burdett A., and Wendy J. Schiller. *The Contemporary Congress*. 7th ed. Boulder, CO: Rowman & Littlefield, 2018.

Mackaman, Frank H., and Sean Q Kelly, eds. *Robert H. Michel: Leading the Republican House Minority*. Lawrence: University Press of Kansas, 2019.

Mann, Thomas E., and Norman J. Ornstein. *The Broken Branch: How Congress Is Failing America and How to Get It Back on Track*. New York: Oxford University Press, 2006.

Mann, Thomas E., and Norman J. Ornstein. *It's Even Worse Than It Looks: How the American Constitutional System Collided with the New Politics of Extremism*. New York: Basic Books, 2016.

Mayer, Frederick W. *Interpreting NAFTA: The Science and Art of Political Analysis*. New York: Columbia University Press, 1998.

Mayer, Kenneth R., and David T. Canon. *The Dysfunctional Congress? The Individual Roots of an Institutional Dilemma*. Boulder, CO: Westview Press, 1999.

McPherson, James Brian. *The Conservative Resurgence and the Press: The Media's Role in the Rise of the Right*. Evanston, IL: Northwestern University Press, 2008.

Mervin, David. *George Bush and the Guardianship Presidency*. New York: St. Martin's Press, 1996.

Miller, Judith, and Laurie Mylorie. *Saddam Hussein and the Crisis in the Gulf*. New York: Times Books, 1990.

Mitchell, George J. *The Negotiator: A Memoir*. New York: Simon & Schuster, 2015.

Morrissey, Katherine G. *Mental Territories: Mapping the Inland Empire*. Ithaca. NY: Cornell University Press, 1997.

Northouse, Peter G. *Leadership: Theory and Practice.* 8th ed. Los Angeles: Sage, 2019.

Nugent, Walter. *Color Coded: Party Politics in the American West, 1950–2016.* Norman: University of Oklahoma Press, 2018.

O'Neill, Tip, with William Novak. *Man of the House: The Life and Political Memoirs of Speaker Tip O'Neill.* New York: Random House, 1987.

Page, Susan. *Madam Speaker: Nancy Pelosi and the Lessons of Power.* New York: Twelve, 2021.

Palazzolo, Daniel J. *The Speaker and the Budget: Leadership in the Post-reform House of Representatives.* Pittsburgh: University of Pittsburgh Press, 1992.

Peters, Ronald M., Jr. *The American Speakership: The Office in Historical Perspective.* Baltimore: Johns Hopkins University Press, 1990.

Peters, Ronald M., Jr., ed. *The Speaker: Leadership in the U.S. House of Representatives.* Washington, DC: CQ Press, 1995.

Petersen, Keith C. *River of Life, Channel of Death: Fish and Dams on the Lower Snake.* Lewiston, ID: Confluence Press, 1995.

Pitzer, Paul E. *Grand Coulee: Harnessing a Dream.* Pullman: Washington State University Press, 1994.

Polsby, Nelson W. *How Congress Evolves: Social Bases of Institutional Change.* New York: Oxford University Press, 2004.

Prochnau, William, and Richard W. Larsen. *A Certain Democrat: Senator Henry M. Jackson.* Englewood Cliffs, NJ: Prentice-Hall, 1972.

Putnam, Robert D. *Making Democracy Work: Civic Traditions in Modern Italy.* Princeton, NJ: Princeton University Press, 1993.

Rohde, David W. *Parties and Leaders in the Postreform House.* Chicago: University of Chicago Press, 1991.

Rollins, Ed, with Tom DeFrank. *Bare Knuckles and Back Rooms: My Life in American Politics.* New York: Broadway Books, 1996.

Rozell, Mark J. *In Contempt of Congress: Postwar Press Coverage on Capitol Hill.* Westport, CT: Praeger, 1996.

Schneider, Bill. *Standoff: How America Became Ungovernable.* New York: Simon & Schuster, 2018.

Scott, George, ed. *Turning Points in Washington's Public Life.* Folsom, CA: Civitas Press, 2011.

Sinclair, Barbara. *Legislators, Leaders, and Lawmaking: The U.S. House of Representatives in the Postreform Era.* Baltimore: Johns Hopkins University Press, 1995.

Smith, Jean Edward. *George Bush's War.* New York: Henry Holt, 1992.

Theriault, Sean M. *The Gingrich Senators: The Roots of Partisan Warfare in Congress.* New York: Oxford University Press, 2013.

Theriault, Sean M. *Party Polarization in Congress.* New York: Cambridge University Press, 2008.

Thomas S. Foley, Late a Speaker of the House and a Representative from Washington,

Memorial Addresses and Other Tributes. Washington, DC: US Government Printing Office, 2014.

Triumph without Victory: The Unreported History of the Persian Gulf War. Edited by the staff of U.S. News & World Report. New York: Times Books, 1992.

Walsh, Lawrence. *Firewall: The Iran-Contra Conspiracy and Cover-Up.* New York: W. W. Norton, 1997.

Wattenberg, Martin P. *The Decline of American Political Parties, 1952–1996.* Cambridge, MA: Harvard University Press, 1998.

Wright, Jim. *Balance of Power: Presidents and Congress from the Era of McCarthy to the Age of Gingrich.* Atlanta: Turner Publishing, 1996.

Wright, Jim. *Worth It All: My War for Peace.* Washington, DC: Brassey's, 1993.

Zelizer, Julian E. *Burning Down the House: Newt Gingrich, The Fall of a Speaker, and the Rise of the New Republican Party.* New York: Penguin Press, 2020.

Zhou, Baodi. "Thomas S. Foley and the Politics of Wheat: U.S. Wheat Trade with Japan, China and the Soviet Union, 1965–1986." PhD diss., Washington State University, 1999.

INDEX

INDEX

AUTHOR BIOGRAPHIES

R. Kenton Bird is a professor in the School of Journalism and Mass Media at the University of Idaho. He was director of the school for twelve years, followed by two years as the university's director of general education. He received his PhD in American studies from Washington State University in 1999, writing his dissertation on Tom Foley's congressional career. Before pursuing his doctorate, Bird was the managing editor and editorial page editor at the *Idahonian* and *Daily News* of Moscow, Idaho. Earlier, he worked at newspapers in Sandpoint and Lewiston, Idaho. Bird coauthored a textbook on covering government and public issues and has written articles for journals dealing with media law, editorial writing, and environmental policy. In 1988–1989, he was an American Political Science Association Congressional Fellow, working in the offices of Senator Timothy Wirth of Colorado and Representative Lee Hamilton of Indiana.

John Pierce is an affiliate professor in the School of Public Administration and Affairs at the University of Kansas, where he also has taught in the graduate program in museum studies. Prior to his position at Kansas, he was executive director of the Oregon Historical Society, vice chancellor of academic affairs at the University of Colorado at Colorado Springs, and dean of liberal arts and chair of political science at Washington State University. Pierce has published numerous articles, chapters, and books dealing with the role of political values in public opinion and public policy, including in a cross-national context. He was named a distinguished alumnus of the University of Puget Sound, an Alumnus of Notable Achievement at the University of Minnesota, and an outstanding faculty member at Washington State University. He was an American Political Science Congressional Fellow in 1970–1971, serving in the offices of Senator Frank Church of Idaho and Representative Tom Foley.